WARS WITHOUT END

*Recipient of the
University of New Hampshire
Book Prize for 1989*

WARS WITHOUT END

The Political Economy of
a Precolonial African State

S. P. Reyna

Published for University of New Hampshire
by University Press of New England
Hanover and London

University Press of New England
Brandeis University
Brown University
Clark University
University of Connecticut
Dartmouth College
University of New Hampshire
University of Rhode Island
Tufts University
University of Vermont
Wesleyan University

Printed in the United States of America

∞

Library of Congress Cataloging-in-Publication Data

Reyna, Stephen P.
    Wars without end : the political economy of a precolonial african
state / S.P. Reyna.
        p.   cm.
    Includes bibliographical references.
    ISBN 0–87451–505–X
    1. Bagirmi (African people)—Wars.   2. Bagirmi (African people)—
Politics and government.   3. Bagirmi (African people)—Economic
conditions.   4. Chari-Baguirmi (Chad)—History.   I. Title.
DT546.445.B34R53   1990
967.43—dc20   89–40233
                        CIP

5   4   3   2   1

Contents

Illustrations

Preface

This book reconstructs certain of the politics and economics of the east-central Sudan, especially those of Bagirmi, for the period roughly between 1870 and 1897 and, on the basis of this, formulates a model that accounts for the frequent warfare in the region. Its approach might be called a historical structuralism because it considers events that have occurred over long periods and analyzes them as instances of transformations of different types of social structure.

A number of individuals have offered assistance and comment at different stages of this project. These include Sultan Alipha, E. Brown, C. Bouquet, J. C. Caldwell, J. Chapelle, R. Cohen, D. Cordell, M. Galadima, M. Hamilton, M. Herold, J. P. Lebeuf, J. Middleton, S. Naogban, A. Rosman, Hadji Ngarmorio, J. Voll, and E. Wolf. I am especially indebted to comments of R. E. Downs and N. E. Gratton. Financial assistance for the study has come from the National Institute of Mental Health, the Hill Foundation, the Population Council, and the University of New Hampshire Faculty Scholars Program, as well as its Summer Faculty Fellowship Program.

I would like to acknowledge the assistance of C. Buckley, who translated certain portions of Nachtigal 1880, and G. Beltz, who did the same for Nachtigal 1889. Finally, a note on orthography: I have generally followed V. Pacques's (1977) orthography for Tar Barma words and that of *The Cambridge History of Africa* (1977) for Arabic words. However, where a word has already been well established as spelled according to some other canon, I have let that spelling stand.

This book is for Priscilla Trick Reyna and her grandchildren—Braden, Damon, and Alexander—of whom she was so proud.

S.P.R.

Durham, New Hampshire
April 1989

WARS WITHOUT END

Introduction

Bagirmi[1] was a small kingdom, roughly the size of Connecticut, located in the east-central Sudan immediately southeast of Lake Chad.[2] Its inhabitants associated their sovereign, the *mbang*, with the sun and his officials, *maladonoge*, with planets. The Bagirmi "sun" and "planets" were on full display by the beginning of the sixteenth century. Then in 1897 this political universe disappeared following its incorporation into the French colonial empire. In the interim, however, the sun and planets of Bagirmi made war.

For example, when the German explorer Gustav Nachtigal visited the Bagirmi sovereign Ab Sakin in 1870, he was asked on the very day of his arrival to participate in the punishment of a rebellious village. Nachtigal wrote:

> The village in question, called Kimre, was a half-day's journey to the south-east. On the fourteenth of April, a decisive expedition was undertaken against this refractory population. At half past midnight, the long trumpet resounded; it was the *patcha* who had the privilege of blowing it. Everybody gathered together at the call, albeit without much haste, outside of the town, and one hour later the expeditionary corps, which I naturally joined, set off in commotion.

Kimre was deserted. Its inhabitants had taken refuge in the tops of huge trees. Tree by tree the *patcha*'s troops attacked. Nachtigal described the scene:

> I remember a tall young man inhabiting the first tree, covering himself with his shield, encouraged by the cries of the women who were with him, who released his harmless arrows against us: then after each shot hid behind his reed shield, or rising uncovered to his full height triumphantly made a fist, defiantly menacing his aggressors.

> He was one of the first victims: struck by one of Almas' bullets, he fell without a cry. A second native, when struck, crouched for an instant in the branches, then fell on the ground from a height of 20 meters. The whole band fell upon him, uncontrollable, and in a few seconds he was literally torn apart. A third, also wounded, took refuge with his people in the next level up in the branches, while long threads of blood flowed down the trunk to the ground. This poor fellow was the last adult inhabitant of the tree. So the attackers, in an excess of bravura, decided to climb the tree. A moment later, dogs, chickens and goats came tumbling down; the wounded man was also thrown down in order that he might be done in, and women and children were pulled violently from their refuge: not a cry came from the lips of these unfortunate people . . . .

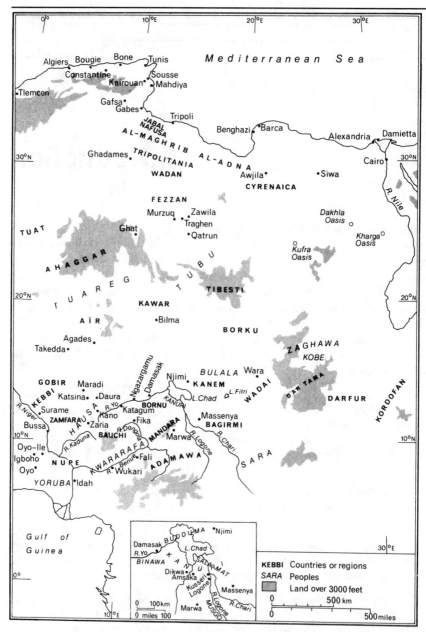

Source: *The Cambridge History of Africa, Vol. 3*, ed. R. Oliver (Cambridge: Cambridge University Press, 1977).

Map 1.1 The Setting of the East-Central Sudan

The cotton tree captured with the most difficulty was occupied by a single man, who, having observed the scene I have just described, had begun hiding in his hut, which then caught fire; he withdrew to the top of the tree, allowing the attackers to climb on the free floating ladder. Finally he was wounded and fell. He was immediately torn to pieces. But at the last moment two young boys, barely adolescent, were retreating to the extreme heights of the cotton tree. They stayed there until one of the aggressors reached them; when approached, with the heroism of despair, they threw themselves down. Their death appeared preferable to slavery. Seeing them roll from branch to branch, I couldn't help closing my eyes . . . one minute later, the two victims were but shapeless forms lying at our feet, beheaded, entrails torn from their bodies (Nachtigal 1880, 391–99).

The high frequency and considerable intensity of Bagirmi war was reported in the 1820s by Denham (1825, 215), in the 1850s by Barth (1965, 564), in the 1870s by Nachtigal (1880, 405), in the early twentieth century by Gaden (1909, 3) and Devallee (1925, 28), and most recently by Pacques (1977, 63). There appeared to be, as the administrator-soldier Lanier put it, some "necessity" that impelled Bagirmi "constantly" to war (1925, 458).

Rather little is known about the east-central Sudan.[3] Equally little is known about precolonial warfare throughout what medieval Arab scholars called the Sudan. Many studies resemble M. G. Smith's (1960) classic *Government of Zazzau*, which reported warfare to be important and thereafter treated it only *en passant*; or Marcel Griaule's *Conversations with Ogotemmeli* (1965), which presented the beliefs of a Dogon elder living in the Bangiagara Hills of Mali to the exclusion of all other topics.[4]

The neglect of Sudanic warfare may indicate how problematics can draw scholarly attention away from phenomena begging for explanation. The historical traditions of the precolonial Sudanic states are full of accounts of "Kings and battles" (Urvoy 1949). However, the need to understand such conflict was absent in the anglophone and francophone structural-functional approaches that have dominated much of the social science research in the Sudan.[5] It was so important to hold conversations with Ogotemmeli in these paradigms that it was appropriate to suppress the clamor of war that drove Ogotemmeli and his people into the hills.

Perhaps for similar reasons, there has been relatively little analysis of warfare in anthropology, and almost none of that in archaic, that is, preindustrial states. Keith Otterbein found in a 1973 survey of anthropological studies of warfare that "although many ethnographies contain brief descriptions of warfare, there are actually few books and articles that are devoted primarily to the analysis of warfare" (1973, 924). This situation has persisted. A search of the *Abstracts in Anthropology* for the decade 1974–84 shows that there were only an average of four articles per year on war by sociocultural anthropologists, which suggests that the study of warfare has been of peripheral interest to anthropology.

If the study of warfare has been of only marginal concern to anthropologists, the study of war in archaic states has been on the periphery of the periphery. Turney-High's (1949) *Primitive War: Its Practice and Concepts* explicitly avoided considering "civilized" war, that is, conflict conducted by states (1949, xiii). This bias continues to the present. Only five of the forty articles in *Abstracts in Anthropology* that dealt with war did so in cephalous societies. In fact, there is presently only a single social anthropological monograph whose topic is in explanation of warfare in archaic states.[6]

Yet warfare among archaic states was a common occurrence that presented, and presents, as Nachtigal had observed at Kimre, the living with the "shapeless forms" of the dead, thereby posing the question, Why? This monograph seeks to discover the necessity that drove the Sun Kings to produce and reproduce shapeless forms over hundreds of years and, in so doing, to contribute to a fuller understanding of the east-central Sudan and to the nature of war.

Approach

This necessity will be sought in the precolonial politics and economics of the east-central Sudan. The thinking of M. G. Smith has been influential concerning these subjects. Smith, following an examination of the state of Zaria, decided, "We cannot therefore agree with such writers as Marx who hold that government change is always a function of other social and economic changes" (1960, 295). He arrived at this conclusion even though he knew that government was "interrelated" with other societal structures (296). Such a view might be called a ships-that-pass-in-the-night understanding of the relationship between Sudanic states and their economies, because it treats the two as if they were independent phenomena that—like ships in the night—slip unaffected past each other. Refusal to explore political and economic interactions when they are known to occur can inhibit discovery of their significance. My approach is the reverse of Smith's. Its central concern is to understand political and economic interrelationships.

The late 1960s and early 1970s were a time of ferment in the social sciences. This was, at least in part, because French structuralism contributed to the structural Marxism of L. Althusser (1970), E. Balibar (1970) and M. Godelier (1972b), which seemed to offer a compelling alternative to the structural-functionalisms of Talcott Parsons, Bronislaw Malinowski, and A. R. Radcliffe-Brown. A mode-of-production school, dominated by the work of Rey (1973) and Meillassoux (1964, 1977), translated the generalities of the three Marxist theoreticians into specific analyses of African societies. Hereafter the work of Althusser, Balibar, and Godelier, together with that of the mode-of-production thinkers, will be referred to as structural Marxism. Today their views have weathered careful explanations (Callinicos 1976), thoughtful critiques (Geras 1972; Glucksmann 1972), scornful polemics (Thompson 1978; Harris 1968), and thoughtful reassessments (Benton 1984; Smith 1984). Certain modes-of-production thinkers have recanted in the *Canadian Journal of African Studies* (1985) and now appear to believe that certain of their views are "surviving dinosaurs" (Dupre 1985, 46). However, rumors of the extinction of structural Marxism are greatly exaggerated.[7]

Two Levels of Social Reality

There is a tendency, especially among certain American anthropologists, to conflate French structuralism with Lévi-Strauss. This is misleading. French structuralism is a far broader theater in which Lévi-Strauss is but one, albeit a leading, actor. A common act in the theater of French structuralism has been to reveal the "hidden" structures in different psychological, social, cultural, linguistic, and literary domains. One way this has been done has been to examine preexisting theories, making explicit their underlying structural properties. This was what Lacan sought to do for Freud (Lacan 1966), and what Althusser and Balibar were about when they were *Reading Capital* (1970).[8]

This work is a development of some and a rejection of other tendencies in the thought of Althusser, Balibar, and Godelier. To understand why, we must develop the notion of structure and of the "levels" of social life in which structures operate. Structuralism—any structuralism—is about structures or systems. Structures consist of parts, or elements, which exhibit relationships. Structural analysis reveals what the parts are in a structure and how they are related to each other. Such analysis is equally interested in how structures came to be (origins), how they maintain themselves (statics), and how they change themselves (dynamics). It has been said of feudal Europe that there was no terrain without its lord. It can equally be said of structuralism that there is no (intellectual) terrain without its structure.

Physics analyzes atomic structures. Social sciences look at social structures. Ultimately, the parts in social structures are individuals, or individuals in groups; and the relationships are the behaviors, or actions, of the individuals or groups. When the actions of individuals or groups regularly interact, there is social structure. However, a distinguishing feature of French structuralism—be it that of Lévi-Strauss (1953) or the Marxists (Godelier 1972a, xix)—has been the observation that social structure exists on different levels.

What these levels are has seemed puzzling. One way of thinking about them is that they are different types of concepts that can be arranged in a hierarchy, with different levels being different positions in the hierarchy. Philosophers of science distinguish concepts in terms of their scope and abstractness (Wallace 1971). Scope refers to the number of phenomena a concept covers.[9] The concept of mother has a narrower scope than that of kinship. Abstractness is the "distance" of a concept to observed events. A classroom is closer to the empirical world than enculturation. Mother and kinship, classroom and enculturation are concepts at different levels of scope and abstraction.

Social structures may be thought of as constructed from concepts occupying at least two levels above the ground, the ground being events occurring in the world. Closest to the ground is the level of concepts built up, in Radcliffe-Brown's terms, from observations of "actually existing social relations" (1965, 90). One talks, for example, of the potlatch, and one understands a specific movement of salmon, coppers, and so on to and from particular persons (*numaym* members and *numaym* chiefs) in a single set of populations (those on the Northwest coast) at a particular time. This level, then, tends to be one of relatively low scope and abstraction. It is, nevertheless, still a level of structure, for a potlatch has parts (*numaym* members and chiefs) and relations (the movements of fish, etc. between *numaym* members). We will call structures on this level institutions.[10]

Then, as Lévi-Strauss insisted, there is a second, higher level that had "nothing to do with empirical reality" and "everything to do with models which are built up after it" (Lévi-Strauss 1973, 375). This level is distinguished from the first by concepts of greater scope and/or abstraction. These are still about individuals or groups and their relations, but they can be applied to more societies because of their greater scope and abstraction. We will term structures on this level models.

Models may be built from institutions. A redistributive system, for example, is a structure consisting of parts and relationships that are greater in scope and abstraction than those of a potlatch. The parts in a redistributive system are any direct producers and redistributors. The relationships are any flow of products from direct producers to redistributors and, then, back again. *Numaym* members are direct producers. *Numaym* chiefs are redistributors. Gifts to *numaym* chiefs are a flow of products from direct producers to redistributors. The potlatch is a counterflow. Clearly, the concepts of direct producer, redistributor, and product are greater in scope and abstraction than *numaym* member, *numaym* chief, and salmon. Thus the potlatch and redistributive systems are constructed from concepts at different levels of scope and abstraction, and a redistributive system may be said to be a model of the institution of the potlatch.

This higher level can be achieved through processes of induction from the institutions of everyday life. So conceived, this level is a product not of observation but of the scholar's inferences from observation. Nobody ever saw or smelt a redistributive system, but some people saw and smelt fish being exchanged from chiefs to commoners in both the Kwakiutl potlatch and the Tikopian *anga*, and then inferred from common properties of these institutions the existence of distributive structures.

It is appropriate, given the preceding, to distinguish lower and higher levels of social structure. The former is constructed from concepts dealing with actually existing social relations. The latter utilizes concepts of greater abstraction and scope. Individuals are to some extent conscious of certain aspects of the lower level because they are aware of the norms and values that prompt their behaviors. No such norms and values prick consciousness on the higher level. So, for example, Kwakiutl chiefs knew they should give potlatches, although they were unconscious that potlatches were a redistributive structure. This second level, because it is largely unconscious, might be said to be the hidden realm of social life.

Such a conception of the two levels of social life suggests that there are two major tasks for structuralist analysis: first, to observe the institutions of social life, and second, to infer models from these. This is, indeed, the program of the present work, for it will first describe the institutions relevant to Bagirmi warfare and then infer that these are parts of a more abstract, hence hidden, model, one of whose properties is a high frequency of warfare. So a crucial question becomes, What will be the nature of this abstract structure? A response brings us first back to the structural Marxists.

Two Structural Marxisms

Structural Marxists have strong opinions about which abstract structure is better for explaining most actually existing social relations. However, a case can be made that their researches really resulted in two structural Marxisms, one explicit—an orthodox version—and the other implicit, with distinctly unorthodox implications.

Althusser, Balibar, and Godelier attempted to make explicit the structural properties that Marx had imputed to the mode of production (hereafter MP) in the *Grundrisse* and *Capital*. The MP school applied this model to actually existing social relations in pre- and postcolonial Africa. What gave this model its orthodoxy was a concentration on MPs and an insistence that "in the last instance" the MP is "determinant" of the entire social structure and its transformations (Althusser 1969, 111; 1970, 99; Godelier 1972a, 95). A consequence of such an orthodoxy is that only a single structure counts, for the properties of the MP alone allow the social scientist to "motor" through all of history (Balibar 1970, 216).

However, Althusser asserted in his classic statement of the "orthodox" position, *Reading Capital*, that a central concern of Marx's later work was the "mode of organization and articulation of the complexity" of the "complex whole" that is society (1970, 201–2). Here he was insisting that Marx was interested in *all* the related structures comprising society. He further claimed that Marx had shown that the component structures in the complex whole might be imagined as levels (ibid., 99). Althusser is using the term *levels* differently from my usage above. Here it is a metaphor for the major, abstract parts of a society. They might be the MP or the superstructure, and they were themselves structures with substructures. Althusser insisted that these levels were "relatively autonomous and hence relatively independent," which meant that each society had an MP with a "peculiar time and history," and a "political superstructure" with "its own time and history" (ibid.). However, these relatively autonomous structures were not independent of each other, because they "had a certain type of dependence with respect to the whole" (ibid., 100). Thus, at the same time that Althusser, the orthodox Marxist, was contributing to a theory of the MP, the unorthodox thinker was developing the distinctly disturbing view, at least to many Marxists, that society consisted of immensely complex, simultaneously dependent and autonomous structures.

Althusser proposed a principle of "structural causality" to guide the analysis of this more intricate structural reality. Structural causality is the proposition that the cause "of the effects" in social structures "is the complex organization of the whole" (Brewster 1970, 310). Put differently, it is a methodological principle that social structures are best explained by their properties. This is not so very different from Durkheim's insistence that social facts are best explained by social facts.[11] What is, however, very different is the conception of the relevant social facts, because the structural Marxist insists that analysts must deal "first and foremost with the relationship of different structures" (Therborn 1976, 359).

Implicit in these notions of society as a complex whole and of structural causality is a far more complex structuralism where the MP is but one structure, though an important one, in a system of interrelated structures. This is precisely the position of the present work, and to develop it further we now turn to notions of process.

Articulation, Reproduction and Contradiction

One criticism leveled at certain structural Marxists has been that they exhibit "a concentration on structure at the expense of process" (Harries 1985, 36). I believe this criticism to be incorrect. Furthermore, the exercise of showing why this is the case will contribute to an understanding of the structural Marxist concepts of articulation, reproduction, and contradiction, terms concerning the ways in which structures are connected to each other.

Process is often conceived of in anthropology as something opposed to, and fundamentally different from, structure (cf. Firth 1967; Barth 1966).[12] This view seems eccentric, because other sciences treat processes as attributes of structures. They are the actions of elements in a structure that produce relationships between the structure's parts and other structures, so as to to achieve certain ends.

Genitalia are biological structures. The structures in this system are prostates, gonads, penises, ovaries, wombs, vaginas, and so on. "Making love" is a process that produces certain relationships between these structures to achieve the end of recreating life. Process is structure in motion, and motion articulates structures, as anybody who has had anything to do with making love will testify.

Structural Marxists have tended to think about process in terms of articulation. This has been an important and perplexing structural Marxist notion because Althusser, as Foster-Carter notes, introduced the term without defining it (Foster-Carter 1978, 217). However, again following Foster-Carter, when he did employ it, it was "as an anatomical metaphor to indicate relations of linkage and effectivity between . . . all sorts of things" (ibid., 216). Mode-of-production thinkers have usually used articulation more narrowly to refer only to relationships between capitalist and other MPs (Wolpe 1980, 41). I use the term in its original, broader sense to mean processes of linkage and effectivity within and between any and all social structures. I understand *linkage* to mean the processes actually joining elements or structures and *effectivity* to refer to the strength of the linkage.

Godelier, Balibar, and Althusser believed that reproduction was an articulatory process that "genuinely sets" structures "in motion" (Balibar 1970, 259). Reproduction was explicitly the actions by which MPs recreated themselves (ibid., 254–70) and by extension any actions by which any social structure in a system recreated itself. Marx and Engels had insisted that the processes by which MPs reproduced themselves were dialectical, and because they were, they provided "the general laws of motion" of society (Engels 1940, 169). We will suggest that there are two types of motion.

The structural Marxists' most innovative work was a reformulation of the dialectic. There are differences between the dialectics of Althusser (1969, 87–129, 161–219) and Godelier (1972a; 1972b, 77–103). However, common to both were an insistence that dialectics pertained to structures, not thought, and a view that articulations within or between structures are contradictory.[13] The import of this last assertion needs clarification.

All dialectics share a common irony: that which keeps structures the same, changes them. Contradictions in dialectics are the source of change. Structural incompatibility, which is the inability of articulations within or between structures to continue, is a source of contradiction in the structural Marxist dialectic. Contradictions occur, among other reasons, because structures consume resources to achieve their goals, so they must recreate the expended resources to reproduce themselves. Articulatory processes must connect structures, either with parts of themselves or with other structures to reacquire the resources needed for reproduction to occur. It is the process of extracting resources to reproduce a structure, either from some part of itself or from another structure, that may produce structural incompatibility.

Contradictions intensify when the quantity of a resource taken to reproduce a structure becomes so great that there is not enough of it left to satisfy both the needs of that structure and those with which it is articulated. When this occurs, structures may be said to be at the "limits to their capacity to reproduce themselves" (Godelier 1972b, 90). Limits are a type of effectivity, for they are a "threshhold" beyond which "a change of structure must occur" (ibid., 90).[14] A group, for example, that cannot supply an average of fifteen hundred calories per day to each of its members is at its limits, and some structural change, perhaps extinction, must occur.

In this structural dialectic a structure in motion implies consumption of resources. This implies the need to reproduce the structure. Reproduction involves consumption, and then reconsumption, of resources, which pushes the structure toward its limits. When a structure is at its limits, it cannot remain unchanged, so there occurs motion of a second kind, one that transforms the structure. If it is assumed that reproduction is a universal requirement of social structures and that all resources used to reproduce structures are finite, then all structures eventually reach their limits and experience transformation. The fundamental contradiction in such a structural dialectic is that the necessity of reproducing a structure eventually destroys the ability to reproduce it further.

Two major types of contradictions are possible: those within and those between structures (Godelier 1972b, 77–92). Capitalist production relations, as described by Marx, may be interpreted as a structure. The elements in the structure are the capitalist and proletarian classes. The two classes are articulated by flows of necessary and surplus labor. Marx used the term *capitalist accumulation* for the process by which these two classes are articulated and reproduced, and he further suggested that a consequence of this process was the eventual reduction of surplus flows to the proletarians. Capitalists and laborers, then, were in contradiction to each other within the structure of productive relations.

According to Marx, in capitalist society the relations of production are in contradiction with the forces of production. Productive forces are a structure consisting of the organization of the factors of production. He further believed that capitalist accumulation reproduced both the forces and the relations of production. As this occurs there is a tendency to overproduce commodities (Marx 1981, 317–79). Another problem emerges because the rate of profit begins to fall for producers. Both overproduction and the falling rate of profit threaten the compatibility between the forces and the relations of production, and grave crises such as depressions occur. There is thus a contradiction between the forces and relations of production.

The structural Marxist reinterpretation of Marx believed that Marx's genius was to discover the reproductive process, capitalist accumulation, whose intra- and intersystemic contradictions were the "motor" of capitalist history. The mode-of-production thinkers choose the analysis of articulations between the capitalist and other MPs as their mission in order to show how the MP was, indeed, the motor of all history.

This book's approach borrows four elements of structural Marxism and rejects another. First, it seeks ultimately to work on the higher level of models. Second, it heartily accepts the Althusserian vision of society as a complex whole consisting of structures articulated with other structures. Third, it accepts the principle of structural causality, that the explanation of systems comes from understanding the properties of their component structures. Fourth, it believes that the articulations within and between these structures produced by contradictory reproductive processes are crucial to understanding both the dynamics and the statics of systems.

However, it believes that mode-of-production thinkers propose an implausible problematic by seeking to analyze only a single structure, the MP. Such a position is what I have previously called an aholistic holism (Reyna 1987). This is a refusal to analyze connections between structures when these are known to exist. Althusser suggested that social forms are "immensely complex" articulations of *many* structures. This work will formulate a model of a complex precolonial social system in the east-central Sudan that was reproduced by a process that articulated its mode of production with other structures.

Predatory Accumulation In Fields Of Empire

R. Cohen, referring to the central Sudan, echoing Tilly speaking of Europe (Tilly 1975), has said that "wars make states, and states make wars." The question, of course, is what model could best address the specifics of state making and war making in the east-central Sudan. Some hints as to just what such a model might consider are provided by Nadel and Smaldane. Nadel said that the central Sudanic kingdom of Nupe had to "guarantee [itself] a dependable, uninterrupted supply of all that it needed—arms, tools, clothes, saddles"—to "uphold" its "huge court" (1942, 294). Smaldane, speaking of another central Sudanic state, the Sokoto Caliphate, observed that "slaves as a form of war booty were used to purchase firearms, horses, and other military slaves" (1977, 147). In a sense, Nadel was suggesting that for the state of Nupe to reproduce itself, that is, to uphold its court, it needed arms, which implied that it had to have a revenue system to supply these means of destruction. Smaldane, for his part, noted that war was used to capture slaves, who were part of a revenue system used to acquire means of destruction. All of which suggests that any model seeking to explain warfare in the east-central Sudan should explore the articulations between state violence, revenue systems, and the accumulation of the means of destruction.

Predatory accumulation in fields of empire is a model that makes such connections. A field of empire consisted of different relations of domination—different varieties of empire, with different revenue systems that engendered different types of contradictions. These contradictions formed grids that articulated all the empires with their MPs, with other empires, and with certain acephalous polities. Fields were reproduced by a process called predatory accumulation. Frequent warfare was an institutional expression of predatory accumulation. Readers may be baffled by unexplained visions of fields, grids, and predatory accumulation dancing in their heads; and indeed, it is the task of this monograph to show how these notions are elements in an explanation of a region's precolonial conflict. To this end, *Wars without End* follows a logic of inductive exposition.

Chapter 1 has set the stage by telling the reader what the model will be about. Chapters 2–8 make the observations needed to construct the model. Part 1, "A Savanna Periphery," introduces the region and Bagirmi's origins in it. Chapter 2 presents the east-central Sudan. Chapter 3 discusses Bagirmi's beginnings and subsequent development.

Part 1 has a double purpose: to propose the necessity for a model that is of a region, not of a particular society, and to show why this model should be one of predation.

Part 2, "The Sun Kings' Realm," presents in chapters 4–8 the institutional pieces of the fields of empire model. It is based on information from the period roughly between 1870 and 1900, because a considerable amount of data pertaining to this time was gathered both during my own fieldwork in Bagirmi in 1969–70, 1973–74, and 1980, and by other ethnographers and scientists, Islamic scholars, Islamic and European travelers, colonial soldiers, administrators, diplomats, and scientists. (A general discussion of sources is contained in the Appendix.)[15]

Bagirmi discourse about farmers' families and the Sun Kings' court classified both institutions as fundamentally important and similar. Both were described as households (*bege*), so a reconstruction is made of these two forms of the household. Chapter 4 presents an overview of the Sun Kings' realm. Chapter 5 describes the structure and functioning of farmers' households, showing how these were a form of the domestic MP. Chapter 6 portrays the business of the Sun Kings and their officials. Here the analysis reveals what might be termed a household state. Chapter 7 describes the structure and functioning of this state's revenue institutions. Chapter 8 does the same for its military institutions. The analysis in chapters 7 and 8 articulates the domestic MP with the household state and exposes how the latter structure is exploited by the former to reproduce itself.

Part 2 lays out the pieces. Part 3, "Predatory Accumulation," puts them together. Chapter 9 assembles the model and tests it against certain facts of late-nineteenth-century Bagirmi history. Chapter 10, finally, speculates briefly about certain implications of this model.

Though readers do not yet know what grids or fields are, they may sense that these involved empires forcibly articulating with their domestic MPs, which tried to fend them off; while at the same time these very same empires grasped at other empires, which in turn grappled with their domestic MPs, while seizing at still other empires or stateless peoples. The metaphor of ships that pass in the night hardly seems appropriate for such a drama. Rather, this situation evokes an image of some enormous field in which structures linked in violent electric grids of predatory accumulation twitch to galvanic dances. Predatory accumulation, however, was a curious electricity, one that nourished the very structures it threatened to tear asunder. It was the reason for the gutting of Kimre's young teenagers. It was the "necessity" for war—and we begin to develop in the next chapter just how this was the case.

PART I

A SAVANNA PERIPHERY

Chapter 2

The East-Central Sudan

The bird of prey abides in open and wild places. . . . Kingdoms are held by the sword. . . . Do not part with your coat of mail and weapons. . . . Have near to guard you at all times a band of faithful and gallant men, sentries, bowmen, horse and foot.

"The Obligations of Princes" Sheikh Muhammad al-Maglili, (1492–1503)

Social anthropology has often analyzed societies as if they existed in splendid isolation. However, there was nothing isolated about Bagirmi. It took al-Maglili's precept, "Kingdoms are held by the sword," to heart and was an aggressive meddler in the affairs of other societies within and beyond the region in which it was located.

Bagirmi's bellicosity came about in part because it existed in a region where there was frequent conflict. So to begin to understand Bagirmi, one must become familiar with this war-worn region. This is the task of the present chapter, which introduces the region's geography, languages, peoples, societies, and their histories. Attention is focused upon the different kingdoms whose affairs dominated the region. The second most powerful of these at about the time of Bagirmi's founding (c. A.D. 1522) was Gaoga, whose location has long been a source of speculation. A solution to this "puzzle of Gaoga" is proposed that has implications for Bagirmi's own origin. A goal of these analyses is to suggest that an interpretation of the precolonial history of the east-central Sudan based on the notion of predatory accumulation may be desirable, thereby paving the way for such an interpretation in the remainder of the volume.

Geography

The eastern region of the central Sudan is roughly Chad's portion of the Chad Basin.[1] This nearly circular basin covers approximately 2,500,000 square kilometers, of which about 1,280,000 are in the Republic of Chad. Intermittent mountain ranges surround the basin on all sides: the Tibesti Mountains are to the north, the Air and Bauchi plateaus to the west, the Mountains of Lam to the south, and the Wadai Massif to the

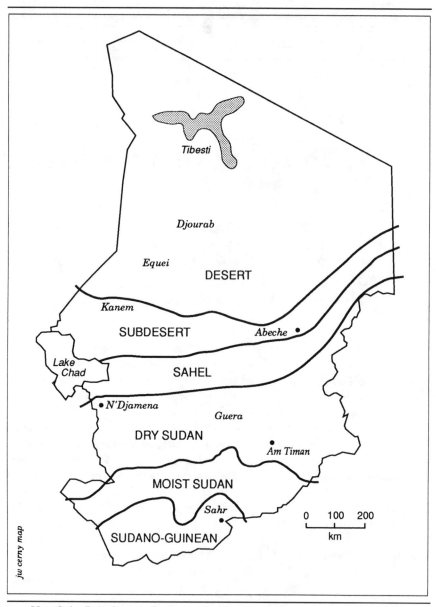

Map 2.1. East-Central Sudanic Bioclimatic Zones.

east. The topography within these boundaries is flat, although there is a gentle incline toward the basin's low point in the Djourab. Lake Chad is in the south central portion of the basin. It is a large, shallow body of water varying between 15,000 and 25,000 square kilometers in area, with no outlet to the sea.

The basin's most important recent ecological events have been an alternation between wetter and drier periods. These are indicated by changes in the size of Lake Chad, with wetter periods revealed by "transgressions" when the lake was larger in size than is now the case. The prevailing view of southern Saharan paleoecology is that "the final desiccation set in about 4000 B.P." (Bakker 1976, 53). It was thought that this drying out occurred later in the Chad Basin—circa A.D. 200 (Pias 1970, 34). However, Maley's (1977) work postpones even this "final desiccation" until much more recent times.

It is now believed that between 55,000 B.P. and A.D. 1200 the lake experienced four expansions called transgressions. The Chad Basin was far moister than at present during the first and the second transgressions, which ended by circa 22,000 B.P. and when a veritable inland sea covered 850,000 square kilometers, inundating much of the northeastern portion of the east-central Sudan. The next period, between 20,000 B.P. and 12,000 B.P., was one of greater aridity than that of today. This was followed from 12,000 B.P. to 4,000 B.P. by a third transgression, when the climate was moister than at present. Then a gradual drying out to roughly contemporary conditions began. However, a fourth transgression (1,600 B.P. to A.D. 1200) interrupted the decline to contemporary aridity. During this time the lake again extended north into the desert.[2] The crucial point is that the "final desiccation" appears to have begun about A.D. 1200, only three hundred years prior to the traditional date of Bagirmi's founding (Maley 1977).[3] There is a tradition, at least among some, that when the long drying out started, "the people followed the water" (Chapelle 1980, 10).

As a result of these climatological perturbations, two river systems, one largely extinct, one active, exist today. Rivers north of the lake generally flow in a southerly direction toward Lake Chad, while those in the south flow northward. The northern streams, however, are for the most part dry beds. There are two major river systems in the south. The Logone drains much of the southwestern portion of the basin. It flows for approximately one thousand kilometers until it meets the Shari River at N'Djamena. The Shari, after receiving the Bahr Sara, Bahr Aouk, Bahr Keita, and Bahr Salamat, drains the southeastern portion of the basin. It is the basin's major river and, after receiving the Logone, flows another hundred kilometers to empty into Lake Chad. The lake receives 98 percent of its water from the combined flow of these two rivers. Seen from a satellite, this hydrological system might be likened to two coral fans whose broad ends face away from the lake. The northern fan is for the most part a dead latticework of empty channels. The southern one, at least during the rains, is alive with water.

Climate was and is the basin's most crucial ecological variable. It is brutally hot and arid, with a long dry and a short rainy season. During the height of the dry season (April-May) temperatures throughout the basin soar to well over one hundred degrees Fahrenheit; while at the peak of the rains (July-August) they are still in the eighties and nineties. However, there are very considerable variations in precipitation within the basin, which are controlled by the intertropical front. This front, propelled by southerly winds off the Atlantic, brings precipitation. During the winter it is situated south of the basin, and the prevailing basin winds are dry northerlies—the harmattan. Starting in the spring, the front moves north, bringing southerly winds and rain. By August it is at its northern limits near the Tibestis, and then, almost immediately, it returns south again. The harmattan generally prevails throughout the basin by December. The longer the front is at or north of an area, the longer there will be rains. It is over or north of the southern part of the basin for more than five months. It hovers about the extreme north for a matter of a few days. Thus different areas of the basin annually experience very different rainfalls, and because of this they exhibit different vegetations adapted to different moisture conditions. Ecologists distinguish four bioclimatic bands: the desertic and subdesertic; Sahelian; dry and moist Sudanic; and Sudano-Guinean zones. In sum, the geography of the east-central Sudan consists of vast, dusty, and generally arid plains surrounded by rocky uplands. Two hydrological fans cross these plains to empty into Lake Chad.

The overwhelming sensation one receives when standing somewhere in the basin during the dry season is of a horizontal slash of bleached ocher, which is the land. Piled on top of this is another slash of sun-blanched blue, which is the sky—and that is all, save for a few buzzards gliding in the blue. But climate is a trickster in this landscape, a trickster because it is unknown from year to year how much rain there will be, and because over the centuries and millennia different areas of the basin are subject to drying and moistening trends. Sometimes the trickster brings rains and sometimes it doesn't— one never knows. When it doesn't rain the ocher becomes even more bleached, and there is only the deadening, shimmering heat.

The east-central Sudan was characterized by five areas where different groups of languages were spoken in the nineteenth century: to the north in the desert were the Saharan speakers; to the west were Chadic and Adamawan speakers; in the east were the Maban, Tama, Dajo and Mimi; then in the center was a veritable Babel in the Guera, as well as, slightly to the west, the Bongo-Bagirmi speakers. Crosscutting these in the Sahel and dry Sudan were Arabic and Fulfulbe speakers.

There were hundreds of different ethnic groups speaking these languages. This complexity, however, may be reduced to four broadly different types of societies in the nineteenth century.[4] These societal types were arranged in north-south layers that roughly corresponded to the bioclimatic zones. Camel pastoralists were farthest north in the desert and subdesert. Immediately to the south in the Sahel and dry Sudan were a string of states. South of the states in the moist Sudan and the Sudano-Guinean zone were cereal producers. Finally, in certain environments that were not widespread in the Chad Basin, were people whom we might call micro-environmental specialists.

The Teda and Daza were the major camel pastoralist ethnic groups.[5] They herded camels, sheep, and goats, but not cattle, whose pasture and water needs exceeded those available in the desert. They practised irrigated agriculture and traded. These activities were performed in different areas separated from each other by vast distances, sometimes as much as thousands of kilometers. The location and amounts of pasture and water for camels, sheep, and goats varied enormously with the time of year. During the rains they might be in the desert near the Tibestis, whereas during the dry season they might be eleven hundred kilometers farther south in the Salamat. Irrigation agriculture was

Table 2.1. East-Central Sudanic Languages.

Groups	Principal Languages	Principal Speakers	Location
1. Saharan	Teda-Daza	Teda, Daza, Kreda	Desert
	Kanuri	Kanuri, Kanembu	Bornu, Kanem
2. Chadic	Buduma	Buduma, Kuri	Lake Chad
	Kotoko	Kotoko	North of N'Djamena, between the Shari and Logone rivers
	Mului	Musgum	Between the Shari and Logone rivers, east of Guelendeng
	Massa	Massa	West of the Logone River, around Bongor
	Mussei	Mussei	East of the Logone River, around Bongor
	Somrai	Somrai	Between the Shari and Logone rivers, northwest of Gundi
	Ndam	Ndam	Upper Ba Illi River, near Ndam
	Miltu	Miltu	Middle Shari River, near Miltu
	Tumak	Tumak	Near Goundi
	Saba	Saba	Guera, near Melfi
	Sokoro	Sokoro	Guera, near Melfi
	Djongor	Djongor	Guera, near Melfi
	Mubi	Mubi	Guera, southeast of Mongo
3. Bongo-Bagirmi	Tar Lisi	Bulala, Kuka, Medogo, Babelyia	Batha, near Lake Fitri, immediately south of Lake Chad, east of Shari River
	Barma	Barma	Bagirmi
	Kenga	Kenga	Guera, near Bitkine
	Sara	Sar, Nar, Gulay, Ngambay, Mbay	Southeastern Chad
4. Maban	Bora Mabang	Maba, Kodoi	Wadai
	Massalit	Massalit	Northern Wadai
	Runga	Runga	Salamat

Table 2.1. — *continued*

5. Tama	Tama	Tama	Biltine
6. Dajo	Dajo	Dajo	Near Goz Beida and Am Dam and Mongo
7. Mimi	Mimi	Mimi	Near Biltine
8. Adamawan	Tupuri	Tupuri	Southeastern Chad, near Fianga
	Mundang	Mundang	Southwestern Chad, near Lere
	Mbum	Mbum	Extreme southern Chad, near Baibokum
	Koke	Koke	Guera, near Melfi
	Fanian	Fanian	Guera, near Melfi
	Bua	Bua	Middle Shari, near Korbül
	Niellim	Niellim	Middle Shari, near Niellim
	Tunia	Tunia	Middle Shari, north of Sahr
	Dai	Dai	Southern Chad, near Bedaya
	Bunda-Ngbaka	Bolgo	Guera, near Melfi
		Gula	Southern Chad, near Lake Iro
9. Fulfulbe	Fulfulbe	Fulani	Southwestern Chad, near Lere Bagirmi around Massenya
10. Arabic	Arabic	Arabs	Arab groups are spread in an east-west band across all of Chad in the Sahelian and dry savanna zones

Source: Cabot and Bouquet 1972.

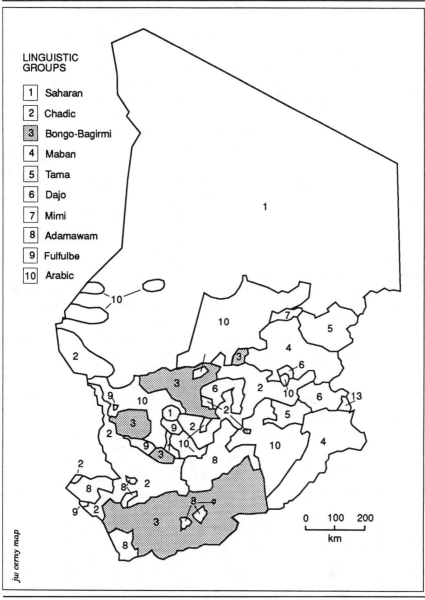

LINGUISTIC GROUPS

1 Saharan
2 Chadic
3 Bongo-Bagirmi
4 Maban
5 Tama
6 Dajo
7 Mimi
8 Adamawam
9 Fulfulbe
10 Arabic

jw cerny map

Map 2.2. East-Central Sudanic Languages.

21

conducted in oases in the valleys of the Tibestis or in Borku, where usually there was only enough water and fodder for animals for a short time during the rains. Trade occurred at marketplaces to either the north or south of the desert. Because these different activities depended on resources that were immensely far apart and scarce, they were, as Nachtigal observed, "always on the move . . . to ensure the means of existence for themselves" (1974, 1:394). Subsistence depended upon mobility, and mobility was assured by the camel. Hence these peoples' designation as camel pastoralists.

The family and the descent group were camel pastoralists' major social groups. Families tended to be female-headed for much of the year, with wives staying at the household's permanent residence, in some permanently watered area, managing its servile personnel. The latter did its more menial chores—especially irrigation farming, and perhaps extracting salt, collecting dates, or producing other goods traded against southern peoples' cereals.[6]

Clans controlled the resources (valleys, oases, wells, and pastures) necessary for this production. They were also the basis for recruiting men for common action—especially for raiding. Camel pastoralist groups tended to be acephalous. Small chiefdoms did, however, emerge, based on clans that were particularly effective in controlling resources. However, nowhere in the desert was there enough water and pasture to support more than a handful of horses and men. This meant that, so long as the camel pastoralists stayed in the desert, they could not organize standing armies; and without a standing army, large-scale, centralized states were not possible.

Immediately south of the desert were the states. Bornu, Bagirmi, and Wadai were the most important of these in the nineteenth century. This habitat permitted production of drought-resistant millets and sorghums, but only under conditions of uncertainty, which meant that mixed farming was a sine qua non of survival. There were two major mixtures that provided some protection in cases of drought. The first combined cereal production with cattle raising. Crops cannot be moved but animals can. Should there be drought in one area, animals could be herded to another. A second insurance against drought combined cereal production with foraging, especially fishing. Crops might fail, but dried fish offered a margin of security in lean years. Ethnic affiliation tended to follow economic specialization, so that states—as opposed to other societies in the east-central Sudan—were composed of different ethnic groups. For example, the Kotoko states were dominated circa 1800 by the Kotoko, who concentrated upon flood recession sorghum and fishing (A. M.-D. Lebeuf 1969), and the Arabs, who emphasized cattle raising, but who grew some millet (Reyna 1984). Similarly, Wadai was largely populated by the Maba, who combined cereal production with hunting, and Arabs, who tended to be more mobile pastoralists than those to the west.

A few words need to be said about states to distinguish them from chiefdoms, which were also found in the east-central Sudan. I largely follow Carneiro's definition of a state as a "political unit, encompassing many communities within its territory and having a centralized government with the power to collect taxes, draft men for work or war, and to decree and enforce laws" (1970, 733). A key part of this definition is that states are centralized. This means that they have a center, a hierarchy of offices with different amounts of power and authority with which to collect taxes, and so on. Wadai, for example, was ruled by a sovereign, a *kolak* (sing.) with power and authority over officials called *ḳamḳolaḳ* (sing.) and *agid* (sing.), who in turn enjoyed certain powers and authority over large territories in which there were different tribal chiefs called *tandjaḳ* (sing.), who themselves exercised several powers and authority over village and descent group chiefs called *mandjaḳ* (sing.).[7] A *ḳolaḳ* could issue an order to an *agid*, who could transmit it to a *tandjaḳ*, who could tell a *mandjaḳ* to have his villagers do such and such a thing. It was in this fashion that the center could control the lives of all the inhabitants throughout the state of Wadai.

States and chiefdoms were not differentiated from each other on the basis of the presence or absence of hierarchies, for both had them. They differed, however, with respect to the role of kinship and redistribution in these hierarchies and with respect to the power and authority of their offices (Sahlins 1968, 20–27). The hierarchy in chiefdoms tended to be an aspect of some kinship structure. This was not the case in states, where there was no kin organization of political offices that included all persons in the society. The Abu Krider, who resided about twenty kilometers north of the present capital of Chad, Ndjamena, and who at different times were tributaries of Bagirmi and Wadai, were an example in Sahlin's terms of a petty chiefdom. The entire tribe consisted of twelve patriclans (*ḳhashim bayt*) whose founders were stipulated to be the patrilineal descendents (*ahl*) of Musa Abu Krider, who was the founder (*jid*) of the entire tribe. One of the patriclans provided the tribal *sheiḳh*. This worthy was normally the eldest son of the previous *sheiḳh*'s first wife. So the chiefly hierarchy among the Abu Krider was, indeed, petty. There was only one *sheiḳh* over a number of clan elders. But this is, nevertheless, a hierarchy, and one based on kinship, because the *sheiḳh* and clan elders were agnates. Hence, *sheiḳhs*, elders, and ordinary male clan members might all legitimately refer to each other as brothers, whereas there was absolutely no pretense that the sovereign and village leaders were related in Wadai.

Office holders tended to be generous in chiefdoms, because chiefs and clan elders were conceived of as being like household elders whose responsibility was to collect their kinfolks' goods and then give them out again. Such redistribution was largely absent in the states. Wadaian officials, for their part, believed they had a religious duty to collect their subjects' goods, consume them, and demand more.

Power and authority are relatively restricted in chiefdoms. Abu Krider *sheiḳhs* had no standing armies. Their closest supporters were their male agnates, who did not have to obey them. *Sheiḳhs* were expected to suggest solutions but never to impose them. They further enjoyed the privilege of leading battle charges mounted on conspicuous white camels. Thus a *sheiḳh*'s authority amounted to cajoling and dying first in battle, which might be considered an example of conspicuous destruction. The east-central Sudanic states, on the other hand, had large standing armies that were highly professional organizations. When a *ḳolaḳ* spoke, he expected to be obeyed, and if he was not, he might send an army of ten thousand or so to impose his will, as Bagirmi discovered to its chagrin circa A.D. 1800.

It is at times difficult to distinguish large chiefdoms from small states. This, for example, is the case with the Dajo, who are remembered as the founders of the first Darfurian state, which was located to the east of Wadai in the Jebel Marra just outside the east-central Sudan (Berre 1984). Those Dajo who reside in Chad are found near the town of Goz Beida in the region called Dar Sila. In the nineteenth century they were a Wadaian tributary. They are described as having been "divided into tribes and subdivided into patrilineal clans. . . . Each tribe was ruled by a sultan, the clans by chiefs giving allegiance to the sultan. While once possessing almost total authority over the tribes sultans today have only nominal authority. . . . Royal clans [*leoge*] enjoy preeminence. . . . The *letuge* are are clan leaders [of nonroyal clans] who assist the sultan" (Berre 1984, 220). There certainly seems to have been a hierarchy among the Dajo running from sultan to royal clan members to nonroyal clan chiefs to ordinary folk. However, it is unclear whether nonroyal and royal clans were segments in a common lineage system. If this was the case, then the Dajo were a chiefdom; if not, they were a state.

Similarly, the first Bagirmi sovereign, Dala Birni, is remembered to have hosted a feast for his followers as part of the ceremonies by which he assumed power. This is a type of generosity associated with chiefdoms. Certainly, for a very long time such remembrances of royal redistributions past are just that—remembrances of things past.

So differences between large chiefdoms and small states were often delicate matters where kinship links between groups were forgotten, or where officials no longer redistributed goods collected by their followers. We shall classify a polity as centralized in the analysis that follows if it is not possible to decide whether it is chiefdom or a state.

It is now time to discuss the cereal producers. The people in southern Chad experienced the least climatic uncertainty. There was usually enough rainfall for some variety of sorghum or millet. This meant that southern people could specialize more thoroughly than northern folk in cereal production.[8]

There were two major ethnic groupings of cereal producers. In the southeast, between the Shari and Logone rivers, were Sara speakers, while in the southwest, on or west of the Logone River were Chadic and Adamawan speakers. There were more flooding and fewer tsetse flies in the southeast than in the southwest. This meant that cereal production could be combined both with fishing and cattle raising among Chadic and Adamawan speakers. It equally meant that cattle raising was not feasible because of trypanosomaisis among the Sara.

Cereal producers generally lacked differentiated political institutions in A.D. 1800. People resided in small villages composed of different neighborhoods, with each neighborhood usually "belonging" to a patrilineal descent group. There were no political offices regulating intervillage affairs, while within some villages, E. Brown observed: "No formal or informal political institutions existed. . . . Even within the clan the elders held no politico-jural authority over their kin. These same elders did not have the ritual means with which to coerce people either" (1975, 33). In general, from the perspective of the colonial administrators, cereal producers committed the sin of "living in anarchy," as one 1913 report expressed it (Dumas-Champion 1983, 31). From our perspective, they were merely highly acephalous.

The religions of cereal producers often conceived of departed ancestors and spirits of various natural phenomena as divinities. Religious specialists tended to perform rituals that were thought to allow them to interact with these forces, and sometimes because of their intimacy with these divinities they were believed to acquire supernatural sanctions over their kin. In general, these religions were lumped together in the early literature as "animistic," which leads us to another crucial criterion that distinguishes cereal producers from camel specialists and the states.

For the most part, by the beginning of the nineteenth century, the two latter types of societies were Islamic. This did not mean that all their members were strict Muslims; it did mean that Islamic piety was important to many influential persons. This piety involved the notion that all non-Muslims, and especially animists, were drunken, naked louts, who were called *kirdi* by Bagirmi and Bornuans. When Bagirmi used this term it was as a frightful curse, one that classified someone as semihuman. Cereal producers were emphatically *kirdi* in their eyes.

So too were the microenvironmental specialists. These ethnic groups had ventured into environments in which survival could be difficult. There were two types of microenvironmental specialists in the east-central Sudan: those adjusted to the lacustrine environment of Lake Chad and those who extracted a living from the rocky hills of the Guera.

Lake Chad itself is habitable because it is dotted with islands. Ethnic groups who lived on these islands called themselves Yedina. Those Yedina who lived on the northern islands were called, by their neighbors, Buduma, and those who lived on the southern ones were called Kuri. Both groups spoke a language similar to that of the Kotoko, their immediate southern neighbors. Very little is known about Yedina.[9]

However, their economy appears to have been dominated by fishing, herding, and raiding in the nineteenth century (Talbot 1911, 249). Many of these economic activities showed ingenious adaptations to their watery environment. For example, they had special boats that made transport possible. They had bred a breed of cattle, called Kuri, who were able to swim in the lake, and they had developed a system of pasture rotation that moved animals from island to island, which allowed them to feed these animals. Yedina were generally acephalous, and for the most part in the nineteenth century emphatically non-Muslim.[10] Offerings were regularly made to a gigantic supernatural serpent that was said to be the "Master of the Lake." Those who ventured near the lake in the 1800s did so with extreme caution, because the Yedina's "daring raids made them the terror of the mainland" (Talbot 1911, 249).

The ethnic groups that lived in the Guera Hills were called Hadjeray by their neighbors. The most numerous Hadjeray were those who spoke Chadic languages and included the Djongor, Dangaleat, Sokoro and Saba. The largest single Hadjeray group, however, were the Kenga, who spoke a Bongo-Bagirmi language and who were believed to have had a role in Bagirmi's founding. Finally, the least numerous were the Adamawan-speaking peoples, the Koka, Fanian, and Bolgo, as well as a few Dadjo speakers.[11]

All Hadjeray, regardless of language, tended to be economically and culturally similar. Most groups had developed a form of farming based upon terracing and manuring. This intensive farming system resembled that of other hill peoples throughout the Sudan, and, as was the case with these peoples, it may be seen as an adjustment to the land scarcity that prevails in a hilly habitat.[12] Hadjeray tended to be acephalous, or, as was increasingly the case by the nineteenth century among the Kenga, Sokoro, and Saba, to have small chiefdoms. Religion provided a cultural unity for these small polities.

Hadjeray, like Yedina, were emphatically non-Muslim. A cult of the *margai* was central in their religion. *Margai* were supernatural forces that exercise certain powers over such natural events as harvests, animal and human fertility, and storms. *Margai* inhabited different places such as trees or mountains. The bigger a place occupied by a *margai*, the bigger its powers over nature. The largest places inhabited by *margai* were mountains. Each *margai* had a priest, and, as might be imagined, those persons who were priests of *margai* resident in mountains tended to have greater religious authority and influence than others.

Some idea of the relationship between religion and polity can be gained from a brief description of their arrangement among certain Kenga near Ab Tujur (Fuchs 1973–74). This Kenga chiefdom occupied the land around a peak called Ab Tujur. These lands were divided into a number of areas of clan settlement. There were two major types of clans in the chiefdom. The first, the *garienge* was the dominant clan and provided the chief (*gar*). The second type of clan was called *jenange*, which meant literally "they of the earth." These were landowning clans, of which there were, in turn, two types, the *tarbitge* and *masaķim*. The former clans were said to be the original owners of the chiefdom's territory, while the latter were believed to have received their lands only after requesting it of the *tarbitge*.

The chief of this chiefdom was a priest of the highest *margai*, *ra Tjeng*, recognized by the Kenga. *Ra* is the Kenga term for their highest supernatural force; *Tjeng* is a boulder on Ab Tujur where this force is believed resident. The chief could intercede with *ra* at this boulder, thereby gaining an indirect influence over natural events. He could also give a sacred spear to his subordinates that contained *ra Tjeng*. It was undoubtedly this relationship to *ra Tjeng* that, it was believed, gave the Kenga chief and his subordinates their legitimacy and influence over their followers. Other Hadjeray groups organized themselves differently, but their differences tended to be different permutations of how leaders were associated with *margai*.

First, this chapter gave the east-central Sudan a geography. Then it populated this landscape with ten linguistic groups and hundreds of ethnic groups. This complexity was reduced by showing how all peoples belonged to one of four social types at the end of the nineteenth century. It is now time to suggest that these types were themselves actors in a regional system. In order to do this, I must now turn to the area's history.

History

Centralized polities continually arose in the east-central Sudan. This process appears to have begun some time before the eighth century A.D., and it continued throughout the nineteenth century. In the reconstruction that follows we shall show how chiefdoms and states formed, warred, and traded, and through these activities forged connections between each of the social types identified in the previous section. First we shall reconstruct certain centralized polities and their doings roughly from A.D. 900 through 1200. Next we shall do the same for the period from A.D. 1200 to circa 1800. Then, in the chapter's final section, we shall propose an interpretation of this history.

History Prior to A.D. 1240

The first centralized polity to emerge in the east-central Sudan appears to have been associated with the Zagawa. Exactly who the Zagawa were is not clear. The word *Zagawa* does not appear in the local central Sudanic traditions, but it was used by Arab scholars resident in North Africa or the Middle East. Arguments can be advanced that the Zagawa were a clan, a tribe, or a dynasty, and at different times they may well have been all three.[13] The first mention of their existence appears to be prior to A.D. 700 (Zeltner 1980, 29). The first observations that suggest what their political structure may have been like come in the ninth and tenth centuries, when they are described as a kingdom (al-Ya'cubi, writing c. A.D. 872, and al-Muhallabi, writing c. A.D. 990 both in Zeltner 1980, 29). Their capital appears to have been at Manan, whose location, a matter of conjecture, may have been in the Equei (Zeltner 1980, 30).

Details of the structure of the Zagawa polity are lacking. However, it is termed "a vast and important kingdom" in the tenth century (al-Mas'udi in Cuoq 1975, 61). Al-Muhallabi speaks of Zagawa religion with some contempt, because it was non-Muslim. He was especially disturbed that "they venerate their king. . . . Their religion is to adore their kings, who, according to their beliefs, bring life and death, send sickness and death" (in Zeltner 1980, 31). Five centuries later such veneration of sovereignty would be an important feature of the Bagirmi state.

Certain students of the east-central Sudan emphasize the role of nomads in the process of state formation (cf. especially Urvoy 1949). The Zagawa do not appear to support this view, because they were not depicted by the Arab chroniclers as nomads. For example, al-Muhallabi, writing in the ninth century, says: "Their houses are huts of reeds. . . . Their country is completely in agricultural fields. . . . Their crops are principally millets and beans, and then wheat" (in Cuoq 1975, 78–79). Such agriculture seems entirely possible because this was the moister time of the fourth transgression, when Lake Chad spilled down the Bahr el Ghazel as far as the Djurab (Maley, in Zeltner 1980, 31). Zeltner, on the basis of such climatological information and al-Muhallabi's account, concludes that the Zagawa were "sedentary or semisedentary" (1980, 30). Of course, it is possible that the Zagawa might have been nomads prior to their sighting by the medieval chroniclers. This, however, would further suggest that nomadism was not crucial in the rise of the earliest central Sudanic state, because state formation would then have occurred only after the nomads had ceased to be nomads.

A more significant factor would appear to be the existence of, and opportunities offered by, the trans-Saharan trade. Trade between North Africa and the central Sudan was "already flourishing" in the ninth century (Fisher 1977, 237).[14] The Bilma Trail led from Tripoli through the different oases in the Fezzan south to the Kawar, also important for its oases, and then on to Lake Chad. This trail appears to have been the most important medieval trans-Saharan route, because it offered the easiest crossing, possibly as a result of having more wells than the other routes (Arkell 1952, 264). The Fezzani town of Zawila was apparently the northern entrepot for the Bilma Trail's goods at this time.

Al Ya'cubi (c. A.D. 891) identified the major commodity in this trade when he reported that at Zawila "they export slaves from the Sudan taken. . . . from the Zagawa. . . . and other Sudanese tribes near to them" (in Cuoq 1975, 49). Again, in the eleventh century al-Bakr said of Zawila: "The caravans assembled from everywhere and left again in all directions. . . . One exports from Zawila slaves" (ibid., 49). Thus, the "flourishing" trade along the Bilma Trail was a slave trade.

It is unclear why the central Sudan specialized in slaves. Fisher has said: "In the mid-tenth century, al-Istakari contrasted Nuba, Zanj and Habash and Beja slaves, all from the Nile countries and eastern Africa, with those passing north through Zawila and from the central Sudan, whom he found blacker and better than any others. The slave revolt in Iraq, late in the 9th century, particularly associated with Zanj slaves, may have given all those from eastern Africa a bad name, and correspondingly heightened the demand for those from the central Sudan" (1977, 262). Regardless of the reasons for its occurrence, the central Sudan's participation in the slave trade, which was to last into the twentieth century, appears established by the ninth century A.D.

Centralized polities played a direct role in this commerce. Al-Muhallabi observed that the sovereign's "hold over his subjects being absolute, he reduces to slavery whom he wishes" (in Lanne 1977, 117). Al-Ya'cubi said, "It was told to me that the kings of the Sudan sell them [slaves] without reason and without war" (in Cuoq 1975, 49). The crucial phrase in this quotation is "the kings . . . sell them," which suggests that the slave trade was largely a state prerogative. However, al-Ya'cubi's claim that slaving occurred "without war" seems improbable. For example, al-Idrisi said that Zagawa slaves were acquired by "kidnapping" (in Fisher 1977, 271). Now kidnapping is rarely a tranquil operation, and when it is done by kings on a level necessary to participate in the trans-Saharan trade, it strongly suggests considerable organization. Large-scale, organized kidnapping performed by kings would seem to imply warfare—exactly, it might be added, the type of war Bagirmi executed nine centuries later in the raid upon Kimre that opened this book.

It appears that the first central Sudanic state was in the business of acquiring and selling slaves in the trans-Saharan trade. It may thus be conjectured that to participate in such commercial opportunities, an organization was necessary to seize the people who were commodities in it. The formation of such an organization could well have been at the origin of the Zagawa state.

Whatever the reasons for the first centralized polity in the central Sudan, the process appears to have begun quickly to repeat itself, because a new kingdom arose in the Kanem at the beginning of the eleventh century. The sovereigns of this Kanem state came from the Magumi clan, whose members were said to be descendants of Saif ibn Dhi Yazan and were thus called Saifwa. Exactly how the Saifwa came to rule in the Kanem and what their relationship was to the Zagawa is unclear. However, by the thirteenth century the Zagawa were resident east of the Kanem and were, according to Ibn Sa'id, "under the authority of the sovereigns of Kanem" (in Cuoq 1975, 210). These Saifwa "sovereigns," called *mai*, were to be one of the longest ruling dynasties in the world, governing from circa A.D. 1100 until 1846. Their capital was at Njimi, apparently near the present Mao. Like the Zagawa, they appear to have originally venerated their ruler, for al-Umari, writing in the 1300s, found him "hidden from view" and shown to nobody, "except at the occasion of great ceremonials" (ibid., 259). However, the Saifwa were to become Muslim circa A.D. 1100, when *mai* Humai adopted Islam.

There were two main periods in Saifwa history. The first was when they ruled a state in the Kanem, and the second was when they repeated this performance once again in Bornu. The Saifwa Kanem state enjoyed two main subperiods: one, when it rose to dominate the central Sudan (c. A.D. 1100–1296), and the other—a "time of troubles" (A.D. 1296–1390)—that culminated in its expulsion from the Kanem. During the first period, the *mais* continually expanded their influence. At its apogee, under Dunama Dibale (1210–48), Kanem extended north to the Fezzan and as far east as the Nile around Wadi Halfa.

Warfare was important during both periods of the Saifwa Kanem state. One chronicler remembered that "Allah had made him (Dunama) powerful multiplying his children and his soldiers" (Ibn Sa'id in Cuoq 1975, 209), who according to one account numbered 100,000 men (*Diwan* 132, in Zeltner 1980, 49). There appear to have been two types of warfare at this time. On the one hand, Dunama would attack other centralized polities, such as those in the Fezzan. This conquest, according to Fisher, "probably reflected the great importance to Kanem of security for trade and travel on the road northwards" (1977, 290). Dunama is also remembered to have warred against certain Tubu groups to the northeast of the Kanem. This warfare may well have been to secure control over a second trade route that went northeastward from Lake Chad to Egypt and was known as the *derb arbain* (Arkell 1952, 264). Conquest along this route would explain the Kanem's influence on the Nile.

Then there was a second type of warfare described by Ibn Sa'id, who reported that "the sultan left on campaign" from the northwestern part of Lake Chad "with his fleet for infidel lands situated on the borders of the lake, to attack their embarkations, to make them prisoners" (in Cuoq 1975, 210). This warfare thus continued the pattern observed for the earlier period, for it involved raids to enslave the "unsubmitted and idolatrous" (Ibn Sa'id in Cuoq 1975, 208).

The region south of the lake at this time was "the great unknown" whose people appear to have been called *anakazar* (Zeltner 1980, 59). The geographer al-Maqrizi, perhaps on the authority of Ibn Sa'id, may have been describing this area when he wrote: "This region is covered with great trees and with pools from the overflowing of the Nile. It was invaded in the year 1252/3 A.D. by the king of Kanem, from Njimi, who killed many of the inhabitants, or enslaved them" (al-Maqrizi in Palmer 1970, 193). Thus the period from A.D. 900 through 1248, the conventional date of Dunama's death, saw the origin and first extension of centralized polities over an area largely to the east and north of Lake Chad. A pattern had been revealed and repeated itself. The states that emerged—Zagawa and Kanem—used their political hierarchies to make war in order to make commerce in the trans-Saharan trade.

History after A.D. 1248

At the height of prosperity the climatic "shoe" dropped for the central Sudan. The final desiccation began after A.D. 1200. Increasingly the habitats of the early medieval states in the Equei, the Djurab, and the Kanem became subdesert or desert. We shall reconstruct certain events first to the west and then to the east of Lake Chad.

The Saifwa "time of troubles," mentioned in the last section, began immediately after Dunama Dibale's reign. This involved both an internal struggle for the throne and an external struggle against a new ruling group, the Bulala. Little is known about Bulala origins.[15] Today they reside around Lake Fitri and speak a Bongo-Bagirmi language. Certain authorities, however, think that they originally belonged to the same Saharan-speaking populations as did other Kanem peoples (A. M.-D. Lebeuf 1959). How they changed languages is unclear and a matter of some speculation (see Carbou 1912). However, they were effective fighters, and the Saifwa *mai* Umar fled with his followers to the west of Lake Chad (c. 1390), where earlier, during the reign of Dunama Dibale, people from the Kanem had settled and created "an independent kingdom" called Bornu (Zeltner 1980, 51). Umar's withdrawal left the Kanem to the Bulala, who ruled relatively undisturbed there for two and a half centuries until circa 1460. This was largely because the Saifwa in Bornu were still preoccupied with civil strife caused by dynastic rivalry.

The rivalry was over by the mid-fifteenth century, when a new capital had been built at Birni Gazargamu (near the present Geidam), and an aggressive state had emerged that sought to crush opposition within and to expand its territories beyond Bornu's borders. The latter policy resulted in a one-hundred-year war against the Bulala from 1460 until 1564, during which eight *mai*s attacked Bulala armies and gradually reasserted Bornuan control over the Kanem. By the end of the sixteenth century, following defeat at the hands of *mai* Idris Alaoma, the Kanem was again in Bornuan hands; and for that matter so was much of the east-central Sudan because, according to Arkell, Bornuan influence extended as far east as Darfur, which, he speculated, may have become a tributary of the *mai*s c. A.D. 1535 (1952, 268).

Little is known of the Bulala state and warfare at this time, but a fair amount is known about that of Bornu under Idris Alaoma (1580–1617) thanks to his chronicler, Ahmed ibn Fartwa. The wars that Ahmed ibn Fartwa describes strikingly repeat the pattern noted earlier for the thirteenth century. Idris Alaoma made wars against other states, the most significant of these being against the Bulala. Equally, he made wars against "pagans" to the south. These pagans, however, instead of being called *anakazar*, as Ibn Sa'id had called them in the 1200s, were now called *sao* by Fartwa (in Palmer 1970b, 30). Idris Alaoma appears to have continually attacked them. When this occurred, often "they turned and fled. Most of them were killed. Some, however, were fortunate to escape by flight. . . . The Muslims captured their women and children as slaves" (ibid., 42). Many of these slaves were then sold into the trans-Saharan slave trade, which by now was seven hundred years old.

Exactly who the *sao* were is a matter of lively debate. One reading of this literature is that they were Chadic speakers resident about Lake Chad who evolved into the Kotoko states (Cohen 1962), which were concentrated around small cities such as Makari, Kousseri, and Logone Birni. Kotoko polities, though they never seem to have been united into a single polity (A. M.-D. Lebeuf 1969), may be classified as states because their hierarchies were neither kin based nor generous. Just when this status was achieved is unknown. However, al Fazari, apparently writing at the end of the eighth century A.D. according to Lewicki, mentioned the "small kingdom of Nakhla or Nkhala," which "owed its name probably to the town of Ngala, the capital of . . . Sao, in Bornu" (Lewicki 1974, 14). Given this ninth-century mention of a kingdom, an appropriate estimate for the first occurrence of the Sao-Kotoko city-states would be at this time.

Certainly, by the time of Idris Alaoma, these states were well established, with the population living in walled, urban centers that even had paved streets. With respect to the *sao*, Idris Alaoma appears to have been interested not only in booty but also in establishing tributary relations. For example, one of the towns Idris attacked was Amsaka. After he defeated it, Ibn Fartwa reported:

> The people of every quarter came to him with many gifts bowing their heads in submission — whoever they were and wherever they dwelt.

> So there was destroyed this stockade which held out against Ali ibn Idris's predecessors. He turned upon it and rendered it barren and deserted.

> The people who brought presents continued to pay the poll-tax as of old every year, and became more and more obedient. (Ibn Fartwa in Palmer 1970b, 28–29)

Warfare in the sixteenth century, at least in Bornu, and probably throughout the central Sudan, was directed against competing states and stubborn "pagans." There is every reason to believe the Yedina were Sao who responded to these predations by withdrawing into the lake.

Turning from Bornu to Kanem, it appears that the situation had become intolerable for the Bulala by the early seventeenth century. This seems in part related to the rise of Wadai in the east, which sent peoples and dynasties ricocheting westward toward the Kanem. This meant that the Bulala now had to address military threats from the east as well as those that continued from the west. To understand this situation, we must look to the east and Wadai.

The history of Wadai during the Middle Ages appears intimately linked with that of Darfur. The latter state first emerged at an unknown date in the Jebel Mara massif. The first rulers of Darfur are believed to have been Dajo. They were, then, replaced by a Tunjur group, who ruled Darfur until the end of the sixteenth century, when they, in their turn, were overthrown by an individual remembered as Dali, who founded the Keira dynasty, which ruled Darfur into the nineteenth century (O'Fahey and Spaulding 1974, 107–17). Arkell believed that Wadai, too, had had a Tunjur period and that it and Tunjur Darfur were coprovinces in a larger state (1963).[16] At roughly the same time that the Keira dynasty began, one Abd el-Karim usurped Wadai's throne and drove the Tunjur west to the Kanem (c. 1635). Abd el-Kerim's dynasty would rule Wadai until 1915, and by circa 1805 Wadai would become the strongest state in the east-central Sudan. However, the immediate impact of Abd el-Kerim's victory would be borne by the Bulala.

This is because the Tunjur, driven westward by Abd el-Karim, seem to have anchored themselves in the Bahr el Ghazel (between Salal and Koro Toro). Here they were exposed to repeated attack from the Kreda, a Tubu group. These predations seem to have motivated them to move westward, which they could only do by assaulting the

Bulala at Mao. When this occurred, Bulala was placed in a vise, between a resurgent Bornu to the west and the Tunjur to the east. Eventually, led by their ruler Djili Esa Tubu, the Bulala migrated, first to a region east of the Bahr el Ghazel and then to Lake Fitri (Hagenboucher 1968, 49). Here, they subjugated an existing polity, that of Kuka, and established their own rule over the Fitri at Yao sometime around 1665. This brings us to the "puzzle of Gaoga."

The Puzzle of Gaoga

Just who were these Kuka conquered by the Bulala? One answer to this question may contribute to the resolution of one the puzzles of Sudanic, medieval history. Leo Africanus, a Moroccan diplomat who visited the Sudan between 1512 and 1514, reported that there were fifteen kingdoms in the Sudan and that the three easternmost were, from west to east, "Bornu, Gaoga and Nubia." He further said that twelve of the kings had submitted to three others. The three most powerful rulers were "the king of Timbuctu, who possessed the major part, the king of Bornu, who had the smallest, and the king of Gaoga, who held the rest in his powers" (Leo Africanus 1956, 9–10). Thus Gaoga appears to have been the second state in the entire Sudan at the beginning of the sixteenth century. The puzzle in all of this was, What people, living where, controlled Gaoga?

At first there seemed to be no puzzle. Gaoga was Gao, the capital of Songhey in the western Sudan. However, Leo had been clear: Gaoga was located between Bornu and Nubia, which placed it to the east of Lake Chad and west of the Nile, precluding Songhey. Since Barth in the 1850s, most authorities have placed Gaoga somewhere in the east-central Sudan. This simply moved the puzzle eastward, for the question of who controlled Gaoga and where it was located still nagged.

There have been seven solutions to the puzzle of an east-central Sudanic Gaoga. The first was Barth's, which identified Gaoga with the Bulala and located it at Yao near Lake Fitri (1965, 545). Modat proposed a second solution: he believed, because Leo had said some of the inhabitants of Gaoga lived "in the mountains," that the kingdom had to be located in the Jebel Mara Massif of Darfur (1912, 79–80). Carbou authored a third position when he proposed that the "Kingdom of Gaoga is none other than that of the Kanem, where the Bulala reigned" (1912, 1:292). Palmer advanced a fourth view by arguing that Gaoga was a Dajo state that ruled over Kuka peoples near Lake Fitri (1929, 283–84). Urvoy raised a fifth possibility, which was that Gaoga was a Nquizim state near Lake Fitri (1949, 59). Kalck, broaching a sixth solution, argued that Gaoga was a Kuka polity of Tar Lisi speakers resident around Wadai and Darfur (1972, 541). Tar Lisi languages were those of the northernmost Bongo-Bagirmi speakers and were spoken by inhabitants of the nineteenth-century Kuka, Bulala, and Medogo kingdoms (Meillet and Cohen 1952, 785). A final view is that of Fisher, who identified "Gaoga with Kaga" (1977, 304), which he suggested was probably a "district southwest of Lake Chad" (1977, 291). We will suggest an eighth, "compromise" alternative, which, like Barth, Urvoy, and Palmer, places Gaoga in the Fitri, but which, like Kalck, suggests that it was a Tar Lisi–speaking Kuka polity. Our approach will be to decide upon Gaoga's location, and then to show how it appears to have been a string of centralized,

Tar Lisi–speaking polities stretching from the Shari in the west to the Wadai Massif in the east. We begin with Barth.

A problem with Barth's position is that if Gaoga had been located around Lake Fitri, then it would not have been a Bulala polity, because, as Carbou noted, the Bulala did not arrive in the Fitri region until Abd el-Kerim had driven the Tunjar from Wadai (c. 1610), and they, in turn, had helped squeeze the Bulala from the Kanem. This, as we reported above, was probably around 1650, which was well over one hundred years after Leo had visited Gaoga. The implications of the preceding are clear. If Gaoga was in the Fitri when Leo visited, it could not have been a Bulala state because the Bulala would only arrive there a century later. Therefore, if Gaoga was a Bulala state, it was not in the Fitri; and if it was in the Fitri, it was not a Bulala state. It is thus essential to discover whether Gaoga was in the Fitri. Attention turns to Fisher's suggestion that this was not the case.

Fisher's location of Gaoga at Kaga, also spelled as Kaiga, to the "southwest" of Lake Chad appears improbable because Leo had said that Gaoga was to the east of Bornu. Further, Fisher appears to have gotten his location of Kaiga wrong, and this is important for the position we are trying to develop. According to Palmer, the term *kaiga* appears to have originally meant "'subject peoples' to the south" ruled over by an official called the *kaigama* in the Saifwa Kanem state (1936, 108).[17] The Fitri is southeast of the Kanem, which is east of Bornu. If Palmer's interpretation of *kaiga* is correct, it suggests they were located to the southeast of Bornu at Fitri (Palmer 1970a, 212). Thus, if Fisher is right and Gaoga was a way of transcribing Kaiga, then Gaoga may have been around the Fitri.

Carbou decided that if the Bulala were not in the Fitri, then Gaoga could not have been in the Fitri because he was convinced that it had been a Bulala state. So he moved Gaoga to the Kanem, where the Bulala resided at the time of Leo's visit. Carbou's arguments for a Gaoga in the Kanem are as follows. Leo had mentioned that the people in Bornu and Gaoga spoke similar languages. This presumably would have been some variant of Kanuric. Bulala today speak Tar Lisi, but they say, and Carbou agrees with them, that in the past they spoke Kanuric. People around Lake Fitri speak Tar Lisi. Thus, if Gaoga and Bornu spoke the same language, and if Bornu and Bulala spoke Kanuric, while the Fitri peoples spoke Tar Lisi, then Gaoga would appear to be a Bulala kingdom, which, as we saw earlier was in the Kanem. There are difficulties with this view.

First, it does not take into account the fact that Kanuric was a lingua franca throughout the east-central Sudan as late as the nineteenth century, and, given medieval Kanuri control over trade, would have been even more of one around A.D. 1500. So, when Leo was in Gaoga he may well have heard Kanuric being spoken even though he was in the Fitri, not because it was the language of the area, but because he was traveling in a body of merchants and diplomats who used it as their market language.

There are two further difficulties with Carbou's equation of Gaoga with the Kanem. The first is that it does not explain why Leo called the kingdom Gaoga. This is curious because Carbou had been careful to explain that if you add the plural suffix -ge to the name of a town, the resulting word can stand for the people of the area in Bongo-Bagirmi languages (1912). Thus, as the major town in the Fitri was Yao, the people would be called *yaoge*. Those familiar with late medieval Arabic script will realize that the symbols for *y* and *g* sounds would have been the same, and that there would have been no symbols for vowels. Thus, what European scholars transcribed as *Gaoga* could have just as correctly been written *Yaoge*. It suggests that Leo's Gaoga meant the "people of Yao," or Yaoge; which is inconsistent with its location in the Kanem.

A second difficulty with Carbou's suggestion of a Gaoga in the Kanem has to do with the strength of the Bulala in the Kanem at the time of Leo's visit. Leo arrived at precisely the time when the one-hundred-year war turned decisively in Bornu's favor. The Bornuan *mai* during Leo's visit was probably Idris Katakarambe (1507–29), who was one of the greatest warrior *mais*. During his reign the Bulala suffered the indignity of losing the old Saifwa capital, Njimi, back to the Bornuans. Such events have prompted historians such as Urvoy to assert that much of the "Kanem fell again under Saifwa domination" during the time of Leo's visit (Urvoy 1949, 73). Now, Leo had been clear about the relative strengths of Bornu and Gaoga: Gaoga was the stronger. However, the Bulala in the Kanem were clearly weaker than Bornu, making it unlikely that Gaoga was in the Kanem.

If Fisher's location of Gaoga to the southwest of Bornu seems improbable, and if Carbou's placing of it in the Kanem seems equally implausible, then Modat and Kalck's vision of a Fur-Wadaian location is the only alternative to Barth's original location of Gaoga in the Fitri. Indeed, there are reasons for suspecting this position to be correct. First, Leo had mentioned that there were Christians in Gaoga, and archaeological evidence suggests the possibility of Christians in Darfur (Adams 1986). Second, Leo had emphasized that Gaoga traded with Egypt, and the trail that led from Bornu to Egypt, the *derb arbain*, passed through Wadai and Darfur. Third, Leo had talked of the existence of mountains in Gaoga, and Wadai and Darfur had mountains.

However, it is quite possible that there were Christians around Lake Fitri. Fragments of pottery of a medieval Christian-Nubian type have been found in the Chadian Bahr el Ghazal near the Fitri (Adams 1986; Arkell 1963). On the basis of such finds, O'Fahey and Spaulding conclude, "it is becoming very likely that there was Nubian activity, possible trade, during the Christian period in the Darfur/Chad region, but the evidence is still very slim" (1974, 114). However thin, the evidence is of Christian pottery in *both* Chad and Darfur.

There is, further, every likelihood that the Fitri region traded with Egypt during Leo's time. The Saifwa in the Kanem, as documented earlier, had gained control over the *derb arbain*, which went from Lake Chad directly through the Fitri, thence in a northeasterly direction to the Dongala area of the Nile, and finally north up the Nile to Egypt by the thirteenth century. Consequently, the Fitri region was in a privileged position to participate in Egyptian commerce, and Christian merchants from the Dongala area might well be expected to trade in the Fitri.

Finally, there were mountains near Fitri both at Moyto and in the Guera. These may not have been as tall as those to the east, but they were strikingly dramatic because they rose from a dead-flat plain. Thus, the Fitri may have had some Christians, as did Wadai and Darfur; the Fitri had excellent opportunities to trade with Egypt, as did Wadai and Darfur; and the Fitri had mountains, as did Wadai and Darfur, all of which make the reasons that compelled Modat and Kalck to assign Gaoga a more easterly location seem uncompelling.[18]

There are three reasons that suggest that Gaoga was farther to the west than Modat and Kalck propose. First, Leo had specified that there was a "Gaoga Lake" (Leo Africanus 1956, 3–4). Remembrance of past lakes implies a certain lacustrine grandeur. However, no large lakes exist in the Jebel Marra or Wadai, while lakes Fitri and Chad both exist, and are imposing, near Yao. Second, Leo also insisted that Bornu was weaker than Gaoga. However, all we know of the Tunjur in the Fur-Wadai region circa 1500 suggests that they were far weaker than Bornu. Third, Leo had said: "When I was in Bornu, the king of that country, Habraam, assembled his entire army to attack the kingdom of Guargara. But when he arrived near this kingdom, he learned that Homara, lord of Gaoga, was preparing to march against Bornu and he immediately abandoned this enterprise to hastily return to his kingdom" (ibid., 479). So Gaoga, wherever it was located, had to be close enough to Bornu to strike at it. Darfur, even at the height of its powers in the eighteenth and nineteenth centuries, was simply too far away to attack Bornu, and it never did. Wadai was the exception that proved the rule. It did attack Bornu's core, just once, at the height of its power in the nineteenth century. But Wadai's logistics were so poor that even a Bornu weakened by a two-front war — to the west against the Fulani and at home against Wadai — quickly and decisively drove Wadai from Bornu. The Fitri being a few days' ride from Bornu's core, was in a much better position actually to attack it. The preceding suggests that it is unlikely that Gaoga was located to the southwest of Bornu, in the Kanem or the Wadai-Fur regions. This strengthen's the Barth/Urvoy/Palmer contention that Gaoga was in the Fitri area.

If, as appears to be the case, Gaoga was in the Fitri in the 1500s, then it could not have been a Bulala, Wadaian, or Furian state. This leaves open Palmer's suggestion of the possibility of a Dajo state in the Fitri. However, Palmer's assertions are strained. He himself provided no evidence of a Dajo presence in the Fitri (Palmer 1929, 282–83). Dajo specialists consider them to be a more easterly population (Berre 1984). Nor is there memory on the part of the people in the Fitri of a former Dajo presence (Hagenboucher 1968).

If Gaoga was not a Bulala, Furian, Wadaian, or Dajo state, then it may have been either a Kuka or Nquizim state. Kalck's insistence that it was a Kuka state ruling over Tar Lisi speakers is plausible. There was a Kuka polity in the Fitri, prior to the arrival of the Bulala, which Barth reported to be "very powerful" (1965, 545), and which Carbou said "exercised a type of supremacy in all this area" (1912, 1:294). Urvoy's view that the Nquizim controlled Gaoga is consistent with Kalck's view of a Kuka Gaoga. This is because Urvoy places Gaoga at Fitri, realizes that Gaoga antedates the Bulala's arrival there, and so associates Gaoga with the people resident in the region. He believed these people were called Nquizims (1949, 35). However, if Nquizims resided at Fitri they would have been Tar Lisi speakers, and the major Tar Lisi ethnic group was the Kuka.

Thus it is plausible that Gaoga was a Kuka, Tar Lisi–speaking state. This state, however, might well have formed to the east of the Fitri. This is because abundant surface water and fertile soils made Lake Fitri an agriculturally attractive area. Nachtigal said, "In the Fitri region . . . (millet) is actually sown twice a year in the neighborhood of the lake, at the beginning of the autumn rains and in the winter or spring" (Nachtigal 1971, 142). The ability to double crop is rare in the central Sudan and perhaps explains why an inhabitant of the area asked of Nachtigal, "Is there any sweeter land than the Fitri region?" (ibid., 36). Nachtigal also observed that the Batha and Buteha rivers, which flow into the eastern part of Lake Fitri, are "the water arteries of the country" (ibid., 138). The years prior to A.D. 1200 were moister than today, and those following A.D. 1200 were ones of desiccation. Barth reports that the original Kuka capital was at Chibina, roughly half the distance between Lake Fitri and the Wadai Massif on the Batha River (1965, 545). This suggests that certain Tar Lisi speakers were originally resident along the Batha River towards the Wadai Massif. If this was the case, then when the desiccation set in after A.D. 1200, they would have "followed the water." This would have been in a westerly direction down the Batha toward Lake Fitri.

There was a second Tar Lisi polity that was called Medogo and was located to the east of Kuka. Very little is known about the Medogo; however, today they reside east of Lake Fitri, south of Ati at El Birni. Their historical traditions give them a common origin with the Kuka, with both groups claiming to have originated to the east of their present location along the Batha and Buteha rivers. It is unclear when Medogo centralized. Medogo traditions, as collected by Carbou, suggest that some hierarchy was created when a person from Wadai, named Mudgo, arrived and established "his sovereignty" (Carbou 1912, 1:348). These same traditions make it clear that this occurred "well before" Abd el-Kerim reestablished his dynasty in Wadai, which was circa 1635 (ibid., 339). The traditions further state that Kuka and Medogo originally were "related tribes" resident in the area around El Birni, and that the Kuka were obliged to move to the west and their eventual location at Lake Fitri (ibid., 339–40). Kuka's as opposed to Medogo's, displacement could have meant that the latter were the stronger group at this time. If, as Leo suggests, Gaoga centralized circa 1400, and if Gaoga was Yaoge, then it is plausible that Medogo was also centralized as early as A.D. 1400.

A third Tar Lisi state, named Babelyia, also emerged. This was situated to the east of the Shari river immediately south of Lake Chad. Its capital was at Dal. Babelyian traditions place its centralization at the end of the thirteenth century. Carbou says that the kingdom was formed when certain people left the Kanem and came to reside in what was to be Babelyia during the reign of *mai* Ibrahim, who ruled at the end of the thirteenth century. This would have been at the beginning of the time of troubles for the Saifwa dynasty. According to traditions collected by Carbou, a "migration took place under the leadership of two princes belonging to a junior branch of the royal family of Kanem" (Carbou 1912, 1:336). This migration may have taken place because of the political instabilities during the time of troubles. It may also have occurred because of the progressive desiccation after A.D. 1200. Finally, the environmental deterioration and the political instability may have been linked. Whatever the reason, the migrants would have diffused Saifwa notions of statehood to the southern lands. It is improbable that this migration could have included many Kanuric speakers, because Babelyia remained a Tar Lisi–speaking state like the Kuka and Medogo.

Leo Africanus gives a remarkable account of when and why Gaoga's centralization occurred that may have implications for the Tar Lisi–speaking polities.

> The people of Gaoga had for a long time lived in liberty. But one hundred years earlier a Negro slave of this country took it from them. He was brought there by his master, a very rich merchant. . . . He killed his master . . . and took this man's goods, which included loaded camels, cloth and weapons. He returned to his house and divided all of these between his relatives and friends. After having purchased several horses from white merchants, he began to undertake expeditions in the lands of his enemies. He was always victorious because his men had modern arms, while his enemies had only poor bows and arrows. He amassed many slaves whom he exchanged for horses coming from Egypt, and, the number of his soldiers having grown, he was obeyed by everybody, who considered him as their chief and lord. (Leo Africanus 1956, 481–82)[19]

What is important about Leo's account of the origin of Gaoga is that only a century had elapsed between the events and his report. Equally important is that Leo was a diplomat, presumably experienced in political reporting, which suggests that his information would be reliable.

Leo's Gaoga was founded some time immediately after A.D. 1400. These were the Saifwa times of troubles. Twelve *mais* ruled between 1389 and 1459 and rather ineffectually flailed out at each other, as well as at Arabs, Bulala, and the Sao (Zeltner 1980, 82). This Saifwa confusion would have left something of a power vacuum among peoples to the southeast of the Kanem. One of these peoples may have been the Kuka located on the *derb arbain* near Chibina.

But, as we suspected for the Zagawa, and actually saw for the Saifwa when they ruled the Kanem, the way to trade was to have an organization, a state, that could conduct war to collect the commodities traded. This is precisely what Leo reported to have happened during Gaoga's founding: the founder "amassed many slaves whom he exchanged for horses . . . and, the number of his soldiers having grown, he was obeyed." This sentence indicates a sequence: first, slaves were acquired; second, they were used to trade for horses; third, horses were used to increase the size of the military; fourth, this increased the number of the "obedient"—that is, the size of the centralized polity. In short, participation in the trans-Saharan trade increased military capacity, or what we shall later call the forces of domination, which extended political domination through state formation. It is possible that Kuka grew in this way, eventually establishing a rough dominion over the other Tar Lisi states, thereby creating what Leo would call Gaoga.

If the period A.D. 900–1248 saw the origin and first expansion of the east-central Sudanic state, then that between A.D. 1248 and circa 1500 saw its diffusion out of what is today desert into the Sudan. When it went south, it went first to Tar Lisi speakers, who were probably subject peoples of the Kanem states. These new polities formed a band of three kingdoms. Barth has said that the Kuka were, prior to the arrival of the Bulala, "very powerful, occupying a great extent of country, from the eastern part of Bagirmi as far as the interior of Darfur" (1965, 545), which suggests a rough hegemony of the Kuka over other Tar Lisi states. This was a veritable Magna Kuka—a vast area stretching well over a thousand kilometers from the Shari River in the west to Darfur in the east, possible larger than fifteenth-century Bornu. Such a Magna Kuka had, in short, just the right dimensions required for Leo's Gaoga.

What is striking about the arid east-central Sudan is that it bred states. Between A.D. 900 and 1800 at least eleven states were formed and survived for extensive periods. These were, moving from west to east, Bornu, Sao-Kotoko, Zagawa, Saifwa Kanem, Bulala Kanem, Babelyia, Bagirmi (discussed in chapter 3), Kuka, Medogo, Tunjur Wadai, and Abd el-Kerim's Wadai.

An Interpretation of East-Central Sudanic History

How is this history to be interpreted? One view that may be developed has to do with the proliferation of trade and markets that was associated with political centralization. There was, as has already been documented, a trans-Saharan trading sector in the east-central Sudan. There were also regional long-distance and local trades, which, while not as spectacular as their trans-Saharan counterpart, may well have exceeded it in volume, and which involved, as Barth noted, "a real exchange of necessaries and wants" (1965, 1:515–16). The long-distance regional trade, for example, involved both north-south and east-west exchanges. Kola nuts were traded north into the Sudan from the forest; salt, dates, and animals were traded south into the Sudan from the desert. The east-west trade involved food, clothes, pottery, hides and leather goods, and metal and metal goods. Local trade allowed peoples exploiting different aspects of a community to exchange their products. Pastoralists exchanged dairy products against farmers' cereals.[20] Commerce in the east-central Sudan "followed the flag" in the sense that, as old states extended their domination or new ones created theirs, trade and markets followed into the newly dominated lands.

Certain conclusions that have been offered for neighboring regions have implications for interpretations of the history of the east-central Sudan. Spaulding has argued that commercial growth in Sennar, in the eastern Sudan, between 1750 and 1850 led "to the adoption of bourgeois institutions" (1985, 150) that were associated with the rise of a "commercial capitalism" (ibid., xviii). He appears to be saying that the growth of states stimulated the rise of markets, which encouraged capitalism. Studies suggest a similar trajectory in the Hausa area of the west-central Sudan in the nineteenth century (Shea 1975; Tahir 1975). What was happening in the east-central Sudan between A.D. 900 and 1800 does not appear, however, to have been the rise of capitalism. Rather it was something quite different.

Capitalism, following its classic exposition in *Capital* (Marx 1981), is the production of goods for exchange on the market by "capitalists," those who combine capital and land, which they own, with labor power, which they buy from free, propertyless workers, the "proletariat." So for capitalism to exist, there must minimally be widespread markets, especially for labor, and there must be production units consisting of capitalists buying the labor of proletarians.

The market was by no means the dominant distributive institution in the east-central Sudan by A.D. 1800. Marketplaces existed, but they were only common where there were states. This meant that markets were relatively rare in the moist Sudan among the largely acephalous cereal producers. Thus, even though markets existed, most agricultural and craft products and services never appear to have reached a marketplace in the east-central Sudan. Studies conducted in the 1950s and 1960s in more accessible regions of Chad suggest that 80–90 percent of the average household's agricultural products were not marketed (INSEE 1967). There is no reason to suggest that this situation was any different in precolonial times. Crucially, there was almost no market for labor, even in the states. Rather, various reciprocities deriving from peoples' social, largely kin, identities circulated most labor services.

The growth of states seems to have had little effect upon production in the east-central Sudan. There were two major productive sectors by 1800. The first, and more important, was food production. The second was crafts, especially textiles. The archeologist G. Connah has excavated a Sao site known as Daima, which is directly south of Lake Chad. He reports that by circa A.D. 1000 "the villagers of Daima III must have been sorghum farmers who employed falling-flood techniques, kept mixed livestock, did a little hunting, fishing, fowling and collecting" (1981, 195). This is precisely the farming system that exists around contemporary Daima, so that Connah concludes that by A.D. 1000 the Sao had "evolved all the essential elements of the mixed farming economy [that exist at] the present time" (ibid., 195). There is no systematic archaeological analysis of east-central Sudanic crafts. The archaeology that does exist suggests that all the metal, clay, and cloth implements that would be produced by the nineteenth century were in production by the Middle Ages circa A.D. 1200. Certainly, the vast bulk of the agricultural or craft products produced in the east-central Sudan by A.D. 1800 came from households organized on the basis of kinship, not from firms hiring wage labor.

Goody used the term *stagnation* to characterize economies throughout the precolonial Sudan (1971). Such an adjective seems descriptive of production and provokes the question, If a capitalism did not arise in the east-central Sudan, then what did?

The historian Anders Bjorkelo, toward the end of his analysis of the central Sudan, was struck by "a close relationship between the military organization, the slave raids and the commercial contact with the Sahara and North Africa, centered on slaves" (1976, 183). Such a close relationship was certainly present in the easternmost portion of the central Sudan, and it cast the previously noted social types as actors with strikingly different roles in a regional structure.

States, as was earlier suggested, warred to trade and traded to war. War and trade drew the other societies in the east-central Sudan into the coils of the states, forming a regional structure. The parts in this structure were the different social types in their respective regions. The relationships between the parts were these types' different activities in war and trade. The states acquired the major commodity exchanged, the slaves, by warring and capturing other peoples. The act of capturing a person transformed her or him into a commodity. War in this sense "produced" commodities. The warfare of the states was an offensive warfare that allowed them to be sellers of products in the trans-Saharan trade.

Generally, slaves were sold by the states to merchants, who transported them across the desert, where they were again sold. The desert specialists—part transportation service, part protection racket—assured the journey of caravans across the desert. They, however, had to be cautious, for the states would attack them when possible. The microenvironmental specialists used their environment as a shield to avoid participation in the trade. Their role, thus, was in a sense no role, at least in the trans-Saharan trade. But in order to enjoy this role they had to war with the states, so they had withdrawn into specialized environments that they could use as defensive weapons against the assaults of states. Cereal producers had no such shields. Thus, even though they waged continual defensive war, they became, at least by the nineteenth century, the major reservoir of products for the trans-Saharan trade.

In this regional system, then, the states conducted offensive warfare, and as a result they became the big sellers in the trans-Saharan trade, while the cereal producers, microenvironmental specialists, and occasionally the desert pastoralists conducted defensive warfare and as result participated in the trade as the items traded. Whatever this system was, it was not the capitalism of Manchester so close to Marx!

Its captains were not metaphorical captains of industry. They were not a bourgeoisie devoted to the calculation of profits and losses. Rather, they were in Sheikh al-Maglili's terms, daring "birds of prey" with bands of "sentries, bowmen, horse, and foot." Theirs was not a capitalist system but one of predatory accumulation. To create such an interpretation of the precolonial history of the east-central Sudan, however, we need a model of this predatory accumulation, and formulation of such a model requires the exploration in detail of one particular predator. It is time to give Bagirmi its place in east-central Sudanic history.

Chapter 3

Origins and Other "Impressive Things"

This chapter speculates about the origins of Bagirmi and then outlines what its traditions insist were some of the "impressive things" that occurred during its history. An ecological argument that modifies Carneiro's (1970) circumscription theory of state formation is presented to account partially for the rise of the Sun Kings' state.

Origins

Bagirmi's place in the Sudanic periphery was in the old first delta of Lake Chad. Its core was along the Shari and Bahr Erguig rivers, roughly from contemporary N'Djamena in the north to Bousso in the south. This dry Sudanic core was surrounded in 1800 by allied territories that extended from Moyto in the north to the Bahr Salamat in the south and from the Batha Lairi in the east to the Shari in the west. In total, Greater Bagirmi occupied an area of approximately seventy-five thousand square kilometers. It might be imagined as a football pointed in a northwesterly direction from what is today moist Sudan toward the more arid north.

Granite peaks were scattered about northern Bagirmi at Moyto and Aouni. There was also a sprinkling of hills in the east at Melfi, where the Guera begins. In general, however, Bagirmi was, and is, a flat plain filigreed by streams winding toward lakes Chad and Fitri. This plain was dusty, blazing hot, and empty of most vegetation during the dry season (October through May), when all waters ceased to flow save for the Shari. But the empty watercourses refilled when the rains came, creating streams and swamps, confounding transportation but transforming the bleached plains into verdant prairies alive with the colors and scents of flowers, butterflies, and birds.[1] This area would have been the southernmost portion of Magna Kuka.

Nachtigal calculated the date when he thought the first *mbang* may have started to rule in this region by adding the total number of years of each sovereign's reign and then subtracting this total from the present. Using this procedure, he suggested that the first *mbang* may have begun his reign about 1522 (1889, 693). Barth, apparently using a similar procedure, said that the kingdom began some three hundred years prior to

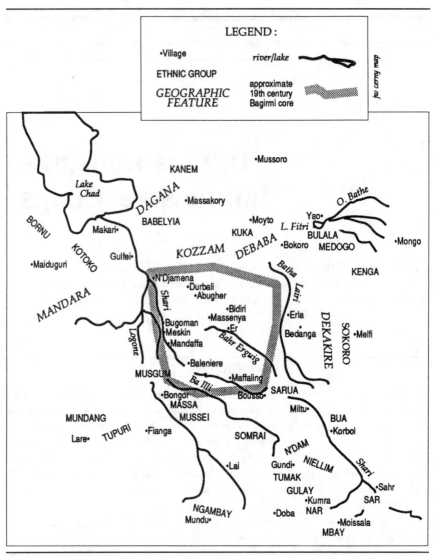

LEGEND :

•Village

ETHNIC GROUP

GEOGRAPHIC FEATURE

river/lake

approximate 19th century Bagirmi core

fw cerny map

•Mussoro

KANEM

Lake Chad

DAGANA

•Massakory

O. Bathe

BORNU

Makari•

BABELYIA

•Moyto

Yao•

L. Fitri

KUKA

KOZZAM

DEBABA

•Bokoro

BULALA

MEDOGO

•Mongo

KOTOKO

Gulfei•

•Maiduguri

•N'Djamena

Batha

KENGA

•Durbali

•Abugher

Shari

•Bidiri

•Massenya

Lairi

•Erla

MANDARA

Bugoman•

Meskin•

•Mandaffa

•Er

Bedanga•

DEKAKIRE

•Melfi

SOKORO

Logone

Bahr Erguig

•Baleniere

MUSGUM

Ba III.

•Maffaling

•Bousso

SARUA

•Bongor

MASSA

MUSSEI

Miltu•

BUA

•Korbol

MUNDANG

Lare•

TUPURI

•Fianga

SOMRAI

N'DAM

NIELLIM

Shari

•Lai

Gundi•

TUMAK

GULAY

•Kumra

•Sahr

SAR

NGAMBAY

Mundu•

•Doba

NAR

•Moissala

MBAY

Map 3.1. Bagirmi.

his visit, which would have placed its origin circa 1552 (1965, 550). Vivien, following a comparison of five genealogies of Bagirmi rulers, placed the origin of the kingdom somewhere between the end of the fifteenth and the middle of the sixteenth century (1967). Furthermore, the sixteenth-century Italian geographer d'Anania mentions the existence of Bagirmi in his world geography (1582, 349). If Bagirmi was important enough to require mention by Europeans in the 1580s, then it had probably already been centralized for some time. How did this occur?

According to certain traditional Bagirmi accounts, their kingdom began when the first *mbang* was brought to earth by a whirlwind (*gugari*) in a pirogue containing himself and his first two wives (Pacques 1977, 34, 42). Whirlwinds skipping across the plains are a common sight in Bagirmi. I believe that certain climatic changes that appear to have occurred in the east-central Sudan in the centuries prior to Bagirmi's founding were an example of what might be termed environmental reversal, and that this, like the mythological whirlwinds, spun out a centralized polity considerably earlier than the traditional dates contained in the accounts of Barth and Nachtigal.

The concept of environmental reversal is derived from Carneiro's speculations about state formation. His theory of the origin of the state hypothesizes that population growth can lead to increased warfare, and that increased warfare can, in turn, lead to the state in circumscribed environments. Important to this view is the concept of environmental circumscription. This is an idea about a confined space, a region where "mountains, seas or deserts . . . sharply delimit the area that simple farming peoples could occupy and cultivate" (Carneiro 1970, 734–35). When there is war in an uncircumscribed environment, such as the Amazon, the losers tend to drift off, out of reach of their victorious opponents. Losing is a radically different proposition, however, in a circumscribed environment. Losers cannot drift off, or they can only do so in small numbers at great risk into hostile deserts and the like. This means that losers must stay and face the music. This music is a situation in which winners have already established their power over losers, thereby creating a power hierarchy, which, according to Carneiro, is at the origin of the state. Carneiro used the notion of circumscribed environment to account for the origin of pristine states, those formed in the absence of other states (Fried 1967).

Secondary states are those formed in the presence of other states. There probably have been states in the Kanem since A.D. 1100. Then circa 1400, the states appeared to the south in the lands along the Shari and Bahr Erguig in southern Magna Kuka. Bagirmi was therefore a secondary state in Fried's terms, and it raises a question as to why secondary state formation occurred when it did. The notion of environmental reversal may help answer this question.

Occasionally, as climate changes, livable environments become less so, while inhospitable ones become more livable. Environmental reversal refers to reversals in the habitable and circumscribed components of a circumscribed environment. Specifically, it is the situation where formerly habitable regions in a circumscribed environment become less so, while formerly circumscribed ones in that same circumscribed environment become more livable. For example, a circumscribed environment might include a habitable flood plain by a river, and an inhospitable, or circumscribing, desert surrounding the flood plain. When rainfall increased in this region, the former flood plain might become too flooded for farming, while its surrounding desert bloomed as an arable savanna. If this occurred, the circumscribed environment would be said to be subject to environmental reversal. The environment in Carneiro's analysis is unchanging. The notion of environmental reversal puts the environment in motion.

Environmental reversal promotes social transformation by geographically shifting the areas where people can subsist, thereby obliging them to move their institutions. It is the diffusion of institutions from formerly into currently habitable areas that results in social changes in the latter area. This is precisely what appears to have been at the origin of Bagirmi. The argument to suggest that this was, indeed, the case proceeds as follows. First, we examine and reject an alternative possibility, which is that the state was brought to Bagirmi by persons who migrated very long distances from the east. Then we show how the area of Bagirmi and the Kanem was part of a common circumscribed environment subject to environmental reversal subsequent to A.D. 1200, which appears to have injected certain northerly state activities into the lands along the middle Shari and Bahr Erguig rivers. It will then be shown how the affairs of northern states may have provoked Bagirmi's founding.

The Case for Eastern Origins

Medieval peoples living around Lake Chad lived in walled cities with paved streets. They enjoyed sophisticated crafts and architecture. They were governed by the state. So they were judged to have achieved the level of "civilization" (Lebeuf and Lebeuf 1950). Earlier scholars often claimed that "high" aspects of east-central Sudanic society were brought by Promethean migrants who brought the fire of civilization from the Near East. In fact almost all Bongo-Bagirmi speakers have traditions of migration sometime in the Middle Ages from Yemen.[2] Such origins are claimed by the Kuka (Carbou 1912, 1:339), the Sara (Kogongar 1971), the Bulala (Carbou 1912 1:300–302), the Medogo (ibid.,) and Bagirmi (Pacques 1977). Bagirmi, in fact, claims two migrations: first, a long one from Arabia, followed by a shorter one from the Kenga region. Such migrations should leave linguistic, paleobotanical, and physical anthropological traces.

Remember that Bongo-Bagirmi speakers inhabit the entire region between the Shari and Batha Lairi rivers. The Tar Lisi speakers (Bulala, Medogo, and Kuka) and the Babelyia are in the north. The Barma and Kenga, who speak Tar Barma and Tar Kenga, are in the center. The Sara speakers are distributed from the Logone to Lake Iro in the south (see map 2.1). An exact comparison and classification of these languages remains to be performed. However, it is clear that they are a set of related but distinct languages.[3]

It takes a very long time, on the order of millennia, for distinct languages belonging to a family of languages to evolve from a proto-language. Thus, unless there is clear evidence of origin outside the present area of distribution, it would appear that the Bongo-Bagirmi speakers in Chad have been in roughly their present location for thousands of years.

There are two possible reasons to consider a more easterly origin of Bongo-Bagirmi languages. The first is that this is what their traditions say was the case, and the second is the existence of Bongo-Bagirmi languages in the Sudan. In fact, when one examines the legitimacy of different traditional claims to an eastern origin, one does find movements, but only of modest dimensions. The Bulala actually seem to have come not from the east but from the Borkou in the north (Chapelle 1980). The Kuka, as we speculated in chapter 2, may have drifted a few hundred miles west to their present location. This also appears to be the case for the Medogo. Similarly, with regard to the Sara, there are only legendary claims of major migrations from the east, while the actual evidence of migration suggests only a gradual drift of a short distance from the northeast to present locations in the southwest (E. Brown, personal communication).

Most of my Bagirmi informants viewed the tradition of a Yemeni origin for Bagirmi as legend. They did think it possible that some Barma could have come from Kenga territory, but this would have meant a mere five-day stroll from the Guera.

There were strong political reasons for groups to claim Middle Eastern origins even, if they were fictitous, because the attachment of a state or a people to a person of importance in Islamic tradition transferred some of that person's prominence to the state or people. Such attachment was established largely through descent from major Islamic ancestors. Thus, Abd el Tukruru, who was claimed as an ancestor of the first Bagirmi *mbang*, was himself stipulated to be a descendant of Hassan, son of Ali, who was both a cousin and a son-in-law of the Prophet Mohammed. This situated Bagirmi in the *shi'ite* tradition, but more importantly it gave Bagirmi a more prominent Muslim heritage than Bornu because the *mais* only claimed descent from Husain. The way Bagirmi saw it, Husain and Hassan were brothers, but Husain was the younger and hence the less important, which meant that Bornu was less important than Bagirmi. Claims of a Yemeni origin make little sense linguistically and a great deal of sense in terms of central Sudanic political realities.

Some Bongo-Bagirmi languages, notably Bongo, are located in the Republic of Sudan, so it is *thinkable* that the proto-Bongo-Bagirmi language was in the east near the Nile. There is, however, no hard evidence that this was the case; and a priori, it is just as plausible that the languages began in the west and spread east. There is evidence for just this sort of movement among the Bongo. The Bongo lived in the Bahr el Ghazel in the Republic of Sudan, which placed them close to the Azande. Evans-Pritchard, who surveyed the area in the 1920s, reported: "Numerous tribal units . . . have been cut off from the main body and swept permanently out of touch with men of their own language and blood. . . . Many tribes have been carried before waves of Zande invasion to distant strands" (1929). The Zande waves are known to have pushed the Bongo in an easterly direction (ibid.). Such evidence does not prove that all Bongo-Bagirmi languages arose in the west and drifted eastward. It does prove that this occurred in one instance, which is evidence that is inconsistent with an origin of Bongo-Bagirmi languages in the Republic of Sudan. So the ball would appear to be in the court of those seeking to make the reverse case.

Certain paleobotanical speculations appear to return the ball to an eastern court of origin for Bongo-Bagirmi languages. Research conducted at the Crop Evolution Laboratory at the University of Illinois concerning the domestication of sorghum suggested that a race of sorghum known as caudatum may have been domesticated between A.D. 350 and 900 (1975:177). The laboratory's researchers, further observed that the "distribution of caudatum sorghums and Shari-Nile speaking peoples coincides so closely that a causal relationship seems probable" (ibid. 182)—that is, that Shari-Nile speakers domesticated this type of sorghum. Further, they believed that "the large number of varieties of caudatum in the Republic of Sudan suggests that . . . [it] may have been developed there" (ibid. 183). Bongo-Bagirmi speakers do grow caudatums. If correct, this hypothesis may mean either that the Bongo-Bagirmi branch of Shari-Nile speakers moved from the east to the west carrying with them their seeds, or that the seeds were diffused, without migration, from east to west. If the former possibility is correct, then Bongo-Bagirmi speakers would have migrated relatively late to their present locations, sometime after A.D. 950.

There are reasons to be skeptical of assertions that caudatum was domesticated in the Republic of Sudan. The only evidence for this hypothesis is the greater number of caudatum varieties found in there than in Chad. However, there was far less botanical research in Chad than in the Sudan during the colonial period. This situation persists in postcolonial times, in no small measure because of the Chadian civil war. Thus, it is possible that more caudatum varieties have been found in the Sudan than in Chad simply because more botanists have spent more time searching for them.

Such reasoning may have occurred to the Crop Evolution Laboratory researchers because they do not give caudatum an origin in the Republic of Sudan in a later article (Harlan and Stemler 1976). Rather, in this article the entire eastern and central Sudan are suggested as the place of domestication (ibid., 475–77). This means that at present there does not appear to be sufficient information to pinpoint exactly where in the eastern or central Sudan the caudatums were domesticated.[4]

A final point: Connah has found caudatum at Daima at a level dated to be circa A.D. 1000 (1981, 190–91). The peoples at Daima were likely to have been Sao, who are likely to have been the population that became Kotoko, who speak a Chadic language. Therefore, caudatum would have had to get to the east-central Sudan before A.D. 1000 if it was developed in the present Republic of Sudan and carried by proto-Bongo-Bagirmi speakers to Chad. This is well prior to the time of Bagirmi's founding, which suggests that Bagirmi speakers were roughly in their contemporary locations before the time of Bagirmi's founding.

Very little research in human biology has been conducted in the east-central Sudan. However, Crognier studied a number of Sara populations and suggested that certain aspects of their morphology were genetic responses to their diet, which, in turn, largely consisted of sorghums that were adapted to their savanna habitat. In short, Crognier argued that Sara populations exhibit genetic adaptions to their environment (1969). This prompted Hiernaux to observe that "the Sara group of tribes . . . have occupied their fairly homogeneous biotope since time immemorial" (1975, 164).

In summary, current linguistic, botanical, and physical anthropological research provide no clear evidence of any long-distance movements by Bongo-Bagirmi speakers, from either the Middle East or the Republic of Sudan. Further, linguistic and physical anthropological evidence suggests that Bongo-Bagirmi speakers have resided for a long time—perhaps millennia—where they do today. Thus it appears that the state was not brought to Bagirmi like some Promethean fire by outsiders from a "higher" civilization. Rather, it seems to have been a product of local forces, and environmental reversal may have been the most important of these.

The Case for Environmental Reversal

Climatological conditions were changing in the regions surrounding Lake Chad subsequent to A.D. 1200 for reasons that are unknown. Maley's work allows us to follow the dimensions of these changes. Figure 3.1, derived from this work, reports fluctuations in the level of Lake Chad over the last one thousand years. It shows a lake at an elevation of 286 meters circa A.D. 1200 a level at which the lake extends into the Djourab. Next the lake declines following A.D. 1200. This is precipitous in the first fifty years of the thirteenth century, with the lake dropping to about 280 meters. Then it rises until about 1500, when it is at about 283 meters, after which it begins another precipitous decline during the first half of the sixteenth century. The curve of lake levels in the 350 years between A.D. 1200 and 1550 rises and plunges, like a roller coaster, but with a downward trend. This decline indicates environmental reversal.

Such reversal occurred because reduction of the lake levels resulted from declines in precipitation in the areas surrounding Lake Chad. Remember that there is a north-south rainfall gradient in the east-central Sudan, with the north getting far less precipitation. Rainfall reduction around the lake meant that certain northern areas that had formerly had sufficient rainfall for farming withered, while certain southern areas that were formerly too inundated for farming became arable plains.

The areas subject to extreme desiccation during this time were the Kanem, the Bahr el Ghazel, the Equei, and the Djourab. Lake Chad covered much of the Bahr el Ghazel as far north as the Djourab in the years immediately prior to A.D. 1200. The areas near this lake were probably Sahelian or arid savanna in climate. There would have been enormous stretches of fertile farmland along the shores of the lake. This old lake might be thought of as a balloon and the desiccation as the letting of air out of it. In the end all that was left of the pre–A.D. 1200 lake was a thin ribbon of moisture threading up the Bahr el Ghazel. Hundreds of thousands of hectares may have been transformed into barely habitable desert or subdesert from A.D. 1200 through 1800.

This same desiccation affected the area immediately to the south along the Shari and Bahr Erguig rivers, the region that was to become Bagirmi. Chevalier described what it was like prior to the desiccation. "All the country stretching from the lower

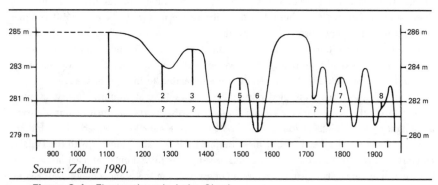

Source: *Zeltner 1980.*

Figure 3.1. Fluctuations in Lake Chad.

Bahr Salamat and Lake Iro to the lower Bahr el Ghazel, more than 300 kilometers wide, was at some time that is impossible to tell, but truly not very distant, covered with innumerable streams communicating with each other by an infinity of arms, sometimes squeezing around granite peaks, sometimes emptying into huge lagoons of which Lake Iro and Fitri are the last vestiges" (Chevalier 1907, 337). The landscape would have been like the Salamat today, too flooded for many people to reside there because it was inundated by "huge lagoons" into which "innumerable streams" emptied. Millets and most sorghum would not grow under such humid conditions, and it is improbable that forest crops were available. Thus during moister times the Shari–Bahr Erguig area might have been attractive to fisherfolk and unattractive to farmers because their crops would literally bog down in the vast swamps.

However, "in our times," again according to Chevalier, "all this country [is] actually threatened by complete sterility in consequence of the extension of the Saharan climate" (1907, 337). Chevalier's sterility might be taken with a grain of salt, because the receding waters revealed rich alluvial soils in previously flooded lakes and watercourses. These would be of especial interest as rainy season fields for sorghum and dry season pastures for cattle. Farther away from the watercourses, sandy soils that in the past had received too much rainfall for millet now received appropriate amounts of precipitation for this crop. Major streams remained along which fishing might continue. Thus the climatic shift affecting the area around Lake Chad between A.D. 1200 and circa 1522 increasingly transformed northern lands into subdesert and desert and southern ones into dry Sudan. These were environmental reversals: the north became far less habitable, and the reverse was true in the south.

We turn now to certain historical sources that suggest some of the effects of the environmental reversals upon the peoples in this area. There are few—and those often debatable—references to Magna Kuka and the lands along the middle Shari and Bahr Erguig rivers in the medieval literature. However, those snippets that do exist hint that centralization was occurring in these lands well prior to the traditional date of Bagirmi's founding.

We begin with the chronicles and praise songs of the medieval rulers of Kanem and Bornu. Palmer, in the third volume of *Sudanese Memoirs*, presented a list of Saifwa *mais* that included, among other things, their burial places. There were 63 *mais* on the list who ruled from circa A.D. 800 to 1808. Strikingly, he reported that three of these, and only three, were buried in the Fitri between A.D. 1377 and 1400 (Palmer 1967, 3:43). It is not absolutely certain that the three *mais* were buried in the Fitri.[5] However, they were buried at exactly the time when Leo Africanus said Gaoga began and possibly in exactly the place where we suspect this occurred. If this was the case, it would be improbable that their deaths were unrelated to the rise of Gaoga.

Further, the three *mais* died during the Saifwa time of troubles when they were expelled from the Kanem by the Bulala. In fact, Barth reports that their deaths occurred after fighting the Bulala (1965, 586–87). If the three *mais* were buried where Palmer reported them to have been, and if these burials occurred after combat with the Bulala, as Barth suggested, then the Saifwa-Bulala rivalry was played out—at least in part—in the Fitri. This suggests that the warfare among polities in the Kanem may have been an expression of the environmental reversals. Specifically, they may have fought to control the *kaiga*—subject peoples—in the increasingly habitable Magna Kuka as their own environment in the Kanem became more arid.

The earliest mention of Bagirmi appears to have been a praise song honoring the first Muslim *mai*, Humai (c. A.D. 1100). A portion of this song, which exults in martial prowess, goes: "Hail all powerful . . . who went to the Wabe wars 330 times . . . You put to flight a warrior Dala, son of Mukka, chief of Mobber, during the freshness of the rainy season. Again and again you put him to flight. . . . And captured [from his following] a thousand slaves, and took them and scattered them in the open places of Bagirmi" (in Palmer 1970a, 161). This song by no means establishes that there was a state in Bagirmi in the twelfth century even if it does refer to twelfth-century events. It does, however, confirm a Saifwa remembrance that the region that would be Bagirmi had been used by the Kanem state for its own purposes as a place of colonization.

The Bornuan king list, called the *diwan*, together with other east-central Sudanic documents, hints at conflict between Kanem and the area that was to become Bagirmi in the thirteenth and fourteenth centuries. The *diwan*, discussing the reign of Dunama Dibale (1210–48), says, "In his time began the war against Ghayu son of L.f.r.d" (in Lange 1977, 72). The passage does not indicate who Ghayu was. Lange, however, suspects that he may have been a Bagirmi "king" (ibid.). Dunama Dibale was the *mai* at the apogee of Saifwa rule in the Kanem. It was he who extended Kanem's rule as far north as the Fezzan and as far east as the Nile. If Saifwa authority extended this far, it is plausible that it could have been felt by their immediate neighbors a few days' easy ride to the south.

Palmer refers to a Bornuan document that includes a phrase to the effect that "in 648 AH [A.D. 1250], Othman Kadeni, the Magumi prince who eventually succeeded as *mai* Othman [Biri] ibn Zeinab, who at that time lived in Bikoro in Begharmi" (1970a, 186). If the document to which Palmer refers is accurate, it suggests that members of the Saifwa royal family resided in "Bikoro" in the reign immediately following Dunuma's, that is, that of Kade (1248–77). Bikoro is probably contemporary Bokoro in the extreme northeastern part of Bagirmi about fifty kilometers southwest of Lake Fitri.

The document mentions nothing about conflict, though it is improbable that Biri was at Bokoro for his health. In fact, the assumption of a residence by a royal official implies a Saifwa interest in southern Magna Kuka. Urvoy has suggested that, before Bagirmi achieved statehood, it was used by Kanem as "a hunting zone for slaves" (1949, 88). The Bokoro area would have been a fine jumping-off spot to conduct such operations. When Othman ibn Zeinab (1288–1306) did come to rule in the Kanem, he did so just before the Saifwa time of troubles and just after the environmental reversals had begun. This raises the possibility that he was in Bikoro because the desiccation in the north motivated Kanemi polities to extend their subject peoples from northern to southern Magna Kuka.

There is a possible sighting of Bagirmi during the reign of *mai* Abd Allah (1315–35), who was the *mai* after Othman ibn Zeinab's son had ruled. The *diwan* says of Abd Allah, "In his time war took place between him and Ghayu son of D.r.gh.z.na" (in Lange 1977, 74). There is controversy as to just who was Abd Allah's opponent. Barth thought him to be an official in the Kanem state whose title was *bagharima* (1965, 585). Barth did not know over what area this *bagharima* presided, though he insisted that it was not Bagirmi (ibid., 591.) Nachtigal suggested he had responsibilities over a region called Bagari sough and west of Kukawa, Bornu's nineteenth-century capital (1889, 1720). Lange thought both Barth and Nachtigal were confused, because he felt that grammatical analysis of the text of the *diwan* indicated Abd Allah's opponent to be the "king of Bagirmi" (Lange 1977, 74).

A manuscript published in Palmer may clarify this difference of opinion. It says of Abd Allah's reign, "In his time, his friend the Baghari-ma [Balakma] waged war against Gayu, the ruler of Dar Massenya" (in Palmer 1970a, 195). Thus the document suggests that Barth may have, indeed, been confused. The *bagharima* was not Abd Allah's opponent; rather, he was the leader of an expedition against Gayu, who ruled where Bagirmi's capital was to be located. It should be noted that no Gayu is mentioned in any Bagirmi traditions.

The *mai* following Abd Allah was called Selma (1335–39). Palmer says: "According to an old tradition, which is recorded in manuscripts . . . [he] died in the Dikwa town called Ren. Three Sultans assembled . . . and found a horn, and within the horn a writing. . . . They read the writing and found two sentences as follows: 'If I die to the east of the Shari, bury me in the land of Abgar. If I die to the west . . . bury me at N'Dif'" (ibid., 196). Abgar is an old Bagirmi town, known today as Durbali. If the tradition does, indeed, refer to Selma's last request, then there had to be some reason to be buried in Abgar, which suggests that it was an important place with Saifwa connections. Whatever the reasons for Selma's last wishes, they suggest a Saifwa political interest in the lands along the Shari and Bahr Erguig rivers.

Bagirmi appears to be referred to in two medieval Arab chronicles written in the Middle East. The first mention is by Ibn Sa'id, writing in the middle of the thirteenth century (c. 1282), who apparently relied upon a lost work by Ibn Fatimat. The latter is believed to have actually visited the Kanem at the beginning of the thirteenth century. Ibn Sa'id says merely that there was a "country of Bakarmi" (in Lange 1977, 74). More explicitly, al Maqrisi (1364–1442), writing roughly a century after Ibn Sa'id and drawing some of his information from him, says: "Kanem is a great kingdom watered by the blessed Nile . . . Near them is another kingdom named Mandara, next to which are the Kotoko, Kungu and Abu Gar [Begharmi]" (in Palmer 1970a, 192). Abgar, as we just saw, is the name contemporary Bagirmi give to Durbali. Al Maqrisi's observation is important because, unlike Ibn Sa'id, who speaks only of a "country," it refers to a "kingdom." The significance of these references is twofold. First, they suggest that whatever was happening in southern Magna Kuka was important enough to attract the attention of Middle Eastern chroniclers fully a century before the traditional date of Bagirmi's founding. Second, they imply that what was happening was centralization.

It is impossible to ascertain, given present information, whether it was chiefdoms or states that were being formed. Perhaps the "kingdoms" were war camps teeming with Kanemi officials and their soldiers, who allied themselves with Bongo-Bagirmi-speaking population centers, whence they mounted raiding operations. Bagirmi officials formed just such war camps in the nineteenth century when they expanded their state southward into Sara territory. Biri's residence at Bokoro hints at such a possibility in the thirteenth century.

Another possibility is that the "kingdoms" were chiefdoms formed about particularily skillful Bongo-Bagirmi-speaking warriors to protect the local population against just such predations from the north. Such polities arose during the nineteenth century among the Bua, Sara, and Hadjeray. Gayu may well have been one of these sorts of leaders. The important point to grasp is that if the traditions are correct, then some sort of centralized polity existed in Bagirmi well before its traditional date of founding, 1522.

How does one interpret the preceding information from medieval sources? Lange, basing his analysis on much of the same material says, "The kingdom of Bagirmi was older than thought" (1977, 74). My view is slightly different. Scholars already had reason to suspect that Bagirmi was older than thought, because its traditions say that "small kingdoms" (Barth 1965, 545) existed in the area prior to the foundation of the state. Thus the state apparently created circa A.D. 1522, which we know as *the* Bagirmi, probably replaced an older polity, much as the Bulala replaced the Saifwa and the Saifwa the Zagawa in the Kanem. There appear, then, to have been two Bagirmis—one prior to A.D. 1522, about which almost nothing is known, and one subsequent to A.D. 1522.

All of the preceding evidence is consistent with the hypothesis that environmental reversals were at the origin of the older Bagirmi. Maley's work establishes that the region around Lake Chad experienced environmental reversals between A.D. 1250 and 1500. The Kanem went from a Sudanic to a desertic environment, while Magna Kuka, now understood to refer to the lands around Lake Fitri as well as those to the south along the middle Shari, experienced the reverse of what happened in the Kanem. It went from a boggish landscape to a dry Sudan.

Political activities shifted southward as these reversals were occurring. There are suggestions that *mai* Dunama Dibale (1210–48) made war in the area to be Bagirmi, that *mai* Othman ibn Zeinab's resided at Bokoro circa 1250, that *mai* Abd Allah (1315–35) made war in the area to be Bagirmi, that *mai* Selma (1335–39) wished to be buried in Abgar in the area to be Bagirmi, and finally that certain Saifwa *mai*s were buried between 1377 and 1400 in the Fitri. It would appear then that environmental reversals intensified the activities of the Kanem state in Magna Kuka and that these may have been responsible for the first Bagirmi polity.

The preceding account of Bagirmi's origins should be treated as tentative, and I stress that it is only a partial explanation of Bagirmi's origins. This is true for two reasons: first, because the account I have given is one of why the older polity might have come about; second, because while an environmental reversals hypothesis furthers understanding of how political activities might diffuse from one location to another, it is opaque to the structural transformations that actually produce the shifts in political activities.

For the moment, however, we might speculate on the perceptions of the inhabitants of the lands along the Shari and Bahr Erguig rivers in the thirteenth and fourteenth centuries. The environmental changes in their habitat would have been too gradual for them to perceive. Such would not have been the case with invading northern armies, whose cavalry would have raised huge dust clouds, which the stiff breezes would have swirled into billowing whirlwinds from which states emerged. So it is possible that the people in southern Magna Kuka might have come to associate the passing of whirlwinds with the coming of states.

"Impressive Things"

Bagirmi's subsequent precolonial history may be divided into three major periods—
formative, offensive, and defensive—when state policy appears to have exhibited different
emphases. A formative period, during the sixteenth century, lasted through the reigns of
the first four *mbangs*. The traditions suggest that this was a time when many institutions
were forged, when Islam was adopted, and when warfare subdued a core and carved
out several tributaries for the fledgling kingdom.

The traditions report memories of an aggressive polity during the seventeenth and
eighteenth centuries. Events described for the reign of the *mbang* Burkumanda I [1736–
41] are illustrative of the times.

> Burkumanda took over from his brother when he was young. He *wanted to do impressive
> things*, so he went to war.

> First, he went to the east against the Sokoros and the Kenga. The Kenga submitted without
> a fight. Then he turned his attentions northward and struck at, in turn the Medogos, the

Table 3.1. Rulers of Bagirmi.

Rulers	Reign
Birni Besse	1522–1536
Lubatko	1536–1548
Malo	1548–1568
Abd Allah	1568–1608
Omar	1608–1625
Dalai	1625–1635
Burkumanda I	1635–1665
Abd er-Rhaman	1665–1677
Dala Birni	1674–1680
Abd el-Kader I	1680–1707
Bar	1707–1722
Wanja	1722-1736
Burkumanda II	1736–1741
Loel	1741–1751
Hadji Mohamed el Amin	1751–1785
Abd er-Rhaman Gaurang I	1785-1806
Bira	1806–1807
Burkumanda III	1807–1846
Abd el-Kader II	1846–1858
Ab Sakin	1858–1877
Burkumanda IV	1877–1884
Abd er-Rhaman Gaurang II	1885–1918
Muhamad	1918–1933
Yusuf	1933–1970

*Note: The dating of the reigns from Birni Besse until Ab Sakin is that of Nachtigal (1889);
from Ab Sakin until Gaurang II, that of Devallée (1925).*

people in the Bahr el Ghazel, those of Borku, and even those around Bilma. From all these
peoples he gathered a rich booty.

He returned from the north by way of Kuri territory beside Lake Chad. Once south of
the lake, Burkumanda crossed the Shari and ravaged the Kotoko and Arabs in the region
between the Shari and the Logone. Not satisfied, he marched to the Mandara Mountain
region. He stopped to engage the Fulani at Binder. Finally, he returned to southwestern
Chad. Here his men complained that they would never return home. So only then did
Burkumanda decide to break off his campaign. After three years he returned to Massenya.

Following three years of rest, he sent his two senior war chiefs on a second expedition. They
attacked to the south in Sarua and Ndam country. Their exploits were not as successful as
those of their *mbang*, who this time stayed home in Massenya.

Wadai had, in the course of a raid on the Bulala, captured the wife of the Bulala sultan.
This woman happened to be a sister of Burkumanda, who, roused by this outrage, went to
war and defeated the sultan of Wadai.

Burkumanda is remembered as being an energetic and courageous *mbang*. [Devallee 1925,
9; emphasis added]

Such traditions suggest Bagirmi's strength vis-à-vis other states in the region. Bagirmi
was supposed to have fallen under Bornu's sovereignty between 1650 and 1675, but
this was certainly "rather honorific" (Urvoy 1949, 89), because Burkumanda warred
with impunity in Bornuan territory around Bilma. Further, Wadai during this time was
not Bagirmi's equal. Clearly, Bagirmi fielded a formidable military machine during its
apogee and may well have enjoyed a rough hegemony in the east-central Sudan.

Military might may have given Bagirmi access to trans-Saharan trade routes. This
is possible for two reasons. First, Bulala had been incorporated into the Bagirmi polity
by the beginning of the seventeenth century. This meant that Bagirmi could influence
events along that portion of the *derb arbain* that passed through the Fitri area. Second,
certain of the military adventures just recounted for the reign of Burkumanda I were
along the Bilma Trail. Military operations in this region would have enhanced Bagirmi
influence along that trail.

Influence over trade routes would have facilitated commerce. Bagirmi participated
in local, regional, and trans-Saharan trade. With regard to the first, Bagirmi was
certainly a major area of pastoral-horticultural exchange by the 1700s. Equally, Bagirmi
merchants were important actors in the east-west long-distance trade, especially in cloth.
Cotton, dyed with indigo, was woven into narrow bands of cloth (*gabak*) in households
throughout the kingdom. These were then traded by Bagirmi merchants in a commercial
network that extended from the Hausa states in the west to Darfur in the east (Burkhardt
1822, 434). But above all, Bagirmi was a longtime participant in the trans-Saharan
slave trade. Traditions suggest that such trade was important at least as far back as the
formative period. In the seventeenth century, perhaps in order to improve market position
and/or profit margins, Bagirmi began to specialize in the sale of eunuchs, who were so
desired that they were even reportedly used to guard Mohammed's tomb in Mecca (Gaden
1907, 443). This trans-Saharan as opposed to local and regional trade was an affair
of state because, as was the case with the earlier east-central Sudanic states, officials

led military units that acquired slaves and then profited from their sale or their labor. In sum, Bagirmi was "an important center of crafts and commerce" in the east-central Sudan by 1800 (Cordell 1985, 40), as it had been in the two previous centuries.[6]

In 1805, Sabun, the sultan of Wadai, went to war against Bagirmi because the *mbang*, Gaurang I, had supposedly entered into incestuous relations with his sister.[7] Sabun captured Massenya and killed Gaurang and the offending wife, together with Gaurang's mother and a number of officials. He left with considerable booty. So the nineteenth century began with Bagirmi succumbing to Wadai and began a defensive phase in Bagirmi history.

Sabun chose *mbang* Bera to replace Gaurang. One of Gaurang's loyal officials assassinated Bera and substituted in his place Burkumanda II. In 1808, Wadaian troops returned to Bagirmi to deal with Burkumanda. An inconclusive battle ensued. Wadai won the battle but lacked sufficient strength to continue, so its forces were retired but returned with the same purpose the following year. This time they were defeated. Sabun acquiesced in this status quo by recognizing Burkumanda II in exchange for the latter's recognition of Wadai's sovereignty over Bagirmi. A decade after these events, Burkumanda entertained an intrigue against the ruler of Bornu, Sheikh el Kanemi. El Kanemi went to war against Bagirmi and, after a number of very difficult campaigns, sacked Massenya for a second time in less than twenty years.

Burkumanda II died in 1846 and was replaced by his son, Abd el Kader. Eight days after Abd el Kader had taken the throne, the sultan of Wadai moved troops into Bagirmi. These were only withdrawn after Abd el Kader had satisfied the sultan of his loyalty to Wadai. Wadai appears not to have insisted on the right to select the *mbang*, only on that of approving him. Abd el Kader's reign was uneventful until 1858, when he was persuaded to attack a huge party of pilgrims, led by a Fulani *mallum*, undertaking the *hadj*. The battle resulting from this attack was a disaster for Bagirmi, which lost the better part of its army. The *mbang* and several of his sons were slaughtered by their Arab escort, who thoughtfully delivered their heads to the pilgrims.

The new *mbang*, Ab Sakin, was feisty and attempted to repudiate Wadaian hegemony. In response, Wadai sacked Massenya yet again. Ab Sakin, however, escaped and set up a temporary capital at Bugoman, from where he was able to defeat all rival contenders for power. After Ab Sakin's death in 1884, Wadai was able to install a son of Abd el Kader who had been raised in Abeche (Wadai's capital) as the new *mbang*, Gaurang II. During the early years of his reign, Gaurang II was preoccupied with defending himself against a rival claimant to the throne.

In the early 1890s a far more dangerous opponent appeared. This was Rabah, the ex-lieutenant of the Sudanese slaver Ziber Pacha who had turned to empire building, and who was at this time entrenched in southern Chad. In 1893, Gaurang was defeated and forced to flee—only one step ahead of Rabah's troops. Bagirmi was defenseless during this time, and it was only when Rabah's interests were diverted to Bornu that Gaurang II was able to return to Massenya, in need of a strong ally to defend Bagirmi against Rabah.

The French appeared to be just such an ally. By the late nineteenth century, France had become interested in adding at least a portion of the central Sudan to its growing

African empire. A mission led by Emile Gentil was sent to speed this process. Gentil reached Massenya in 1897 and persuaded Gaurang to sign a "treaty of protection." Soon after the treaty was signed, Bagirmi was reduced to "shooting off blanks at big festivals" (Lanier 1925, 467).

The nineteenth century was not the best of all possible times for Bagirmi. Nevertheless, it is important to understand that Bagirmi was not obliterated—at least not prior to 1897. The state experienced serious setbacks when it operated outside Bagirmi to the east, west, or north. But within, by and large, Bagirmi officials contin-ued to rule as they had in previous centuries, and a policy evolved that throughout the century increasingly concentrated warfare southward. This southern tilt—so reminiscent of the Saifwa and the Bulala in the centuries prior to Bagirmi's own formation—was actually a southern expansion of the state in the second half of the nineteenth century.

The French judged Bagirmi to be "in complete decadence" during the nineteenth century (Chevalier 1907, 341). This seems too harsh, because even if Bagirmi—like France—endured military defeat in certain areas during the nineteenth century, it was motivated by these defeats—again like France—to develop policies that led to expansion in other areas. This suggests that it is no more appropriate to describe Bagirmi as decadent during the nineteenth century than it is to so describe France.

A more appropriate interpretation, one that applies to all of Bagirmi's history, is that a first kingdom arose out of the whirlwinds of war coming from the north in response to environmental reversals. Then a second kingdom arose circa 1522, and throughout the rest of its history it warred to create a structure whose full dimensions remain to be appreciated and which allowed it to participate in the trans-Saharan and other trades. Finally during its last century history repeated itself, for Bagirmi circa A.D. 1800 was a northern power, like the Saifwa centuries earlier, hurling its whirlwinds of war into southern lands. Wars, according to the chronicle of Burkumanda I's life, were "impressive things," which suggests that Bagirmi's history was a tapestry of such things.

It might seem as if the analysis is complete at this point and that one understands Bagirmi warfare. Certainly, without warfare east-central Sudanic states could assure themselves neither of a supply of commodities to trade nor of access to the trade, so they warred—at least in good measure—in order to trade. Such an explanation appears quite satisfactory, as far as it goes. It explains warfare in terms of its functions. War functioned to facilitate certain forms of trade. However, functionalism explains phenomena in terms of their consequences rather than in terms of what they are. This is a bit like explaining guns by saying that they kill, rather than describing what allows them to perform such a nasty function. A structural analysis provides a model of what it is that is performing a particular function. This allows the analyst to explain why particular functions may be performed. So far we suspect that Bagirmi warred, in part, in order to trade. We do not yet know what the different structures were that made this warfare an utter necessity. The next few chapters describe the realm of the Sun Kings and provide the pieces from which to construct this structural necessity.

PART II

THE SUN KINGS' REALM

Chapter 4

The Social Landscape

This chapter's first task is to understand why the lands along the middle Shari and Bahr Erguig rivers were believed to be a realm of Sun Kings. Then this realm's social landscape is sketched as it was in the final decades of the nineteenth century.

Bagirmi considered their ruler to be sacred and venerated him, just as the Zagawa had done in the earliest days of states in the central Sudan. The reason was many Bagirmi thought that there were two movements in the universe, which they conceived of as animating forces.[1] These gave life to things, in the sense of causing them to be the way they were. It is unclear what these movements were. They seem to have been most often imagined as whirlwinds. There were two rather splendid beasts—*mao*, a snake, and *karkata*, a twelve-legged creature—following each other in these whirlwinds. *Mao* moves from east to west at night and is associated with the moon, the underground world and germination. *Karkata* travels from east to west during the day and is associated with the sun, the above-ground world, and hunting (Pacques 1977, 130).

The *mbang* was the "result and the exponent of these movements" (Pacques 1967, 207); as such he was "electric" with animating force, and this electricity extended even to his spit and feces (Pacques 1977, 63). Consequently, events that happened on the land were a result of his force. So when people spoke of Bagirmi as "the land of the *mbang* at Massenya" (*nange mbang Massenya*), they meant it quite literally. The *mbang* was associated with *karkata*, and above all he was the sun. So it is in this sense that Bagirmi was the realm of a divine Sun King.

One of the ways Bagirmi would explain this realm was to sweep a patch of ground clear with the palm of the hand. Then, on the smoothed patch, they would delicately and precisely make dots with their fingertips. These would indicate the distribution of different ethnic or other groups over the land. It was as a social landscape that certain Bagirmi tended to think about the Sun King's realm. I shall follow this lead, first noting the ethnic groups in Bagirmi's core along the middle Shari and Bahr Erguig, and then seeing how they were distributed in different communities and zones, which zones were themselves arranged a bit like the circular bands in an archery target. The final part of the chapter will present a Bagirmi conception of human relationships, which helped to integrate these parts of the social landscape into a fundamental institution that was at the basis of much of east-central Sudanic society.

Ethnic Groups

Barma believed that, if you asked people in precolonial Bagirmi what they were, they would mention the name of their ethnic group. Then, and only if you pressed them, they might say they lived in "the land of the *mbang* at Massenya." Ethnic groups were important to people in Bagirmi because it was through them that persons acquired much of their access to natural and political resources. There were three major groups at the core of the realm at the end of the nineteenth century. The most important politically, and second most numerous, were the Barma. The most numerous were the Arabs, and the least numerous were the Fulani. These are discussed in turn below.

The Barma considered themselves a single *jili* (kind),[2] composed of people who spoke Tar Barma, who were familiar with Barma *hada* (custom), and whose consanguineal kin were Barma. Barma had founded the second state of Bagirmi, and they reserved for themselves most of its offices. Certain Barma said that the *jili* was divided in two, with there being *barma ba* and *barma kubar*. These were largely geographic categories. The term *ba* meant "river," so *barma ba* referred to those Barma who lived near rivers. The word *kubar* referred to dark, usually hydromorphic soils that were excellent for sorghum production, so *barma kubar* referred to Barma who resided in the interior and cultivated these soils. Most *barma kubar* resided to the east and north of the Bahr Erguig, almost invariably, it should be emphasized, on or near small watercourses or swamps, because it was in these locations that the hydromorphic soils are found. Most *barma ba* resided on the Shari from just south of the contemporary capital of Chad, N'Djamena, as far as Bousso.[3]

Barma kinship terminology was bifurcate merging in the first ascending generation, and generational in ego's own generation. The former terms are suggestive of the previous existence of patrilineal descent groups. Kenga, who are the Barma's immediate neighbors to the east, and to whom the Barma are most closely related linguistically, retain such descent groups.[4] Pacques reported that the term *tarpo* meant "family" (1977, 8). However, *tarpo* means literally "mouth of the fire" (*tar*, "mouth"; *po*, "fire"). Certain informants said that a man's offspring gathered at the "mouth of a fire," which suggests that *tarpo* may have meant "descent group" rather that "family".[5] Perhaps in the past Barma were members of *tarpo*. Descent groups, however, were absent in 1969–70, at least among the Barma along the Shari.

Barma distinguished persons as "free" (*kambe*)[6] or "slave" (*bel*). Free people were descendants of free mothers and fathers. Slaves were persons who had been captured in war, had been purchased, or were descended from other slaves. A person who was the offspring of a slave father and a nonslave mother, an apparently rare circumstance, was also a slave. One who was the descendant of a free father and a slave mother, a more common occurrence as freemen would take additional slave wives, was free but occupied a special category known as *kingi*. Such individuals were ineligible to inherit their father's office. A free person might be either an official or a food producer. The same, however, could be said of slaves, though more slaves were food producers. An official or a food-producing free person might own slaves, though for that matter so could a slave in theory. However, most slaves were owned by free officials.

A Barma believed that he or she had a large number of *tos*. This term corresponds closely to the English term *ƙin*. Some kin lived in the *be*, or household, which was the most important Barma social group from the perspective of production. It was this group that typically performed all food and craft production activities. Each *be* had a head who in the nineteenth century appears to have been called *ngolbe*, though at present the term tends to be *malabe*. This person had inherited rights to land in the city, town, or village in which he lived.

The *ngolbe* tended to be the oldest male who was not *gada*. *Gada* meant a "whitebeard." A whitebeard was conceived of as a person who literally could not sexually or socially "get it up." This meant that when men became too old to participate in everyday activities, they were considered impotent, and they retired from social life, including the headship of their households.

Women, as is described later, were supposed to defer to men. However, because a wife was intimate with her husband, she was believed to be in an excellent position to know whether he was impotent. This meant that wives might declare their husbands to be *gada*, thereby stripping them of their social identities, which was an appalling prospect to men. Thus, one part of Barma culture advised wives to be deferential, while another gave them a tool with which they might control their husbands. Perhaps it was for this reason that the relations between elder husbands and wives seemed roughly equal in the 1970s. Whether such a situation prevailed in the late nineteenth century is unknown.[7]

It was believed that, when a *ngolbe* died or became *gada*, his eldest son should head the household. The type of *tos* who were customarily supposed to be in households were the sons of the *ngolbe*, together with their wives and children. After the old man died, his sons were expected to continue to reside together. Such extended family households were the norm among Barma.

Households were located in larger residence groups, which Barma also called *be*. There were two types of these residence groups, cities or towns and villages or hamlets. Cities and towns were distinguished from villages and hamlets by being, among other things, places of political administration. Cities were walled and situated at places with abundant natural resources that were militarily defensible. The most important city in the nineteenth century was the capital, Massenya, estimated to have a population of circa twenty-five thousand in the 1850s (Barth 1965). Sheikh Ibrahim, who claimed to be of Bagirmi royal blood, told d'Escayrac de Lauture in the 1850s that Massenya was one of the "most beautiful cities in the Sudan" (1855, 90) with houses of "two and even three stories" that compared with those in "Jidda and Mecca"(ibid.,91). Barth has a less enthusiastic description, which still gives some idea of the most important Barma city.

> The town of Mas-ena extends over a considerable area, the circumference of which measures about seven miles; but only one-half of this area is inhabited . . .

> The most characteristic feature of the place consists in a deep, trough-like depression or bottom stretching out at great length, and intersecting the town from east to west, in much the same manner as the town of Kano is intersected by the Jakara; for this hollow of the capital, . . . after the rainy season, is filled with water and on this account is called "beda"

by the natives . . . The principal quarter of the town lies on the south side of the great hollow or beda . . . The central point of this quarter, at least in regard to its importance . . . is the palace of the sultan . . . .

There is a remarkable feature in this palace, which distinguishes it in a very conspicuous manner from all other buildings of the kind in these countries. This difference consists in the wall which surrounds the whole building being built, not of sundried, but of baked bricks . . . .

It [the palace] forms a quadrangle of a somewhat oblong shape, the front looking toward the N.W., and measures from 1500 to 1600 yards . . . It must have once been a very strong building, the walls measuring about 10 feet at the base, and from 15 to 20 feet in height, and the entrance-gate being formed by thick, wooden planks bound with iron . . . .

Adjacent to the royal residence, on the west side, is the large house of the facha, or commander-in-chief, and toward the east a mosque of small dimensions, with a minaret at the northwest corner. The other sides are occupied by the residence of some of the principal courtiers . . . .

Dilapidated as was the appearance of the whole town, it had a rather varied aspect, as all the open grounds were enlivened with fresh pasture (Barth 1965, 517–19).[8]

Other larger Barma towns tended to resemble Massenya. There would be a centrally located ruler's palace, called the *gur*, fronting on an open space where the market would be. Opposite the palace would be a mosque. Then the mosque, market, and palace would be surrounded by different neighborhoods. The term for neighborhood was *gal*, which meant "side."

Neighborhoods were headed by individuals called *ngar*.[9] The head of the largest neighborhood was often the *ngar* of the entire town. The office of *ngar* was the lowest in the state hierarchy. Headships of *gals* could be obtained in one of two ways. Either one could be wealthy and be rewarded with a ward after giving gifts to a political superordinate, or one could be the eldest son of a ward head and inherit from one's father. Gifts would still be given in the latter case. In either case the official upon whom the *gal* depended reserved the final right of selection of its *ngar*.

Cities and towns could be cosmopolitan places. Barth, for example, found a gentleman in Massenya who possessed a copy of "Aristotle and Plato" (1965, 506) and with whom he could spend idle times remembering the "splendor and achievements" of Islamic civilization "from Bagdad to Andalusia" (ibid., 507). Similarly, the town of Bideri had been a "community of scholars and seers" and was "undoubtedly a center of Islamic diffusion" since at least the seventeenth century (Works 1976, 49).

Many Barma did not live in these cosmopolitan centers but in far humbler, rural villages, which were not walled. They were populated at most by several hundred people; they were, however, occupied throughout the year. Barth describes one such village that was located about ten miles west of Massenya. "Our road lay through a fertile country, where the cultivation was divided between millet and sesamun, till we reached the first group of the village of Bakeda, which consists of four distinct hamlets" (1965, 2:481). What Barth called hamlet I believe, in this case refers to different *gals*, because the different sides of a village were often distributed to take advantage of water and arable land.

The prevailing norm of patrilocal postmarital residence meant that neighborhoods were likely to have consisted of a core of agnatically related males to which were attached their wives and children. This meant that a side of Barma would be a de facto descent group. Villages would have a *ngar*, as would each neighborhood.

Barth said that "the headman of the village was called 'gollenange' or 'gar'" (1965, 498). A "gollenange" would have been a *ngolnange*. *Ngol* means "big," while *nange*, as we saw earlier, means "land." Hence, a *Ngolnange* was a "big person of the land." Barth's suggestion that there were both *ngolnange*s and *ngar*s suggests certain possibilities about village leadership. Either the different terms were simply different ways of talking about the same thing, or they referred to different types of offices. Certain Kenga villages, for example, had "land chiefs" and "village chiefs" (Pouillon 1975, 198–99). Perhaps Barma had had a similar situation, with the *ngolnange* being a ritual specialist associated with notions of prospering the land and the *ngar* the village-level officer of the state.[10]

There was a residential unit that was smaller than the village. Barth discovered this when, as be approached Bugoman, he noticed that "the country exhibited signs of . . . numerous farming hamlets, called 'yow eo' . . . [which] at present . . . were tenantless, being only inhabited during the rainy season by the 'fieldhands'" (1965, 477). The term *yoweo* had been lost when and where I conducted fieldwork; however, the memory of temporary farming hamlets remained. Barma remembered two kinds of such hamlets. In some, the field hands were ordinary *kambe* who cultivated their own fields. In others, they were *belge* (slaves) who cultivated the land for their owners. Hamlets tended to be composed not of families but of persons who had left their households back in villages or cities to move closer to their fields.

The mention of slave hamlets raises the question of the implication of the existence of slavery for the organization of the Barma. This question is important because others have insisted that the existence of slavery defined central Sudanic society. Lovejoy, for example, claimed that the nineteenth-century Hausa states were characterized by a plantation economy, because of the existence of slave villages that were owned by officials (1978). The Barma slave hamlet was "owned" by an official in the sense that the official owned the slaves who farmed there. It appears that, at the very end of the nineteenth century, a fair number of these were located in the Abughern region (Chevalier 1907, 45), so that one cannot dismiss out of hand the possibility of a Barma plantation society.

However, further reflection suggests that two requirements should be satisfied before societies can be characterized as plantation. These are, first, that most agricultural output actually came from plantations; and second, that these were the most frequent way of organizing farms.

Slave hamlets certainly existed, but they were restricted to only the most important political actors, those termed court officials (chapter 6). These, according to informants, tended to have no more than one or two slave hamlets, which were inhabited at most by fewer than a hundred persons cultivating fewer than fifty cereal fields. Politically savvy informants thought that there were no more than twenty or so court officials with slave hamlets. However, there would have been many, many thousands of *kambege* fields. Most agricultural output, then, does not appear derived from slave labor.

Furthermore, there were no plantations in the sense of there being large land areas owned by court officials and farmed by slaves who were directed by an overseer employed by the slaveholder. Agricultural production was always performed by some variant of the household. This was as true for slaves as for free persons. Each slave household had two sets of fields: its own and the master's. Each household was supposed to cultivate two days on its own and five on its master's field. Thus most agricultural production came from free persons' fields, and there were no true plantations in Bagirmi, so it seems inappropriate to claim that the Barma were a plantation society.[11]

To sum up, Barma conceived of themselves as either free persons (*kambege*) or slaves (*belge*) who lived in different residence groups (*bege*). These were households, hamlets, villages, towns, and cities. There was a most dramatic contrast between the imposing, cosmopolitan cities, which were seats of power, and the small, rural villages, which were centers of food production.

It is time now to turn to the most numerous ethnic group in Bagirmi, the Arabs. A key to Arab institutions was their use of patrilineal descent to place individuals into descent group hierarchies, such that smaller descent groups were nested within larger ones.[12] An Arab lives in a household (*bayt*) with a head (*syd al bayt*). A child inherits a patrilineal genealogy (*nisba*) from the father and soon learns that, after ascending a number of generations in the genealogy, he or she will find an ancestor (*jid*) who founded a lineage (*khashim bayt*) to which the patrilineal descendants (*ahl*) of that ancestor belong. The child also recognizes that there are other descent groups founded by ancestors who are thought of as "brothers," or patrilineal cousins, of its ancestors that together make up the tribes (*nafar*) to which the child belongs.[13]

Tribes were collections of patriclans that consistently used a particular geographic area (*dar*, "land"). The sole position of leadership within tribes was that of *sheikh*. A *sheikh*, depending upon his leadership skill and wealth, might wield considerable influence, but he had little authority over any persons beyond his household, except the right to goad them to come to some consensus.

Most Arabs in Bagirmi were semisedentary. This meant that they possessed two major residence groups, the village (*hille*) and the camp (*ferik*). Villages were small, often holding fewer than one hundred persons. Usually each tribe would have a central village, which would often be its largest and oldest. It was frequently believed to have been settled by the apical ancestor of either the tribe or the patrilineage providing the tribe's *sheikh*. During the rains many Arabs resided in their villages, which tended to be located in northern Bagirmi along an imaginary line just south of lakes Chad and Fitri, in areas known as the Kozzam and the Debaba. Villages were also located in eastern Bagirmi toward the Batha Lairi.

When surface water and pasture dried up following the rains, many villagers went on transhumance. This might begin as early as November in a year when rains were scarce, and certainly was in full swing by February. Transhumances were usually in a southerly or southwesterly direction. How many times and where the transhumant groups moved and set up camps depended upon the season's rains. Generally, the more rain there was, the fewer the number of camps and the farther north these camps might be located.

Camps had to be sited near water, pasture, and markets. This placed them near rivers or swamps and towns, so that dry season Arab camps tended to surround Barma towns and cities, because the latter were also located near rivers and swamps. Each Barma town or village knew that after the rains certain Arab groups would arrive. When this happened the group's head would inform the Barma authorities in the village or town of its arrival.

Camp members would participate in the village's market, and camp elders would contribute to the village's political life. This usually meant that they attended the daily gatherings at the *ngar*'s residence, which included the *ngar* himself and the different neighborhood heads. Less frequently it might involve participation in judicial cases, especially those between Arab and Barma contestants. Villagers and camp members would participate in each others' life cycle events if they were kin to each other. Successful middle-aged Barma men frequently sought to marry Arab women as second or third wives.

Devallee reported that there were six major Arab tribes in nineteenth-century Bagirmi. These were the Assale, Ouled Musa, Kozzam, Ouled Ali, Yesiye, and Dekakires (1925). The wet season territories of the first three tribes was in northern Bagirmi, in the Kozzam and the Debaba. The Dekakires were located in southeastern Bagirmi, in the region of the same name that was south of Melfi toward the Batha Lairi. The Yesiye, who were the most numerous Arab group, tended to be dispersed throughout Bagirmi, though their home villages tended to be toward the Batha Lairi. A final point: though the Arabs were the most numerous group at the core of nineteenth-century Bagirmi, they had the fewest positions in the political hierarchy, and they may well have been the poorest of peoples.

The Fulani, on the other hand, were the favored pastoral group. They are featured in the traditions as participants in the founding of the second kingdom (cf. Barth 1965, 643: Nachtigal 1889, 693). From their center at Bidiri they often supplied the state with religious and judicial officers. Very little has been written about the Fulani resident in Bagirmi.[14] However, Fulani society appeared to resemble in certain respects that of their Arab neighbors, for like the Arabs they tended to be semisedentary cattle breeders and millet growers who alternated between wet season and dry season residences.

If the nineteenth-century society of Fulani in Bagirmi resembled that of Fulani in Sokoto, as there is reason to believe (Eldridge 1975), then their households were called *wuro* (sing.). Coresident households tended to have a core of patrilineally related men who shared a common ancestor a few generations prior to the living generation (Stenning 1959, 109). Such lineage groups were headed by an individual called the *ardo*, who, like *sheikhs*, facilitated, but did not make, decisions. They also represented it in its dealings with outsiders. Groups of lineages that were stipulated to be patrilineally related lived together during the rainy season in agglomerations that resembled Arab villages, or *hille*. As water and pasture became scarcer during the dry season, there was a general transhumance in a southwesterly direction.

Fulani are described as "disseminated throughout Bagirmi" (Carbou 1912, 2:69), but most wet season residences seem to have been along the Bahr Erguig immediately north and south of Massenya (A. M.-D. Lebeuf 1967, 193).[15] Most dry season camps, which were called *gure*, were around Barma towns along the Shari. Thus, at any time during the dry season, Barma towns along the Shari would be surrounded by Fulani as well as Arab dry season camps, and at any time during the wet season these same Shari towns would have lost these camps, which would have moved to the northeast near the towns along the Bahr Erguig to reoccupy their wet season residences.

Fulani camp members, as did the Arabs, whether in wet or dry season residence, participated in the life of Barma villages. They marketed their dairy products, engaged in life cycle events, and tended to be important in the religious and judicial life of villages largely because of the respect with which Barma regarded their religious specialists.

Communities

The Bagirmi landscape alternated between areas with water, farm and pasture land, and areas lacking such resources. The first two types of area were near streams and swamps, most importantly near the Shari and Bahr Erguig. The third type of area, which occupied far more space, was in the unrelieved plains away from the watercourses. Barma situated their towns, villages, and hamlets near these watercourses. At different times of the year they were surrounded by Arab and Fulani camps, so in the core of Bagirmi an area of Barma towns, villages, and hamlets surrounded by Arab and Fulani camps constituted a community. There does not appear to have been a Barma, Arab, or Fulani term for community, but people knew of their existence and tended to name them after their largest town. So, for example, people spoke in Tar Barma of *nange Bugoman* or in Arabic of *dar Bugoman*, which meant "land of Bugoman," when referring to the community of Bugoman.

Communities exhibited four attributes. First, they were multiethnic, normally including at least Barma, Arab, and Fulani, and possibly some Hausa or Bornuans making the pilgrimage to Mecca. There might also be peoples from tributaries to the south and in the Guera, and perhaps some Sara who originated as slaves. These different ethnic groups tended to have two different food production strategies. Fulani and Arabs, the pastoralists, used the land and water around watercourses to produce cattle and some cereals, while the Barma and other farmers used the same resources to produce cereals and some fish.

Pastoralists were better off moving, whereas farmers were wiser to stay put. Consequently, a second attribute of communities was that they included some people who were more residentially stable, the farmers, and others who were more unstable, the herders. The unstable people, however, were unstable in a most regular way, for they flowed in alternating currents between dry season camps and wet season villages. During the rains herders were in the north and east in their villages. Then with the onset of the dry season, this current turned in the opposite direction, with the lineage groups moving to their southwestern communities. Communities in the northeastern and the southwestern parts of Bagirmi were thus linked by an "alternating current" of pastoral transhumance. Thus communities included a residentially stable nucleus of farmers surrounded by mercurial pastoralists, who, like electrons, would jump to other nuclei in other communities.

A third attribute of communities was the existence of marketing systems, for all Barma towns and larger villages had markets. These were usually held on a single day of the week, with each town and village holding its market on a different day so that a community's merchants traveled from market to market. The major exchange that took place was of pastoral for agricultural products.

Finally, as Malinowski bluntly put it, "propinquity breeds attempt." Neighbors in communities might marry, and when they did they became affines, and as such they had to observe each other's niceties of behavior, and therefore they participated in each other's life cycle rituals. In this manner communities tended to become fields of social interaction, which was their fourth defining attribute.

So far we have been considering Bagirmi at its center, where the Barma live and where the second kingdom was created along the middle Shari and Bahr Erguig. It is time to go further and present the entire realm.

Zones

An insight of the political scientist Jacques Le Cornec is helpful when thinking about Bagirmi on a scale beyond that of a community. He observed that Bagirmi consisted of "three concentric circles" involving the "successive diminution of its political influence and its authority" (1963, 18). At the center was the "core." Here was "the State of Bagirmi." Next there was "a belt of . . . vassals." Finally there was "an exterior sector" comprising "in the north the other empires, . . . in the south a reservoir of captives, a privileged hunting ground of slaves" (ibid., 18–19). Such a way of thinking means that Bagirmi was something of an archer's target, consisting of a bull's-eye surrounded by concentric bands, or zones. There was, indeed, a bull's-eye core surrounded by a band of tributaries, which , then, in its turn was surrounded by a band of predation. The core consisted of different ethnic groups and communities, as did the tributary and predation zones.

However, it was a messy target, messy in the double sense that the bands were not discrete swaths possessing different degrees of authority, nor were they well-defined concentric circles. Generally speaking, the closer one came to Massenya, the greater the authority of the state, but each band at different times had pockets of greater or lesser authority than the band had as a whole, for reasons we shall later see. Further, bands tended to bulge toward the south in nineteenth-century Bagirmi.

Core, tributary, and predatory zones were distinguished from each other in terms of how they were administered, what revenues they provided, what military functions they performed, and what their cultural relationship was to the core. Core areas were ruled directly in the sense that the hierarchy of Bagirmi officials administered decisions that had been formulated in Massenya. Tributary regions enjoyed indirect rule in the sense that their own political structures continued to make many decisions, especially concerning purely local matters. However, their hierarchies were integrated with that at Massenya and, on occasion, served to administer decisions formulated in the latter political structure. No (Bagirmi) rule was the rule in the predatory zones. Here political systems operated that did not tolerate any Bagirmi authority, so that the only way for

Massenya to have influence was through the exercise of force. Here, then, was a zone of frequent military predation.

Core areas paid taxes to the states coffers. Tributary areas provided tribute. Predatory zones provided the spoils of pillage, especially slaves. The core provided the greatest numbers of, and the most operationally essential, soldiers. Core troops fought in all Bagirmi's wars. Tributary areas provided auxilliary troops for some, though by no means all, conflicts. Predatory areas never contributed military personnel to Bagirmi. Rather, their warriors endeavored to obliterate Bagirmi's soldiers.

There was considerable cultural unity in the core. People could understand each other, through the medium of either Tar Barma or Arabic. Many shared notions of how to behave, for they tended to learn the same Muslim *hada* (custom), often taught by the Islamic clerics at Bidiri. People were aware of, and presumably accepted to some degree, an ideology that legitimated the *mbang*'s rule. Tributary areas were culturally distinct from the core, because the ethnic mix was different from that in the core, and these different ethnic groups had their own cultural traditions.

Tributary zones had two sorts of cultural ties to the core. First, court "schools," clerics, and merchants operated to enculturate tributary peoples with aspects of core culture. Male offspring of rulers in allied areas would be sent to the Massenya court. Here, taking a page from medieval European history, they were schooled in the minutiae of Bagirmi statecraft. Clerics from Bidiri and other centers of Muslim learning in Bagirmi traveled to allied areas to give instruction in Islam. But because such clerics were from Bagirmi, their ministrations had a Bagirmi bias. Similarly, Bagirmi merchants plied their wares throughout allied lands, and as they did so, they inadvertently communicated information about Bagirmi ways. Bagirmi merchants and clerics also operated in predation zones, but far less frequently than in tributary areas.

A second cultural bond between the core and tributary areas was the prevalence of a shared ideology of the past. This usually involved past wars between Massenya and the ally, or marriages between the ruling families of Massenya and the ally, and these marriages and wars usually legitimated the acceptability of some core authority over tributary affairs.

Predatory zones were far more culturally "standoffish" to Massenya than were tributary zones. Bornu was dominated by a Kanuri worldview, Wadai by a Maba worldview, and the south by Sara cultural notions. Further, the ideology that prevailed in Bagirmi about predation zones classified them as enemies. The south was full of heathen *kirdi*, fit to hunt. Wadai, which sacked Massenya and slaughtered Barma, was widely perceived as "national enemy number one," as one informant enthusiastically put it.

By the latter half of the nineteenth century, Bagirmi's core consisted of two parts. One was the original core. The other was a part added later, which also assumed the characteristics of the core. The original core was where the state had originally formed around Massenya and was the area of the eight founding landowning (*malanange*) groups. Pacques (1967) identifies this area as a rough trapezoid running from Durbali in the north to Bugoman on the Shari in the west, south down the Shari to Bougoumari, then due east to the Bahr Erguig, and finally northeast back to Durbali. The added core was along the Shari from south of the village of Mandjaffa to Bousso. Here Pacques says the Barma found "three small states"—Bousso, Mapling, and Mondo (1977, 71)—when they arrived in the region. She says that these peoples "made their submission" to Massenya during the second half of the eighteenth century during *mbang* Hadji's reign (ibid., 100). Nachtigal (1889, 699) and Devallee (1925, 34), however, place this submission much earlier, during the reign of the fourth *mbang*, Abd Allah (c. 1569–98). Regardless of when it occurred, by the late nineteenth century the Shari, as far south as Bousso, had become a core area of Bagirmi.

Bagirmi possessed tributary zones at all points of the compass prior to the nineteenth century, but defeat at the hands of both Wadai and Bornu stripped most northern, eastern, and western allies away. There were two southern tributary zones in the late nineteenth century. One was older, and directly south of Bagirmi but north of the Sara populations. This zone included the Sarua, Miltu, Bua, Niellim, Ndam, Somrai, Tumuk, and Gabri. Miltu (also known as Tunia), Bua, and Niellim spoke Lwa languages. The other groups spoke Chadic languages. Three areas south of the Lwa and Chadic speakers had recently become allies by the second half of the nineteenth century. These were the Sara Goulay immediately south of the Tumak at Gundi and Sara Sar (Fortier 1982) and Nar around Bedaya and Koumra (Brown 1975, 1983). This, then, was the second southern tributary zone. In the east, the Kenga remained faithful allies, as did, in a very on-again-off-again way, the Sokoro. Surrounding these tributaries was the predation zone: to the south and southwest, the other Sara, Chadic, and Adamawan groups; to the west, Bornu; to the east, Wadai; and to the north, certain of Wadai's tributaries, including two of Bagirmi's oldest allies, Bulala and Medogo. When Bagirmi is referred to from now on, it will mean the entire target, unless otherwise explicitly noted.

Other states in the east-central Sudan had target organizations in the nineteenth century, and these targets were messy in the sense that their bands might become intermingled. Bornu, for example, had a core located to the west of Lake Chad, with a capital for most of the century at Kukwa. Surrounding the core was a band of tributaries in parts of the Kanem, among the Kotoko and in the Mandara. Finally, beyond the tributaries was a predation zone that was, throughout much of the nineteenth century, to the southwest of the Bagirmi predation zone among people whom Bornuans, like Bagirmi, called *ķirdi*.

Wadai had its core on the plateau bearing its name. The core was centered at Abeche, which for most of the nineteen century was the capital. This was surrounded by a large band of tributaries. There were , to mention only the most important, tributaries in the lands of the Zagawa, Tama, Sila, Runga, Bagirmi, Kanem, and Bulala. Finally, beyond the tributaries, especially to the south, was a land the Wadaians called *dar Fertit*. *Fertit* meant to Wadaians what *ķirdi* mean to Bagirmi. *Dar Fertit* was Wadai's major predation zone. Note how the targets of two states might become messy in the sense that at the same time that Bagirmi had its own target, this was part of Wadai's tributary band.

What we have just described might be imagined as a series of pointillist landscapes. In different parts of each canvas were vast, interconnected, southward-drooping targets.

Scattered throughout the targets were communities, concentrations of points with bigger dots representing cities and towns and smaller ones hamlets and camps. Color is added to the canvas because each point would be a different color for each ethnic group. We must insist, however, that it is a *series* of landscapes we are imagining, for with the passage of time, the landscape assumes new configurations as targets expand or contract and communities disperse or become more dense. This, then, was Bagirmi's, and the east-central Sudan's, social landscape in the late nineteenth century.

Officials and Food Producers

I would pose "textbook" questions designed to fathom Bagirmi conceptions of their society during the initial phases of my fieldwork. One of these was whether there was an ancestor of all the Bagirmi. The first person to whom this question was posed — a teenager who tended to act out — responded by successively bursting into laughter, falling to the ground, and rolling back and forth in a spirited imitation of Saint Vitus' dance. Similar responses to similar questions suggested that descent was not a major organizing principle.

Then one day two elderly gentlemen who had been observing this ethnographic foreplay said that if I really wanted to understand Bagirmi I would have to understand *tashkipage* and *maladonoge*,[16] and they proceeded to distinguish between the two. *Tashkipage* were *dono eli*, which meant that they "lacked power." A *tashkipa* was supposed to be *kinji bena*, which meant that he or she was to "stay at the household," where he or she was to *cao baya* and *noko koshkanje* — that is, "hoe a field" and "fish a lot." *Tashkipage* thus were domestic food producers.[17]

Scholars might be tempted to gloss *tashkipage* as "peasants." I refer to them as food producers for two reasons. First, informants told me that they farmed or fished before they told me anything else about them. Second, the term *peasants* often refers to food producers who are thoroughly integrated into markets. This was simply not the case with *tashkipage*, as is made clear in chapter 5. So the term food producers reports what appears to have been uppermost in Barma notions of *tashkipage* while not conflating them with farmers producing for markets.

Maladonoge, on the other hand, were *debge an mbang*, "people of the sovereign." I was told in no uncertain terms that they *cao baya eli*, *koshkanje eli*," "didn't farm or fish." Rather, they were proud *debge an sinda*, which meant literally "people of horse," or cavalry, who *tad way*, *noko ojo*, that is, who "make war, very much." *Maladonoge* thus were officials who as cavalry made war. Every food producer, they said, was attached to an official.

There was an understanding as to the basis for this attachment. A food producer owed *hormo* to an official. The concept of *hormo* denotes "deference," and deference seems to have been an important aspect of a number of relationships among Bagirmi.[18] Men were supposed to defer to Allah. Women were expected to defer to their men, as their men deferred to Allah. Finally, juniors deferred to elders among kin.

A meaning of *deference* in American usage of the term is that one person "gives in to" another. The Bagirmi notion of deference went farther. *Tashkipage* were expected to defer to *maladonoge*, and if that meant obliging a *maladono* by giving her or him products or labor, so be it, because this was a *ngas hada*. *Ngas* meant "thing"; *hada* meant "custom." Thus a *ngas hada* was a "customary thing." A *tashkipa's* giving to *maladono* was a "customary thing." This is precisely what was expected of a *tashkipa's* relationship to a *maladono*. *Hormo* thus meant that food producer and officials were in a state of negative reciprocity.

Why did *tashkipa* show deference? One cultural reason was expressed in a nineteenth-century proverb that went, "*Hormo* is like a white robe" (Gaden 1909, 52). A white robe is a pure thing, so the proverb implies that a *tashkipa* who exhibits deference to his or her *maladono* is in a state of purity. This explanation, I believe, was a petty deception that helped cloak an unpleasant reality that a model of fields of empire reveals.

However, the elderly gentlemen revealed a fundamental institutional structure that day. Its parts were the *tashkipage* and *maladonoge*, who were articulated to each other by *hormo*. This institution was fundamental because it was the basic, "atomic" unit from which were constructured all the other parts in the contradictory fields model.

Much of the history of Bagirmi and the east-central Sudan is, I believe, one of the expansion, contraction, and transformation of core, tributary, and predation zones. Many changes in these zones occurred through different forms of predation. The fields of empire model explains these changes. However, before we can formulate this model and appreciate the deception worked by the pretty proverb, we must understand food producers and officials. These topics are explored in chapters 5, 6, 7, and 8.

Chapter 5

Food Producers
and Their Households

The agronomist Auguste Chevalier described how Bagirmi farming appeared circa 1900.

> The Bagirmi villages followed after one another without interruption. . . . All resemble each other and aren't very different from Sara villages. At the approaches of these villages one first distinguishes the bare tops of large acacia albida exclusively confined to fallow fields. Next one advances upon land cleared by fire, covered with semi-burnt, dry trunks that are still standing. It is here that millet will be planted in one or two years. . . . Finally a large clearing appears: this is properly speaking the location of the fields, cleared since time immemorial, and on which one plants a part, leaving the rest in fallow until a favorable year. There are more trees here, but shade trees distributed in a random fashion. . . . Soon the silhouette of the village appears. (Chevalier 1907, 326–27)

Chevalier said that just before the harvest, "the fields . . . present a magnificent aspect. The cereals have grown to twelve feet forming an immense, somber green belt around the villages" (ibid., 331). This chapter enters into these villages and considers those who produced this magnificent bounty, the food producers in their households.

In so doing, it analyzes the Barma mode of production, a mode of production that, it is suggested, they shared in large part with other east-central Sudanic peoples. The chapter is in two sections. The first discusses the Barma relations and forces of production, showing how they constituted a domestic mode of production. The second section considers certain contradictions inherent in the reproduction of this mode of production. Sahlins suggested in an influential analysis that such modes of production were not "brilliant" [1972, 99]. This chapter insists, among other things, that sometimes, not to be brilliant was brilliant.

Mode of Production

A mode of production, according to Godelier, is:

> the combination of two structures: . . . the productive forces and the relations of production. The notion of productive forces designates the set of factors of production, resources, tools,

men, characterizing a determined society at a determined epoch which must be combined in a specific way to produce the material goods necessary to that society. The notion of relations of production designates the functions fulfilled by individuals and groups in the production process and in the control of factors of production. (Godelier 1972b, 335)

Events at the institutional level of households are those upon which the more abstract one of relations and forces of production is modeled. So attention now focuses upon these domestic units.

Relations of Production

The Barma household, depending upon whether it was that of an ordinary or more comfortable food producer, was surrounded and thus demarcated by a woven grass fence (*boko*) in the former case or a mud brick wall (*gur*) in the latter case. Within this enclosure lived some, through by no means all, of a person's kin (*tos*). When one asked a person what the word (*tos*) actually meant, they often responded that it referred to "my people" (*debimgay*). This is exactly how a white middle-class American might answer the same question; but what "my people" meant was far different for Barma than for middle-class Americans. Realizing how this was the case is a key to understanding production relations.

A letter to the editor in an American paper announced, "The family unit consists of father, mother and children under God!" (Reyna 1976, 184). Barma saw the matter differently, for they had preferential rules that a son should "sit together with his father," and that "brothers should sit together with brothers." The verb *sit* meant in this instance "staying" together.

Such rules implied household domestic cycles involving movement toward and from two types of extended families: those consisting of a married man and his married sons, and those consisting of married brothers. The cycle might be thought of as beginning with a married man and young children residing in a household. As the children grew, the daughters married and moved to their husbands' households, while the sons acquired wives and "sat" with their fathers, creating the first type of father-son extended family. This structure might in its turn be transformed into a brother-brother extended family when the father died. Then, as sons or younger brothers matured, they often sought greater independence from their elder fathers or siblings, which they expressed by moving out and founding their own households. When this happened, the domestic cycle began anew. Added to this core of regulars might be some more distant—often elderly—kin, fostered children, or a slave.[1]

The physical layout of households reflected the particular family structure occupying it. A general principle seems to have been that nuclear family units, or fragments of such units, had their own place within a household. This meant that behind the major wall that demarcated a household from others in its neighborhood there would be further less substantial ones that separated the nuclear families, or their fragments, from each other. Thus interior walls would divide a married man and his wife or wives from his married son or sons, while further walls would divide married sons from each other. Still other walls would separate unmarried householders—normally children, widows, or widowers—from the nuclear family units. Within these labyrinths would be separate huts for males and females, perhaps an open shelter for entertaining, certainly some sort of granary, pens for livestock, and near the women's huts a place for cooking. Such households were warrens of activity, especially in the early morning and evening hours, when all chores were set to the womens' rhythmic pounding of the daily grain.

Male eldership was an important status around which household activities were organized. Age differences were reckoned within and across generations. Thus one had older or younger fellow household members in one's own generation (brothers, sisters, and cousins), and one had relatives in older and younger generations. Other people looked down upon their younger relatives as "small" (mbassa). Conversely, younger folk looked up at their seniors as "large" (ngollo). "Small" and "large" relatives of different generations might be glossed respectively as juniors and elders. These might be either female (ne) or male (gaba).

Male eldership was, and still is, an informal, largely achieved status. Barma lacked an age-grade system such as is commonly found among East African Nilotic peoples in which men formally acquired eldership as they passed to senior age-sets. Rather, a man who did a good job at what men were supposed to be good at came to be thought of as "big." Men were supposed to become farmers, marry, and have children. Eventually they were supposed to set up their own households in which they were the heads (malabe). Any middle-aged or older gentleman was an elder. But only a person who was a skilled farmer and who was head of a household bursting with dependents—wives, wives' children, fostered children, aged relatives, brothers and their families, and perhaps a slave or two— was though of as really "big." That is, more was "bigger," in the sense that the more dependents a man had, the more prominent he was thought to be.

Eldership was desired because prestige derived from it. The discourse in which prestige was conceived centered around deference (hormo). This notion, previously introduced in chapter 4 to discuss behaviors in the political arena, also specified those in the realm of kin and neighbors. Junior male relatives and neighbors paid deference to elders. Women owed deference to their men.

Eldership was not only desired; it was strongly desired, because there was really no other way men who were food producers could gain renown. Honor was lavished upon officials; but it was improbable that a food producer would ever become an official, for reasons discussed in chapter 6. Certain merchants acquired wealth, and wealthy folk were "big" folk. But wealthy merchants were those in long-distance trades, and to enter these one had to be part of the network of long-distance traders. Access to this network appears to have been largely a matter of possessing kinship with others in it, or possessing capital that was of interest to those already in it. Food producers were not related to the great traders, and they were too poor to motivate them to support their entry into trade. The only other avenue leading to prestige was to become an Islamic specialist (mallam). However, to be a mallam one had to be a devout lad, prepared to leave one's family and to spend considerable time and wealth studying far away with a learned specialist. Many food producers were not especially devout Muslims, so their young boys were unlikely to have been motivated to seek Islamic callings. Further study with a mallam could be expensive, especially because of the loss of the son's labor. Going away to study Islam for a Barma from a food producer's family was a bit like the son of a New York construction worker going off to a fancy prep school, an unrealistic reverie.

So eldership to a Barma food producer was like money to an American, the key to good things! This meant that when a boy in a food producer's household fancied being "big," he dreamed of being old in a household bustling with his dependents. Then he knew he would have, as one ambitious Barma lad expressed it, "his people" lavish the *hormo* that was his rich due each and every moment of the day.

Deference could be paid in a wide variety of goods and services, so long as its payment did not violate some fundamental social rule. Thus if an elder craved his daughter, she would not have to acquiesce to this desire to show her *hormo*, because it was a monstrous demand that violated the incest taboo. Persons owed deference in a household might expect some of the labor or the products of the labor of those persons owing deference. It is important to understand that there was no formal schedule of what and how much should be given. Rather, it was known that it was a "thing of custom" (*hada*) that a "straight" (*tal*) person would want to show deference to the appropriate people. A straight person was moral, and a "unstraight" one was immoral.

Barma conceptualized immorality differently than is the case in middle-class American culture. To Americans an immoral person is naughty, wicked, or even evil; but regardless of the vastness of the transgression, an immoral person is still a person. Americans have reservations about Hitler's morality, but nobody therefore classifies him as nonhuman. This is precisely what many Barma might do. To them an immoral person is biologically distinct from a moral one and is classified as of the "kind" (*jili*) that is or becomes a witch or a sorcerer. Such notions of "straightness" meant that if one really wanted to feel good, rather than loathsome, about oneself, one should pay deference, which meant it was important that a son should help his father, or a wife her husband.

On the other hand, a man owed deference was supposed "to aid" [*kuma*] his dependents. The notion of aid was broad, meaning both "coming to the assistance of" and "seeing to the well-being of" dependents. The belief that a "big" person was a nourisher of dependents introduced an ambiguity in the deference payer and receiver relationship. A father, for example, might ask his son to work for three days on his field; and out of deference, the son might agree to work—but only for one day, because his own fields needed weeding. The son might even ask his father's assistance on his own fields. There was thus a flexibility that characterized the deference payer and receiver relationship. Payers should give, but how much was problematic.

It is time to return to the Barma view of kin as "my people" and, in so doing, to come to a preliminary understanding of production relations. Barma perceived the institution of the household as a place of kin. Further, they knew that every member of a household either owed or paid deference to every other member. Thus the institution of the household was a structure with two elements exhibiting two relationships. The elements were payers and receivers, who were related to each other because the former gave *hormo* to the latter. This structure was that of householders' relations to each other in all social domains, including those of production, so it was, among other things, their relations of production.

Next we consider the role of this structure in the process of production. Barma households farmed, fished, and practiced crafts, and so they participated in three distinct production processes. Considerations of age and gender influenced participation in these processes. Neither boys nor girls seriously worked in production until their teenage years. Adults gradually withdrew from it starting in their mid-60s. Fishing was an entirely male activity, whereas both men and women farmed and practiced crafts. Barma produced two sorghums, *jarto (sorghum caudatum)* and *wa (sorghum durra)* as well as one millet *tenge (pennesitum thyphoideum)*. These were normally cultivated by men. Women produced the vegetables (okra, squash, peanuts, onions, cowpeas). Cotton was also cultivated in fields that appear to have been those of either men or women. Men manufactured the craft products required for farming and fishing and also performed much, though by no means all, of the construction of buildings. They produced the hoes and machetes used in farming, the nets, spears, and pirogues needed for fishing, as well as the adobe bricks and thatching used in buildings, walls, and roofs. Women appear to have made the mats used for sitting upon and the various containers for storing and serving food. Men seem to have done much of the weaving, while both sexes tailored cloth into garments.

There is a tendency to think of domestic production as entirely communal. For example, Pacques, speaking of Barma farming, said, "The father cultivates his field with his children" (1977, 174). This suggests that each household possessed a single field worked in common by all its members, and hence that farming was a purely communal activity. This is, and was, simply not the way the agricultural production process appears to have been organized, for it was a communalism based upon an individualism.

It was individualism in the sense that, if a person undertook some production activity, it was understood to be his or her enterprise. It was a person's activity in two ways. First, the person was responsible for managing the actual production process. This meant supplying the factors of production, that is, in farming, arranging that there be seeds, land, and workers to cultivate a crop. Second, it was understood that the products of the production process belonged to the person whose enterprise it was. This did not mean that he or she actually consumed all these products. It did mean that they were treated like a gross product to which others might have some claims. Thus, if a junior had a field, its harvest was seen as his, even though a portion of it might go to his household's elder or to those who helped him harvest it.[2]

Many of the activities that composed a person's enterprises were performed by that individual. However, especially in agriculture, some types of collaboration might be required. There were two types of cooperation in farming. The first was when there were young and inexperienced persons in the household who might not yet be fully competent farmers. In such cases a younger person might agree to work with an older, more experienced one. Usually the two people working together lived in the same household, and often sons worked with their fathers. Such persons were said to "work one" (*tadchita kede*). This situation, however, was considered temporary, for a son or brother would secure his own field when he had learned to farm well.

A second type of cooperation occurred on a person's own field or fields during operations that were particularly labor intensive. There were six major activities that had to be performed for sorghum and millet production: clearing, planting, weeding, harvesting, threshing, and dividing the harvest. Clearing and planting could be done by a single person because clearing occurred during the dry season when there were fewer competing chores and people thus had extra time. Planting for its part simply required very little effort. Weeding and harvesting were another matter. They had to be performed very quickly or the harvest would be compromised, they required heavy investments of labor, and they occurred at times when there were other agricultural chores requiring attention. This produced what have come to be called in the literature labor bottlenecks (Norman, Newman, and Ouedraogo 1981, 29). Such bottlenecks meant that farmers had to have assistance if their yields were not to be compromised. Those providing it normally came with their own tools, so that assistance involved the provision of both capital and labor to different activities. Most help came from members of a person's own household.[3]

Household members looked upon each other as the closest of "my people" and as such were under a strong obligation "to aid" (*kuma*) each other. This meant that any person in a household might expect help from any other person. Some persons, however, might reckon on more help than others. An aged widow who supported no one and who herself was nourished out of another's granary might anticipate little help in her garden. Women might be aided by their husbands, and more frequently by other of the household's women, as well as by their children.

Clearly, elders had the strongest claim on other household members' labor because their dependents owed them deference in addition to assistance. A household might be thought of as exhibiting a hierarchy of men owed different amounts of assistance because they were owed different amounts of deference. The head (*malabe*), who was owed deference by all, expected assistance from all. Married sons, who owed deference to the household head, and who in turn were owed deference by their nuclear families, expected to give assistance to the household elder and to receive it from their wives and children. Unmarried sons were at the bottom of this heap. They might be able to cadge some assistance from others on the basis of the principle that a household's members owed each other help, but not on the basis of deference owed, except possibly from some of the household's younger women.

The individuals within each household were thus bonded together by the provision of mutual assistance, which was supplied as circumstances dictated. For example, a father working his field might discover weeds that he could not remove alone. That evening he would discuss this situation with other household members, and a junior son might be dragooned into helping with the weeding out of deference to his elder father. In this manner each person in the household benefited from reciprocal bursts of labor services, with the elders' enterprises benefitting from the most, and the most prolonged, bursts.

However, some aspects of the agricultural production process normally required extrahousehold labor. This was often true for weeding bottlenecks. It was also true of the harvesting, threshing, and the final division of threshed sorghums and millets. This labor was supplied by kin and neighbors. The kin who provided it might be consanguines or affines, for example, brothers who had already left the household or wives' brothers, who were never in it. A person feels such kin to be "my people" and requests their labor on this basis. These kin are considered more distant than those in the household, and associated with this belief is one that their assistance should be more immediately recompensed. Thus if a man's wife's brother helps him, he will carefully try to balance this generosity with one of his own, usually in the form of food or labor. Such compensation is likely to take place as quickly as possible.

This balancing of compensation with services rendered is even more marked when non-kin neighbors help. A person's neighbors lent a hand most often during harvest, when a village's young men formed work parties that went from field to field harvesting. At the end of their efforts on each field, its owner would provide them with the wherewithal for a hearty meal. There was a sense that more distant kin, or neighbors, who were not quickly compensated might "forget" them.

Once a harvest had been threshed, as was noted earlier, it belonged to the person from whose field it came: if a husband had a field of sorghum, it was his, just as, if his wife had one of okra, it was hers. There was no custom that junior male or female household members' harvest should become the property of elders. This raises the question, How was food circulated within households?

Different people within, and sometimes even between, households "eat one" (sa kede). This did not mean that they all sat down and ate a common meal. Men in such an eating group have their meals first and are then followed by women and young children. What "eating one" did mean was that those who did so pooled their food resources. Theoretically anybody could participate in an eating group; and in principle, the entire household should "eat one," because the elder was responsible for nourishing everyone.

However, as a household head's younger brothers or sons matured and married, there was a tendency for them to withdraw from the larger family and to form smaller eating units consisting of their dependents. Men did so because this was a sure sign that they were becoming "big." Thus each and every meal was a pooling of food from the different granaries in each eating group within a household.

Though the food in a household belongs to its producers, the elders—because they are owed deference—may ask and expect to receive some of it. Household heads thus acquired extra amounts of food, which they used to meet some of their obligations. There were three major obligations: to nourish nonproductive household members, to pay taxes, and to offer gifts to extrahousehold members, especially gifts forming the basis of bridewealth. Thus the elder was not so much an accumulator of foodstuffs as their circulator outside the household.

We are now in a position to summarize our understanding of Barma production relations. These were kinship relations, especially within households. Households were composed of subunits, men and their dependents usually in a common eating group. These were arrayed in an informal hierachy of males, with the senior male the household head. He was owed deference by all household members but, in turn, was responsible in the most general way for their nourishment. Other married males with their own dependents were less "big" than the head but were nevertheless on the high road to eldership. They owed deference to the household head but were owed deference by more junior males and women. Such "middle" men were responsible for nourishing their dependents. The most junior males were those who had not yet married. They were still "small." They owed deference to all married men in the household and had no dependents to whom they were responsible.

Within this structure individual men and women ran their own enterprises. All kin within the household were expected to help each other perform the productive processes involved in their enterprises, and to a certain extent they did. However, elder kin were deference receivers. Junior men and women were deference payers. This meant that an elder had an additional right to some of his dependents' labor and instruments for his enterprises. It equally meant that elders might expect some of the products that were the fruits of their juniors' enterprise.

Production relations, it will be recalled, refer to the functions fulfilled by individuals or groups in the production process. Elders, because they could command more of their dependents' labor, tools, and products than vice versa, were more controlling of the allocation of factors of production and output than others. This suggests that two groups may be distinguished in the production process: those dependent kin whose productive forces and products were more controlled and those elders who were more controlling. Thus when Barma talked about kin (tos), they were talking about the parts to the production process in their society. This is far from what a middle-class American has in mind when talking about kinship.

Forces of Production

Two related questions are basic when considering productive forces. The first is, How much can be produced with what factors of production? The second is, How much of those factors are actually available to produce with, that is, what is the relative scarcity of different factors of production? Answers to these two questions indicate the force in a mode of production by revealing the limits to its productive capacity and to its productivity. We first consider the relative scarcity of different factors of production. Attention is restricted to farming because agriculture was the most important production sector and because the productive forces in farming were not greatly different from those in other sectors.

Barma combined land, capital, and labor in their different farming enterprises. Land is understood to be the natural resources employed in a production process. Land in Barma farming was, of course, land; and the same area could at different times be either abundant or scarce. The reason for this apparent paradox is explored below.

Land abundance or scarcity is related to human population density. People resided in the old core of Bagirmi under densities of circa four people per square kilometer in the early 1960s (SEDES 1966). Under these densities they tended to treat land as if it were a free good. People said that it was there for the taking and that it could be taken as anybody saw fit, provided they asked permission of their village leader.

If the 1960 population density was low, that estimated for the 1920s was even lower. Colonial reports had it at 1.5 people per square kilometer in 1924 (NA: W, 15, 36). This statistic is important because it is the earliest fairly reliable population density figure that exists for Bagirmi and would appear to approximate the region's density only twenty years earlier in 1900.[4] If it is correct, it meant that there was about a square kilometer of land for every one and a half persons. Perhaps as little as one-fifth of the land is suitable for farming in dry savanna habitats such as Bagirmi (Kowal and Kassem 1978). This meant that there were about 1,333 hectares available to feed each person. It takes about 0.5 hectares of arable land to produce enough food to nourish a person using Barma agricultural techniques. This meant that there was available 2,666 times the amount of land necessary to support the population. Land may not have been available in an infinite supply; it was certainly, however, in abundant supply, as the previous statistic suggests; and perhaps for this reason it tended to be treated as a free good in the 1960s, as we have every reason to believe it would have been at the end of the nineteenth century.

Even though there was abundant land, under certain conditions it could be rendered unproductive. There was a host of reasons for this. Plants could be destroyed by types of parasitic herbs called striga, which attach themselves to their hosts' roots, sucking their nutrients from them. A field could be destroyed by insect pests, such as locusts. Equally, it could disappear under the darting attacks of birds, such as the *quelea*. Further, I saw fields ruined by hippos and monkeys. The former used them as trysting spots for mating, and the latter exploited them as granaries thoughtfully left for them by people.[5]

Rainfall, however, was by far the most important devastator of lands' productive capacity, with both the total amounts and the timing of precipitation influencing whether a field would yield. The dry Sudan, it will be remembered, receives between 400 and 900 millimeters of rain per year. This is generally adequate for most millets and sorghums. However, annual deviations from the mean precipitation may be considerable, ranging between +25–40 percent and −25–40 percent [Matlock and Cockrun 1974, 75]. This means that farmers will receive in any year 25–40 percent more or less rainfall than the average. Parts of northern Bagirmi get in the range of 450 millimeters of rainfall, so that each year they could experience as little as 240 millimeters of rain or as much as 560 millimeters. The former figure is too little for most sorghums and millets. Southern Bagirmi, on the other hand, receives a mean approaching 900 millimeters, so that each year farmers could experience as little as 540 millimeters of precipitation or as much as 1,260 millimeters. The latter figure is too much for many millets.

Further, rain must fall in specific amounts at specific times, which vary from crop to crop, throughout the growing season if fields are to yield. In general, too much rain too early or late in the season deprives plants of moisture when they are maturing, thereby dooming their yields (Kowal and Kassem 1978). However, the timing of rainfalls from year to year is as chancy as the total amounts that fall.

Farmers were acutely sensitive to the hard reality that striga, locusts, birds, hippos, monkeys, or rainfall, among other things, could destroy their harvests. They have, however, utterly no idea when such disasters will strike and tend to say that they are a "thing of Allah" (*ngas Allah*).

It is certain, in a capricious fashion, that some harvests will be obliterated by the normal variations of different components of the dry savanna ecosystem. When this happens to an area, the amount of land that can produce a harvest is temporarily, but often greatly, reduced. This means that land has become scarce. Thus land can be, and was, both abundant (in the sense of there being a great deal of it capable of producing under certain conditions) and scarce (in the sense that, when those conditions were not met, productive areas became unproductive).

Attention now turns to the capital used in the production process. It should be first realized that no money capital was used in agricultural production, only tools. With this understood, it can be suggested that the capital that did exist was the least forceful of the productive forces. The only agricultural implements regularly employed were an ax for clearing the bush, a short hoe for working the soil, a machete for cutting, and a digging stick to help with planting. These implements were necessary to the production process, because land could not be cleared, soil prepared, weeds removed, or plants harvested without them. However, a field's yield would be unaffected if the farmer decided to use two hoes, two machetes, or two axes instead of one on the field, in the absence of other concommitant increases in land or labor. The farmer might look rather spiffy hefting a pair of hoes, but he or she simply could not speed up weeding or any other agricultural activity by so doing. Further, there were no other agricultural implements to which a farmer might turn to increase productivity. As a result, the addition of capital to the agricultural production process, in the absence of additions of land or labor, did not increase agricultural output. This output, however, could be increased when one added more labor and land, without adding new tools. This is to say, using the same tool, a farmer could decide to work longer on enlarged fields. It was in this sense that capital was the lease forceful of productive forces.

When farmers expanded old or began new enterprises, they might find that they needed tools. When this was the case, one either made them, purchased them at affordable prices from blacksmiths, or borrowed them from a relative or a friend. Such tools were technically not free goods. They certainly had their costs in time, money, or reciprocity debts; but many Barma felt that if you needed tools you just went out and got them, and this seems to have been the case. It is in this sense that capital did not constrain production and may be though of as abundant.

So land and capital could be abundant. Labor, on the other hand, relative to land and capital, was scarce. Each worker in a household, as we earlier learned, could be absolutely certain only of his or her own labor. He or she should under certain conditions receive additional labor, but this was not absolutely guaranteed. This meant that, unless a few people were "working one," agricultural enterprises' output was limited to the tools and land that a single person might handle. This was a hoe, ax, and machete working on about a maximum of 1.6 hectares (Guillard 1965, 188). Thus farmers were faced with the knowledge that there was an abundance of land waiting to be farmed with plenty of tools to do it with, if only they could get the workers to put the land and tools into production—which is another way of saying that labor was the most limiting factor of production in the Barma domestic mode of production.

Readers may now appreciate why the relative scarcities of factors of production dampened any enthusiasm for capitalism among Barma food producers. Fields, tools, and people were needed to farm. In this sense, each of these was a necessary productive force. However, all three forces were required if production was to actually occur.

Thus all three in conjunction were the necessary and sufficient conditions of agriculture production. Land and capital, as has just been shown, were abundant, while labor was scarce, which implied that if you had labor, you could get the land, which was there for the asking, and the tools, which were equally easily acquired. This meant that labor was in effect both the necessary and sufficient condition of agricultural production, because if you had labor you could automatically secure land and capital, while you could not do the reverse if you had land and capital. In such a situation a rational person forgoes the accumulation of capital to concentrate upon that of labor.

Attention now turns to how much could be produced, and to how much could be produced per expenditure of labor, that is, to productive capacity and productivity. Generally, the more land, capital, and labor loaded into a production process, the more it can produce; and the greater its output, the higher the level of its productive forces.

Barma farming used production inputs sparingly. Generally each worker in a household farmed about 0.99 hectares. There were an average of 3.6 workers in each household, and—using a few hoes, axes, and machetes—they cultivated a mean of 3.04 hectares, of which about 80 percent was devoted to sorghum and millets. In short, each household put little labor, land, or capital into the production process.

Outputs reflected this input situation. The different sorghums seem to have averaged about 880 kilograms per hectare. Millet seems to have yielded about 550 kilograms per hectare.[6] Households had average yields of about 1000 kilograms of sorghum and 227 kilograms of millet. Of course this was not their total food production, for they also produced fish and certain vegetables. The grain crop, however, was the most crucial one for subsistence and averaged about 1,227 kilograms per household.

The households from which the above statistics were obtained had on the average 5.1 people who had to be fed. Each of these people would require an average of 210 kilograms of grain for minimum adequate nutrition (Clark and Haswell 1964, 59). This means that a household had to produce about 1,071 kilograms of cereal to satisfy its minimum nutritional requirements. As households in the year under study produced 1,227 kilograms per household, its suggests they exceeded their minimum household subsistence requirements by about 156 kilograms per household, or 13.7 percent.

Direct measures of the productivity of Barma cereal production are unavailable. However, estimates are possible. Haswell conducted a study of agricultural production in the Gambia and concluded that, for each hour worked, a person produced circa 1.06 kilograms of sorghum and 0.48 kilograms of millet (1963). The Gambia's habitat and agricultural techniques resemble those in much of Bagirmi, so it is plausible that the labor productivities of Barma cereal production resembled those in the Gambia. By any measures, such a low productive capacity and labor productivity indicate a low level of agricultural production.[7]

The low level of productive forces in conjunction with the conditions of uncertainty meant that food products had to be produced even when variations in the environment created circumstances that were adverse to agriculture. There were at least three important ecosystemic variations addressed by different agricultural practices. These include variations in precipitation, soil fertility, and animal pests. Fluctuations in rainfall were managed through either ridging, intercropping, or multiple cropping. We begin with the first of these. Barth reported that "it seemed very remarkable" to him "that here, as well as in other parts of the country . . . the . . . [cereal] was generally cultivated in deep furrows and ridges, or *deraba*" (1965, 525). What Barth called ridging is the working of the soil into rectangular mounds on top of which, and in the furrows between which, crops are sown. Ridging is not particularly important as a way of controlling variations in total annual rainfall. It is, however, useful when dealing with rainfall distribution. Years of poor rainfall distribution are ones with times of precipitation followed by long dry spells. Ridged crops can better withstand these droughts because mounded soils hold moisture better than unmounded ones (Kowal and Kassem 1978, 178).

Crops may be grown alone in a field, in which case they are known as sole crops; or they may be sown in combination with others. The latter practice, intercropping, is currently widely practiced and equally widely reported to have been an ancient custom. Farmers seemed most often to mix a crop that grew high above the ground with one that grew close to it, often intercropping millet and sorghum with cowpeas, squash, peanuts, or cucumbers. There seem to be a number of advantages to intercropping in the dry savanna (Normal, Buntjer, and Goddard 1970), and at least two of these appear related to precipitation.

It might be said of Bagirmi that it never rains but it pours. Rain comes in powerful, wind-driven torrents. Sole crops tend to dislodge in the runoff of such deluges, because there is considerable distance between the plants. However, the vegetation in intercropped fields is often so closely packed that each plant is woven with its neighbors into a small dam. This can break the runoff into trickles, which reduces erosion, for the gentler trickles do not rush from a field before they can be absorbed. This enhances infiltration, which puts more water in the ground where it can nourish the plants.

Farming systems tend toward either mono- or multiple croppings. In the former the emphasis is upon a single crop; in the latter it is spread among a number of crops. The Barma, as we have seen, were multiple croppers. A reason for this is that, by planting more than one crop, they were protecting themselves against normal variations in precipitation. *Tenge, pennisetum typhoideum*, was planted early on lighter soils and required the least moisture of any cereal to reach maturity, for it can produce under conditions of around 300 millimeters of rainfall. However, it cannot tolerate waterlogged soils (Kowal and Kassem 1978). *Jarto, sorghum caudatum*, was also planted on lighter soils, just after the *tenge*, often intercropped with it. *Jarto* requires more rainfall than *tenge*, at least 600 millimeters (Cabot and Bouquet 1974, 42), but can better tolerate waterlogging. Both *tenge* and *jarto* tend to be planted early (late May or June) and accordingly to be harvested early (late September or October).

Wa, sorghum durra, is often cultivated using flood recession techniques. These require heavier soils and plants that take a considerable time to mature. When cultivated as a flood recession crop, *wa* is first planted in nurseries for approximately 40 days and then transplanted to fields, where it grows for a further 140 or so days. These fields are located by the sides of existing rivers or in old riverbeds that no longer run but become bogs during the rains. Planting occurs in these spots after the flood has began to recede to a level that young *wa* can tolerate. Moisture is not supplied to the plants by rains, which have largely stopped by the time of transplanting, but by the ever receding flood.

The first planting of *wa* in nurseries begins in July, well after the *tenge* and *jarto* are maturing. Transplanting occurs in mid to late August, and harvest occurs well into the dry season at the end of January and into February.

The planting of three different cereals appears to assure farmers of a harvest under strikingly different rainfall regimes. First, if there is very little rain (less than 500 millimeters and more than 250 millimeters), both *wa* and *jarto* are likely to fail, but there will be *tenge*, which tends to thrive under such conditions. Second, if there is normal rainfall (roughly between 600 and 800 millimeters) but it is poorly distributed, there are likely to be problems for the *jarto* and potentially the *tenge*. This is because sorghum yields in the dry savanna drop severely when rains either begin later or end earlier than normal (Kowal and Kassem 1978, 243). *Tenge*, however, has a very short growing period and thus may be less affected by an early end to rains. However, a late start, especially one where there is initially some rain followed by a month with almost none, can considerably depress *pennesitum* yields. *Wa* yields are far less influenced by such pluvial antics because, as long as there is a total amount of rainfall to fill the low spots where it is grown, then these can act as watering cans supplying moisture for proper plant growth. Consequently, normal *wa* harvests might be expected even when there are poorly distributed rains and the *tenge* and *jarto* have been damaged. Third, there is likely to be a bumper harvest of all three cereals if there are normal rains, well patterned throughout the growing season. Finally, however, if it is a year of extraordinary rainfall, it is possible that the *tenge* harvest will be reduced because of waterlogging. Such excesses, however, are far less likely to hurt *jarto* and *wa* yields. The point to grasp is that Barma multiple cropping will produce some harvest come dry years, come wet ones, with well or poorly distributed rains.

Soil fertility was a second source of uncertainty in the Barma environment. Two practices addressed this. The first was the practice of fallowing. My informants' statements varied as to how long a field was cultivated and how long it was fallowed. A number of farmers indicated that fields should be worked for five to six years and then, after they had become "tired" (*orega*), allowed to rest for up to ten years. Dumont, who worked in southern Bagirmi, said that fields were worked for two to three years and fallowed for three to five years (1970, 69). Such discrepancies concerning the length of fallows probably reflect variations in soil conditions and, hence, differences in the amount of time required to return land to fertility levels suitable for cultivation.

Nitrogen is often lacking in savanna soils (Anthony, et al. 1979, 126). Chevalier reported that there were *acacia albida* trees in Bagirmi fields (1907, 326), a plant that returns nitrogen to the soil. Bagirmi did not cultivate acacia. They did, however, try to locate their fields around them, and in the past they appear to have scrupulously tried to preserve them. This meant protecting them from fire when fields were prepared for planting. It also meant resisting the temptation to cut them for firewood.

Marauding animals were a third source of uncertainty. The pattern of land use described by Chevalier at the beginning of this chapter was a way of addressing animal pests. This pattern, widespread throughout parts of the west and central African dry savanna, has been called concentric ring cultivation (Allan 1965). At the center of the ring, in and encircling the household, are its gardens. These tend to be continuously cultivated and semifertilized with the household's refuse. Gardens are often planted with vegetables. A few hundred yards to a kilometer away from this center is a second ring of cultivation. This is what Chevalier said was "properly speaking the location of the fields" (1907, 326). Here were the villages' main sorghum and millet fields. Each person with a field tended to have it contiguous with somebody else's, often with that of some other household member. There were only the smallest paths that separated different plots. Thus the fields of an entire village tended to be "an immense, somber green belt" (ibid., 301). Finally, surrounding this second ring was a third, often far less noticeable, one. Here would be freshly cleared land awaiting cultivation interspersed with cultivated fields, often planted with *tenge*. It should be noted that the rings in this system of land use were not always as neatly situated as they are described. Rather, they tended to conform to each village's supply of land resources.

Placing the first ring of cultivation in households located it near to people's domestic activities. The clamor of these tended to frighten off foraging animals. Then by marshaling the bulk of the village's production in one "immense belt" in the second ring, it was made far easier for a relatively few people to be at these fields at all times to frighten off determined pests. Shepherds with animals to protect assemble them in easily defendable flocks or herds. The ring system did for plants what flocks do for sheep—it concentrated them close to their protectors.

The processes of ridging, intercropping, multiple cropping, fallowing, conserving *acacia albida*, and constructing ring systems allowed farmers to produce under varied environmental conditions. So if it is accurate to characterize the level of Barma productive forces as low, it is certainly equally accurate to classify them as risk aversive, for the different production risks provoked by environmental uncertainty were all reduced by the agricultural practices just described—but at a cost. What this cost was, and how it may have been exacted, are revealed in the following section. To do this, however, we need to understand a major process helping to reproduce the mode of production.

Reproduction and Contradiction

Barma productive forces produced little. They did so only when supplied with labor, which was scarce. This meant that a crucial reproductive problem faced by the Barma mode of production was that of labor resupply. I have earlier argued that Barma households followed an extending strategy. This was one that "extended" the family in a household by replacing and increasing the number of adults in it [Reyna 1976, 184]. Certainly, when elder and junior males plotted to become "big" or "bigger," they contracted marriages to add wives; they had as many children by these wives as possible; they sought to foster their kins' children; they sought to attract to their households other relatives who were no longer children; and in the past they sought slaves. A man seeking "bigness" sought to replace and increase the number of his dependents.

However, calling such a strategy an extending one to a certain extent obscures its nature because, when a man acted to add to his household, he really sought to increase the number of workers in it: extending was really about labor accumulation. Hence the extending strategy was, in fact, a process of labor accumulation.

Frequently both elder and junior men strove to accumulate labor within the same household. Fathers acquired wives, children, and other dependents at the same time that their married sons and brothers busied themselves at the same enterprise. The fact that men in the same household concommitantly added to their dependents meant that these households were sites of multiple labor accumulation. So perhaps it should be said that the Barma mode of production reproduced itself, in part, through a process of multiple labor accumulation.

Multiple labor accumulation involved what might be termed simple and extended reproduction. Mandel defines simple reproduction as "a succession of production cycles which make possible the *maintenance* of social wealth but not its increase" (1968, 322; emphasis in the original). He termed extended reproduction "a succession of production cycles which make possible an increase in social wealth" (ibid., 324). The amount of labor available for the production process largely determined the amount of land and capital that could be deployed, which—in combination with this labor—largely determined how much was produced. The quantity thus produced was the amount of social wealth in a household.

Activities that sustained the existing amount of labor in a household maintained the amount of social wealth it could produce and so might be classified as involving simple reproduction. Activities that increased the amount of labor in a household increased the amount of social wealth it generated and so should be considered to be those involving expanded reproduction.

Men with dependents in households participated in simple and extended reproduction. Both processes involved the distribution of some output from their, or their dependents', enterprises. Using output to feed existing dependents nourished them and allowed them to continue to reside in the household as active members. So a man was engaged in simple reproduction when he gave products to his existing dependents. A man giving his products in the form of bridewealth gifts to acquire a wife sought to add new dependents. This would increase a household's capacity for labor. Similarly, a man who gave his products prodigiously to kin and neighbors to impress upon them his generosity in the hope that they might chose to reside with so liberal a person also sought to add new dependents. Such distributions, because they increased the household's labor supply, were a form of extended reproduction. Thus nourishing existing dependents within households and making gifts to potential new ones were respectively processes of simple and extended labor accumulation. They were the way the mode of production resupplied itself with the force for its productive forces.

It is now time to speculate upon two contradictions engendered by such a mode of production. It is proposed that there were two contradictions within the Barma mode of production—an internal one within the production relations, and an external one between the latter and the productive forces. It is further suggested that intensification of the external contradiction might drive the internal one toward its structural limits.

The first contradiction was that between male elders and juniors. It emerged as a result of these men's motivations as they conducted their domestic affairs. Elder status was greatly desired by junior men because, as was earlier mentioned, it was the sole source of prestige open to them. There was, or is, no ritual that transforms a junior into an elder. Rather, it was a gradually acquired status that followed from a man doing manly things, such as marrying and having children. What usually confirmed that a man had arrived at eldership was that this labor accumulation had reached a point where it was appropriate to set up his own household, with himself as its head (*malabe*). Thus juniors wanted to leave households in which they were juniors, for only then would they achieve the deference available to them.

Juniors who became elders soon found, however, that not all elders were equal. Some, they discovered, were accorded more deference than others. Generally, the larger one's household and the greater one's dependents (both junior males and females), the more elevated one's eldership. This meant that elders, to maintain or to achieve greater deference, were predisposed to hold existing dependents in households while adding new ones.

Readers will recall from chapter 1 that structures consist of elements articulated with each other; that contradictions exist when there is structural incompatibility between elements within a structure or between elements within a structure and those in other structures; and that effectivity refers to the strength of articulations between elements in the face of contradiction. Clearly the two elements to the structure of production relations under analysis are in contradiction. Elders dearly want to hold deference-paying juniors within their households. Juniors equally dearly want to leave. Hence, as their interests are so opposed, the effectivity of the articulation between elders and juniors might be frail, that is, extended family households might easily fission, with junior sons and brothers moving off to found their own establishments.

This first contradiction was at the institutional level. Men knew that they wanted to be "big" (*ngollo*) and accorded deference (*hormo*). They knew that to acquire this status they should, among other things, become household heads (*malabe*). People were sensitive of the fact that at times fathers will be against sons and "big" brothers against "small" brothers. Some spoke of there being anger between juniors and elders. So to some extent Barma were aware of this first contradiction, and it is for this reason that it can be placed at the institutional level. However, they were oblivious to the second one.

It is now time to discover how the articulation of the productive forces with the productive relations generated this second contradiction. When the productive forces operated, they did so by consuming different factors of production, including the labor of elders, juniors, and females. This meant that the productive forces were articulated with production relations because, when the former produced and then reproduced itself, it did so by consuming labor supplied by the latter.

It was this labor consumption that created structural incompatibility between the two structures. Capital and land could be supplied to the productive forces with few problems. They were abundant. Labor, however, was scarce. The two structures had passed the limit of their articulation when the amount of labor required to operate the productive forces exceeded that available in the production relations. This would occur, for example, when a household required the services of four persons to meet its subsistence requirements and could only secure two workers. Under such conditions it would not produce enough food for its members, which meant that the household's productive forces demanded an amount of labor that exceeded that available in the production relations. So productive forces and relations were in contradiction in the sense that the former's demands for labor could reach a limit beyond which both structures' operation was threatened.

Now it is time to consider certain costs of the risk-aversive agricultural practices described in the preceding section. These costs were in labor. Four of the six risk-aversive practices increased the amount of labor demanded by the productive forces. First, consider ridging. Unridged fields are either not hoed at all or simply hoed once over lightly. Ridging requires that the farmer first turn the soil, then work it into a finer texture, and finally scoop it into mounds. Such work is arduous and time consuming. Marchal has shown for dry savanna conditions in Burkina Faso resembling those in Bagirmi that, as soon as labor becomes especially scarce, people no longer have the time to ridge, which causes the practice to fall into disuse (1983). Second, consider intercropping. This practice requires careful planting of plants and more careful weeding and harvesting—all of which take time. Norman, working in a dry savanna area of northern Nigeria, found that intercropping required 62 percent more labor than did sole crops (Norman et al. 1981). Next, consider acacia albida. These are wild plants, so it would not be expected that they would impose additional labor demands. However, acacia can only enhance soil fertility if they remain growing: they must not be cut for firewood, which obliged women, who collected the wood necessary for all domestic uses, to forgo them. They thus had to walk farther to gather fuel. Most fields with acacia in them were about a kilometer from villages. Most other firewood species were located five to ten kilometers from villages. It takes more labor to walk five to ten kilometers rather than one.

Finally, consider multiple cropping. This increased labor demands by including more labor-intensive flood recession agriculture in the cropping pattern. In the production of tenge and jarto, the farmer plants once, and then the plants mature quickly. Wa must be first planted in nurseries, next replanted, and only then does it slowly mature. Cultivation of the young plants in nurseries is toilsome. Their transplanting is equally so. Further, their longer growth cycle means that weeds have a longer time to get established. Thus when farmers choose to grow wa as well as tenge and jarto, even if they do not increase the total area they cultivate, they choose to work harder (Guillard 1965).

The increased labor required by these risk-aversive practices meant that there was more work to be performed during the same short bottleneck of time in which farming was possible. This, of course, worsened labor bottlenecks. Multiple cropping, especially, had this effect because it demanded that farmers be in two or three fields of different crops in different locations, each demanding attention at the same time. For example, it happens that a farmer will have a field of tenge needing harvest, one of jarto demanding weeding, and one of wa requiring immediate transplanting. This is a critical situation, which is uniquely produced by multiple cropping and can only be resolved by the supplying of labor, lots of it, fast!

The preceding suggests the following general point. Reduction of production risks imposed by environmental uncertainty required the addition of greater amounts of labor than would have been the case if the productive forces were insensitive to these risks. This meant that the contradiction between the productive force's need for labor and the production relations' ability to supply it was more intense than might otherwise have been the case and that it became most intense during labor bottlenecks produced by multiple cropping.

We are now in a position to speculate about how events in this second, productive force–productive relations contradiction might influence those in the first, elder-junior contradiction. There are certain unpredictable circumstances that necessitated risk-reducing agricultural practices in the production process. These increased the total amount of labor demanded by the productive forces, especially during bottleneck times. Such risk-reducing practices might be imagined as surges of demand for labor. They were surges in the sense that the need for additional labor was temporary, but great. If, for example, rains had been poorly distributed and a household was in danger of losing all its planting, then it had to find some way to recoup its anticipated losses immediately. Flood recession agriculture was an obvious possibility in this situation, but such an enterprise required considerable effort. This additional work usually fell when labor had to be supplied to other crops maturing in other fields, which meant that there were temporary, but sizable, surges of labor demand.

Such labor demands had to be supplied by the production relations. This was done, among other ways, simply by having elders request assistance from their juniors. Such appeals were made in the discourse of deference. Elders would inform juniors of their great need for help to begin or enlarge some risk-reducing production enterprise. Juniors would be expected to defer to their elders' requests. Deference payers, in short, would be expected to pay up.

However, juniors have only so much labor that they can supply, so there were clear limits to their deference. Clearly, increased demands for their services had to drive them toward these; and it was well known that such appeals could create ill feelings. A junior who felt imposed upon by elders or an elder who believed he had been needlessly rebuffed by his juniors was often said to become a "master of anger" (*malabungo*). This was a person who in American parlance was "ticked off." The crucial point is that, when people found themselves unable to conform to expectations of them as deference payers or receivers, it was believed appropriate for them to express frustration and become "masters of anger." A chief reason given for households fissioning was that they harbored "masters of anger."

The tirades of "masters of anger" were likely to have been more severe if an elder appealed for labor from a junior who was embarked upon a process of labor accumulation during a time when the junior was experiencing a bottleneck in his own enterprises. The junior in this situation might have a number of agricultural activities that had to be performed immediately for the more than one wife, the fair number of children, and the other dependents for whom he was responsible. He would simply have very little time to spare from his own chores and would be inclined to ignore the elder's request. This would mean that the junior would feel bad about not being deferential. It would mean that the elder would feel cheated of his deference. This was clearly a tinderbox situation capable of producing towering "masters of anger."

Thus it is proposed that risk-reducing activities were made necessary by the uncertain environmental conditions. These generated surges of labor demand, which, especially during bottleneck times, intensified the contradiction between the productive forces and the production relations, because the former now required an additional surge of what the latter had in only scarce supply. This intensification of the production relations–production forces contradiction was experienced by elders and juniors as increased attempts to exact deference. Elders and juniors were likely to face off at each other as "masters of anger" when deference could only be incompletely supplied. This would be the case when elders requested labor from juniors who themselves faced labor bottlenecks and who had a number of dependents for whom they were responsible. The anger elders and juniors evinced in such situations expressed that the contradiction within the production relations of a particular household was edging toward its limit—when everybody would be mad at everybody else and somebody would move off.

Conclusion

The mode of production just described appears to have been widely distributed throughout much of the east-central Sudan. Most societies' production relations were an aspect of their kinship relations. The level of these societies' productive forces was low.[8] Labor was everywhere scarce. Most production was food production, most of which was consumed within the household.[9] All food production processes were performed by household members, with some help from kin and neighbors. Consequently, as production was largely by, and for, household members, it seems suitable to call such economies, as did Sahlins, domestic modes of production. He, however, believed that such systems were "not organized to give a brilliant performance" (1972, 99).

My judgement is different. This mode of production could never be "brilliant" with the productive forces available to it. In fact, it would seem stupid for a single person on a tiny plot with a few, pitiful tools to dare the region's savagely quirky environment. But this, of course, is what farmers did; and for at least a thousand years—come drought, come flood, come whatever the environment had to threaten food producers with—the mode of production squeaked through, providing its practitioners with enough food to survive, and then some. They were able to do so because of a number of "remarkable" (Bunting 1975, 322) agricultural practices, such as mounding, intercropping, and multiple cropping, which parried the thrusts of their habitat. In such a place, with such productive forces, to be less than brilliant, but to survive, was brilliant.

Permit a final vignette that contributes to understanding an as-yet-unrevealed property of this mode of production. One day an elder pressed a small coin in his delighted grandson's fist. He then inquired what the boy would do with the money. "Buy candy," the child answered. This was a wrong response. Without a further word, the old man pried the boy's grubby hand open and retrieved his coin. The boy looked up at the elder, as if he thought a joke was being played. The elder dismissed him, with some curt words that I could not follow. Crushed, the boy rushed off.

"My God," I thought, as the boy dashed past, "they're teaching kids to make investments." Later, when I spoke with the elder, I found I was correct; though the type of investments the grandfather wanted his grandson to make were far different from those that dance in the heads of those expecting to cash in on the pleasures of capitalism. The elder said he wanted his descendant to continue his ancestors' customs. To do so, he said, the boy should use his wealth, most of which was not money but food stuffs, to nourish those in his household. He should use it to marry wives and to be generous to kin and neighbors.

The grandfather was teaching his grandson the norms that facilitated the process of multiple labor accumulation. By providing food to nourish his household dependents, the boy would be performing a process of simple reproduction. By giving gifts to kin and neighbors, he would be performing that of extended reproduction. Such processes maintained and added to a household's labor supply. They were a major way these domestic modes of production reproduced themselves.

One consequence of such reproductive processes was that little boys should not race out to buy candy, not because the money should be invested to make more money but because it should be circulated among kin and neighbors to "make" more kin and neighbors to resupply households with labor. As a result, domestic modes of production tended to be closed in the sense that their products circulated, as much as possible, to those who could provide households with the scarce labor they needed to accept the risks hurled at them by their environment.

So the domestic mode of production tended to be closed to all those who would not supply it with labor. However, officials—that other unit in the atomic structure of Bagirmi society, those who dressed in elegant robes, supped on the most succulent foods, and raised rare and fiery horses—never farmed. This presented them with a sticky problem—breaking and entering into the food producers' closed world. Exactly how they did so is the subject of chapters 6, 7, and 8.

Chapter 6

The Sun King and His Court

Bagirmi, as we know, referred to the *mbang* as the sun and his officials as the planets. This chapter describes how Bagirmi conceived and operated political offices and shows how they were organized, how persons were recruited to them, what types of estates were attached to them, how they made decisions, and what their principal officers were like. Thus, in a sense, the chapter presents the institutional "solar system" of the Bagirmi state. Chapter 7 derives a stately model from this cosmology and then shows how it was materially reproduced.

The Nature of Office

A Bagirmi official, as was noted in chapter 4, was called *maladono*. The word *mala* means "master," not in the sense of someone who lords it over others but in the sense of someone who has mastered a skill and in the process become an adept. For example, a fine fisherman is called a *malakoshkanje*, a "master of fishing." The word *dono* was defined by Gaden to mean "political influence" (1909, 77). Barma expressed matters more bluntly, for they said someone with *dono* was a person who "directed" (*jojigiga*) people. Thus a *maladono* was a master of the art of direction.

Barma sometimes substituted the word *debngollo* for *maladono*. A *debngollo* was a "person" (*deb*) who was "big" (*ngollo*). However, you could not be a "big person" just by being a giant with a flair for organization. Rather, you had to occupy some office of the state. The verb used to describe assumption of an office was "to eat" (*kesa*). To eat an office you had first to go through a process of recruitment and then a ritual of investiture. Recruitment processes varied. However, a person was never termed *maladono* or *debngollo* until he or she had undergone investiture and had "eaten" the office.

Barma never spoke of the office of this or that person, the way one might speak of the office of the presidency. Rather, they talked in terms of households. They believed that there were some households whose occupants were *tashkipage*—who farmed— and others whose occupants were *maladonoge*—who directed. Households, whether of farmers or officials, were known over the years to grow in size, become crowded, split into additional households, and eventually become neighborhoods or even villages. This meant that the offices seemed to have been associated with residence groups. Hence the office of the sovereign often was referred to as *be mbang*, "household of the sovereign."[1]

Devallée and Lanier observed that there appear to be two types of officials, whom they usually referred to as "Great" and "Small" (Devallée 1925, 24, 26; Lanier 1925, 468). Lanier contrasted them as follows: "Each of these great officials . . . is surrounded by a numerous following. His . . . [household] is a veritable fortress where he maintains his wives, his servants, his slaves and a personal guard. He has under his authority subalterns to execute his orders and to command the warriors in combat who serve under his banner" (1925, 468). "Great" or, as we shall hereafter call them, court officials were household heads who participated in deliberations at the court, possessed estates that they administered and from which they drew revenues, and had "small" or, as we shall henceforth refer to them, staff officials to work for them. A court official's staff could be called his *aljema*.[2]

Staff tended to be jacks-of-all-trades who acted as judges, trusted advisors, tax collectors, and above all soldiers. Staff lacked estates and specialized in administering and not in formulating policy. There were two types of staff whose functions were differentiated enough to be distinguished by name. Staff called *ḳada*, as in the *ḳadigaladima*, served as deputies or "preceptors" (Gentil 1902, 81) to court officials. Those called *agid*, as in *agidbugoman*, communicated decisions taken at court to the communities within the estate of the court official whom they served. Usually *agid*s were named after the village, ethnic group, or community to which their court official had appointed them. Frequently, *agid*s were slaves. Normally both free and slave *agid*s' most significant task was revenue collection.[3] Court officials, surrounded by their staffs, constituted the basic building blocks of the Bagirmi state hierarchy.

A Barma instructing me about how these offices had been organized would begin by smoothing a patch of sand clear of debris. He would trace a circle on this cleared patch and then say that inside this circle was a "place" (*got*) where the *mbang* had his household. This was his "palace" (*gur*) at Massenya. Beyond this circle was an "outside" (*agela*) place. Once my instructor was confident that I had grasped this distinction, he would make lines, either inside or outside the circle, naming for each line an official. This distinction between "inside," or court, and "outside," or estate officials was important in the hierarchy of the state.

Most court officials lived in or near the *mbang*'s residence, though by no means all did. For example, the *patcha* and *alifa ba* normally resided away from Massenya. However, what made an official a court official was that he or she directly served the *mbang* at Massenya. Such an official had certain rights to participate in policy formation and the administration of those decisions taken at the *mbang*'s palace.

Estate *maladonoge* lived in the different communities that were part of the estate of court officials, which might be in core or tributary territories. Estate officials' decision-making and administrative duties were normally restricted to these communities. Such officials were officers in political structures that might govern communities, towns, villages, or ethnic groups. They might be *mbang*s in their own right, as was the case with *mbang* Bousso. They might be *sheikh*s or *lawan*s, as was the case with the heads of different Arab or Fulani ethnic groups. The degree of centralization in estate political structure varied greatly. *Mbang* Bousso headed a hierarchy that approached *mbang* Massenya's in size and complexity. *Sheikhs* of Arab tribes, on the other hand, were usually the sole political officers in their ethnic group. Estate officials who headed centralized polities, as did the *mbang* at Bousso or the *alifa* at Korbol, might thus be powerful in their own right.

However, all estate officials recognized the authority of *mbang* Massenya to "direct" certain of their affairs. This authority often derived from some tradition of submission and marriage alliance. Massenya's authority over a community might change. Indeed, it frequently did, but there was always some sense that Massenya had the right to direct certain affairs in the community. Thus, from the perspective of a court official, those officials who were "outside" had only community responsibilities, while from the vantage of an estate official, those at Massenya were grandees with multiple community responsibilities. Thus the hierarchy of Bagirmi offices was based upon the direction of estates by court officials. In order to understand how this hierarchy worked we discuss the *mbang* and his court in the following four sections.

Recruitment

Barma said that at the end of the nineteenth century, the *mbang* "chose" (*kus*) court officials and that they in turn "chose" their own staffs. Other sources suggested that those chosen were the wealthiest, who in effect bought the office (Pacques 1977, 60; Devallée 1925, 26; Lanier 1925, 468). This suggests a system of recruitment based on the stimulation of the *mbang*'s cupidity by the candidate's pocketbook. In fact, however, appointment of court offices was more complicated than the preceding suggests, in ways that allowed for considerable flexibility in the choice of an official. This helped to fit the person to the job.

The *mbang* chose all court officials in the sense that he, with his advisors, did have to approve them before they underwent investiture and assumed office. However, the *mbang* was constrained to consider three sets of factors before arriving at a choice: whether the candidate satisfied the "custom" (*hada*) for occupying a specific office; whether the candidate possessed the ability to perform the office's responsibilities; and whether the candidate possessed wealth. These factors, according to informants, weighed differently for different offices. Thus for some offices a candidate's ability counted for more than the possession of customary attributes or wealth. In others, the reverse appears to have been true.

Perhaps the most fundamental customary rule regulating recruitment to court office was the allocation of some offices to free persons and others to slaves. Traditionally there were three types of free offices. These were royal, master-of-the-earth, and free person offices. Recruitment to these free offices was based upon the possession of customarily correct types of kinship links to the previous officeholder.

Royal officials were called *tosmbang*, which meant literally "kin of the *mbang*." The most important of the royal officials, aside from the *mbang*, were the *magira*, the *mbang*'s mother; the *mbang*'s first four wives, who, in order of their marriage, were the *gumsu*, the *bedangul*, the *lel murba*, and the *lel daba*; the *mbang*'s first four sons, who were the firstborn sons of the first four wives, the *chiroma*, the *ngar murba*, the *ngar daba*, and the *ngar keleo*; and finally the eldest of the *mbang*'s daughters by the *gumsu*, the *chikotima*. The *mbang*'s brothers, his cousins, and his uncles were unimportant as royal officials, though they might well be candidates for other offices. The new *mbang* should be the *chiroma*, the first son of the first wife of the previous *mbang*. Then the new *magira* should be the new *mbang*'s mother; and the new *gumsu* should be his first-married wife, and so on. Royal recruitment clearly depended on being the mother, wives, sons, or daughters of the previous or present *mbang*.

Master-of-the-earth (*malanange*) officials came from communities that were believed to possess the land of which the second kingdom of Bagirmi was founded. There were four such officials: The *ngar birkete*, *galadima*, *ngar mweymanga*, and *mbarakudu*. Recruitment to these offices was traditionally based on descent from previous officehold-ers, with the office in principle going to the oldest son by the first wife of the previous officeholder.

Finally, there were certain free officials who were of neither royal nor master-of-the-land origin. The most important of these were the *milma*, the *mange*, the *naib*, the *imam ngolo*, the *arkali*, the *alifa moyto*, and the *alifa ba*.[4] Recruitment to these offices was traditionally through some form of patrilineal descent from the previous officeholder.

The term *slave* official meant an official who occupied an office that, during the nascent period of the state, had been originally filled by a slave. In 1870 the office might or might not be filled by a slave; if the occupant normally resided within the *mbang*'s palace, then it was more likely that he was a slave. Thus the most influential of the slave offices in 1870 was that of the *ngarman*, who was a eunuch as well as a slave. The offices of the *kirema* and the *katourlil* were filled by individuals who resided within the palace and were thus usually filled by slaves. Finally, there were the *mbarma*'s and the *patcha*'s offices, which were filled by individuals who did not reside in the *mbang*'s palace. They were supposed to be slave offices but were often filled by free individuals.

Custom thus preserved certain offices for free and others for slave officials. With regard to free offices, it further reserved some offices for royalty, masters-of-the-earth, and ordinary free persons. Tradition said with regard to slave offices that they could be offered to slaves, eunuch slaves, or free persons.

However, the *mbang* could ignore custom and appoint to an office someone lacking the traditional qualifications. This seems to have occurred more frequently with the appointment of freemen to offices that were in principle reserved for slaves. But when he made such appointments, the *mbang* had to have some reason to do so. One reason for appointing an "inappropriate" candidate to court office was that such a person would be good for the office.

For example, one day I asked an aged Barma gentleman from a family that had supplied court officials whether the *patcha*'s office was hereditary. I was told, "When the son of a *patcha* was a good fighter, then the son became *patcha*; when not, then we took another slave from the slaves." A major responsibility of the *patcha* was as a general, so *patcha*s had to be skilled fighters. This meant that *mbang*s generally chose men they knew to be fine soldiers regardless of their wealth or their kinship connections.

Similar considerations of finding the right man for the right job appear to have operated when a *mange* died in the 1960s. Traditionally, descent regulated recruitment to this office, for it should be awarded to the deceased's eldest son. In fact, the *mbang* at the time offered the office to this son, who was a *mallam*. However, he was devoted to Islam and apathetic toward the *mange*'s duties, and so the *mbang* chose another, who was the son of the *mbarakudu*. The *mbarakudu*'s and the *mange*'s offices perform similar functions. By selecting the son of a *mbarakudu*, informants said, the *mbang* selected someone who was already familiar with the *mange*'s office. Thus it appears that first and foremost, the *mbang* and his counselors were constrained by custom when recruiting officials; but if tradition turned up somebody lacking in ability, then regardless of tradition, what the *mbang* needed was somebody with the "right stuff."

Offices tended to be sold for money in the early twentieth century. Barma did not know the age of this practice.[5] Informants' statements suggest that the purchase of office could have evolved out of gift giving between officials because, some informants insisted, these "payments" were merely "gifts" (*ngaskirege*).[6] Further, they made a distinction between "gifts" and "payment" that turned on the symbolic value of the items disbursed. Gifts, usually foods, were given on social occasions — births, deaths, marriages. They were also given when relationships were established or maintained, and they were tokens of those relationships. Their symbolic scope was great because they could represent any relationship, be it with kin, official persons, communities, or polities. Payments, on the other hand, symbolized nothing. When you went to a market you gave money, you got something, and that was that.

Officials exchanged gifts during investiture rituals. Such gifts seem to have in a general way symbolized the hierarchical nature of office. For example, during the investiture of the *mbang*, a cow was sacrificed and portions of the animal were given to various court and estate officials. This symbolized a sacrifice that Dala Birni, the first *mbang*, was supposed to have performed to create the state (Pacques 1977, 15–16). So the new *mbang*'s gift of meat to his officials was not a payoff for acquiring office. Rather, it was part of a political "theater" in which the meat given represented the meat that Dala Birni gave in the original sacrifices during the founding of the state; these sacrifices had in their turn legitimated the *mbang*'s authority over court officials.

Just as the *mbang* served ritual meals as part of his investiture, so did the court officials. Food in these sacrifices was distributed to political inferiors — staff and estate officials — and to superiors — such as the *mbang*. Such meals were understood within the general Barma view of the significance of gift giving. Hence the food given during investiture symbolized the relationship of offices to each other in the hierarchy of super- and subordinate offices.

Similarly, all staff were given some sort of turban during their investiture during the nineteenth century by the official elevating them to office. Again the turban was not a payoff for becoming a member of somebody's staff. Rather, it was a badge of official position. It symbolized the possession of *dono* (influence).

These gifts may have been transformed into payments because the amounts of foodstuffs that court officials gave to the *mbang* as part of their "eating" office grew to include increasing amounts of money. Larger gifts, however, were symbolically emptier gifts. Originally, when a court official gave a portion of meat to the *mbang* during investiture, this symbolized the relationship between the two. However, when some court officials began to add to this portion of meat a "dash" of money, the dash was a delightful, "sweet thing" (ngas lel) that meant absolutely nothing. As gifts became larger and larger, a greater percentage of their total value appears to have been occupied by "sweet things." This implied that candidates came increasingly to buy offices as their gifts became increasingly meaningless.[7]

We are now in a position to present an overview of the political recruitment process. Recruitment to office was based upon the possession of the appropriate traditional qualifications, ability, or wealth. Royal, masters-of-the-earth, free, and slave persons who possessed one or more of the above attributes constituted a political elite, because they were part of a pool of candidates for office. The mbang and his counselors, however, did not automatically choose someone who had wealth or the right traditional connections from this pool. Rather, they seem to have taken pains to search for the individual who was both traditionally acceptable and suited for the office's duties. Sometimes, especially when colonial rule was starving the mbang's coffers, "well-suited" meant rich and willing to pay.

Estates

Normally the mbang bestowed different authorities on a court official at his or her investiture. One of these was the right to "direct" what one authority has called estates (O'Fahey 1980, 49) and others fiefs (Urvoy 1949; Cohen 1966b; Brenner 1973). We shall explore the nature of estates in this section, suggesting that they alternated between being fiefs and benefices.

A fundamental meaning of estate is "property in land," of which two views might be considered. The first and narrower notion would be of a large farm given to an official when he or she "ate" an office. When court officials acquired many slaves, they located them in villages to farm for them. However, they were not awarded slave villages as prerogatives of office. Nor do they appear to have been given farms at investiture. Further, they do not appear to have been rewarded with these during other times when they were in office. Thus court officials' estates were not large farms in the nineteenth century.

A broader view of estate would be of any territorial unit or units awarded to an official. There is evidence supporting the view that court officials were awarded such estates. Barth, for example, talks of court officials as the "governors of principal places" (1965, 562). Nachtigal speaks of their being awarded "districts" (1889, 610). Pacques says they were each given a "territory" (1977, 59). My informants spoke of this "place" (got) or that "place" as having been the land of this or that official. Hence Mandjaffa was "got mbarma," while certain Sara areas were "got katourlil."

Estates awarded to court officials, however, were not neatly packaged, discrete territories. Rather, they were a hodgepodge of towns, neighborhoods in towns, villages, ethnic groups, and even marketplaces in both core and tributary zones. Most estates seemed to have been composed of both villages or ethnic groups. Such holdings might be thought of as a "portfolio" of places.[8]

When I explicitly asked Barma whether estates were geographic units, I received conflicting answers. Whether one was descended from officials or food producers was crucial in influencing how one answered this question. For example, descendants of officials tended to describe estates as if they were a "place" (*got*). Food producers, however, tended to see their villages as full of kin or the dependents of kin, so they didn't see them as places but as the relatives of this person or that person. Thus, from the vantage of the political hierarchy, a village was a place in an estate, while from that of the villagers themselves it was the kin of such-and-such a person.

Similarly, most ethnic groups who were assigned to particular officials viewed themselves as in some way kin groups. Consider, for example, the case of the Arabs. They considered themselves to be the patrilineal descendants of a founder of a descent group. Their names for their groups were the name either of the apical ancestor who founded the group or of some significant event in the history of the group. Descendants of Barma officials, on the other hand, rarely called these groups by the names they called themselves. Rather, they insisted upon referring to them by the names of the places they happened to be when, during their transhumances, they were dealt with by officials. For example, different Walad Musa clans grazed in the Debaba when it was the time to pay taxes. These clans were never called by their proper names but were simply given the generic of *Shuwa Debaba*, which meant "Arabs resident in the Debaba." Here again officials tended to conceive of groups as territorial entities when they perceived themselves to be groups of agnatic kin. Thus estates were both kin and territorial groups depending upon whom you asked.

The rights that the court officials held in their estates had little to do with agricultural production. Generally, officials exercised neither allocational, use, nor managerial rights over farmland. This meant that they did not control access to land or to the production processes on it. Rather, they enjoyed rights to direct (*jojigi*) its affairs. The notion of direction had broad connotations. It meant to execute decisions taken at court, which is roughly what M. G. Smith meant by *administration* (1960, 16). It also meant to formulate policy within the estate, which is what M. G. Smith had meant by *politics* (ibid.). However, court officials did not dictate the politics or the administration of their estates.

Rather, there was a give-and-take between court and estate officials over the formulation and administration of policy. Powerful court officials tended to have their way on their estates. Weak ones had trouble performing elementary administrative duties. Gluckman long ago suggested that high officials in centralized African polities enjoyed "rights of administration" (1948). This seems a bit too restrictive for Bagirmi. Rather, as was already suggested, they had rights of direction.

Attention now turns to whether or not estates were fiefs. Lanier asserted that a court official was a "veritable feudal lord having fiefs" (1925, 468). However, before accepting this judgment, it is important to make a distinction between fiefs and benefices, and then decide whether Bagirmi estates might have been the latter rather than the former. Max Weber defined a benefice as the remuneration of an officeholder that was an attribute of an office, and not of its occupant (1968, 1:235). For example, in medieval Europe an estate given to an official for doing the work of that office only during the official's tenure was a benefice. Fiefs, in the sense that Weber used the term, were an attribute of the occupant of the office, not of the office itself. Thus fiefs in medieval Europe were inherited estates that a person enjoyed regardless of what office he or she enjoyed (Weber 1968, 1:255; 3:1073–74). Benefices are nonhereditary remunerations for holding particular office. Fiefs are hereditary attributes of a social position.

A crucial difference between hierarchies based upon benefices and those based upon fiefs is the degree of control of higher offices over lower ones in the hierarchy. An official remunerated with a benefice must be more attentive to the desires of superiors because they can remove the benefice, whereas an officer enjoying a fief can afford to take a somewhat breezier attitude toward superiors because they cannot repossess the fief. Power is clearly more centralized in systems based upon benefices than in those with fiefs.

The following evidence bears upon whether Bagirmi estates were fiefs or benefices. Barth was struck in the middle of the nineteenth century by the absence of "an aristocratical element such as we have found in Bornu" (1965, 562). Barth does not explain what he meant by *aristocratical*, but it is likely that he was employing the term in its ordinary nineteenth-century sense, which referred to a hereditary landowning class. Twenty years after Barth's visit, Nachtigal speaks of the court officials possessing "districts" (1889, 610). However, Nachtigal nowhere says that these were hereditary. Devallée, writing in the early years of the twentieth century, seems for the first time to have sensed that *maladonoge* may have been different from medieval European nobility, but he says nothing about whether their estates were hereditary, strongly implying that they were not (1952, 72). Of the four European chroniclers of the nineteenth-century state, only Lanier actually said there were fiefs. However, he never mentions which court officials possessed which fiefs, and he describes no cases of their inheritance. Because inherited estates were so important in medieval and postmedieval Europe, I believe that European observers would have readily recognized them had they existed in Bagirmi. However, four Europeans observed Bagirmi between 1850 and the early twentieth century, and not one reported the existence of inherited estates.

Barma who had trained to be officials stressed the vastness of the *mbang*'s powers. One evidence of this, they said, was that it was he who gave and took away the different prerogatives of office, including estates. One said, for example, that the *mbang* "took the *katourlil* and gave him Sara places." The absence of firm reporting of hereditary estates by the European chroniclers, coupled with informants' insistence upon the *mbang*'s ability to confer estates, suggests that these may have been benefices.

However, just when the nature of estates appears to be resolved, it should be noted that there is evidence of the inheritance of official estates during the twentieth century and a suggestion that this occurred in the 1800s. In the 1960s the *galadima*, Muktar Ngollo, inherited his office as well as the estate that went with it, the communities around Bugoman, from his father, Ngar Kemkaka. The latter was a son of the *ngar keleo*, who was a son of *mbang* Ab Sakin. Prior to *galadima* Ngar Kemkaka, the office had been filled by an individual from another family. The present *galadima* fully believed that the office could go to his son and that the estate could be attached to it. I asked if the inheritance of this office and its estate was a practice instituted by the French during their administration and carried on by the independent Chadian government. The response was that the French had acceded to Bagirmi custom in this matter and allowed the office and its estate to be inherited.

Most striking was the assertion by some that sometimes a court office and its estate would be hereditary for a number of generations, but then the *mbang* might choose somebody of a completely different family, and it would be hereditary in that family. This seems to have been exactly the case with the office of *galadima*, which was moved from one to another family following the reign of Ab Sakin. This suggests that estates alternated between being benefices and fiefs.

One reason that this alternation may have occurred has to do with differing, yet in Barma eyes entirely legitimate, notions of the *mbang*'s and the *maladonoge*'s possession of land. We consider first the ideas about the *mbang*'s relation to the land. According to certain traditions of Bagirmi's founding, Dala Birni, the first *mbang* lanced and killed a rhinoceros in a swamp where an old woman, called Nyonnyon, was making charcoal. In most versions of this tradition, Dala Birni then undertook a retreat, after which he offered a sacrificial meal of the rhinoceros to the eight chiefs who represented the masters-of-the-earth communities at the time of the founding of the second kingdom. The right shoulder went to the Mweymanga, the left to the Guledimari, the right flank to the Kutu, the left to the Birkete, the right ribs to the Murba and the left to the Keleo, the back to the Chilomari, and the lungs to the Dabara. It was after this sacrifice that the chiefs of the original landowning communities granted the status of "master-of-the-earth and *mbang*" to Dala Birni (Pacques 1977, 16).

A crucial point to grasp is what "master-of-the-earth" (*malanange*) actually meant. It will be remembered from chapter 4 that the *mbang* was conceived of as "the result and exponent" of the two forces, *mao* and *karkata*, which "animate the world" (Pacques 1967, 207). The *mbang* was thought of as "of the earth" because he incarnated the very forces that animated the land, in the sense of giving it life and causing things to occur. This implied that if the *mbang* were to cease being *malanange*, then the very forces of nature would be imperiled—a rather sobering proposition. Thus, when an *mbang* granted land to a court official, it was not believed for a moment that he suddenly ceased to be the force that animated the land. So there was no real severing of his relationship to the land with the awarding of estates. Rather, the granting of estates merely allowed his officials to use for themselves part of the land that was there as a result of the operation of the forces of (his) nature.

On the other hand, there was, and is, a strong sense in Bagirmi that the use of natural resources confers rights over them, including those of their patrilineal inheritance. A farmer who had cultivated a field for the first time fully expected that it would be passed on to his sons. Court officials seem to have seen their rights over estates much as farmers saw theirs over fields. Thus, if a *maladono* used an estate in the sense of sensibly administering it, then his sons should inherit the same right. However, the inheritance of a field was unequivocally guaranteed to males in the direct line of descent of the first man to put it into cultivation. If a man had not been a first user of the land, then his sons should ask permission of some individual with the right to allocate the land. This might be a village head or the direct descendants of the first person to cultivate the plot.

Normally this permission would be granted. The situation of court officials with regard to their estates was similar to that of a farmer who was not the first user of land. The official had used the estate, so his or her sons might fully expect to use it in their turn, which, if they did, meant that they had inherited it. However, as a result of the sacrifice of the rhinoceros, the *mbang* had become *malanange*. This placed him in the position of first user, which meant that he always had the right to decide the disposition of estates.

There were thus contradictory principles governing the allocation of estates. A first principle allowed the *mbang* to distribute them. A second principle allocated them to the descendants of previous estate holders. This allowed estates to alternate between being fiefs and benefices. When a court official inherited his father's office and its estate, it was as if the estate were a fief. When, on the other hand, a court official inherited his father's office and was awarded a new estate, or if a court official was awarded an office and its estate who was not patrilineally descended from the previous occupant, then it was as if the estates were a benefice.

Just as there was flexibility as to official recruitment, so there was flexibility with regard to the allocation of estates. Pacques has said that "the sovereigns did their utmost to ride astride their [court officials'] prerogatives and the resources which they drew from them" (1977, 43). This suggests that when there were more vigorous *mbang*s, there were more benefices, and when there were weaker ones, there were more fiefs.

Policy Formation

H. J. Fisher, the eminent historian of the precolonial central Sudan, judged Bagirmi to be a despotic state (1975, 63). Perhaps Fisher's judgment reflected the views of Barth and Nachtigal. The former had said that Bagirmi was an absolute monarchy that lacked an "assembly" (1965, 562). The latter had reported that the state lacked a "parliament or other control" over the *mbang* (1889, 609). This suggests that only one voice counted, that of the *mbang*, when policy was formulated, which, if it were true, would indeed make Bagirmi a despotic state.

Policy formation in any polity may be thought of as a process involving two phases. During the first phase individuals or groups make demands upon political actors. This phase may be termed one of interest articulation. Then in a second phase these actors make decisions upon the demands that have been placed before them. This second phase may be termed one of decision making.[9] If the demands of different individuals or groups in a polity cannot be articulated, or if only a single actor makes decisions about these demands, then policy formation may be truly said to be despotic. The *mbang* may have been a glorious Sun King resplendent in fine robes. He was far, however, from being a ruler with absolute power and authority to formulate policy.

There were two major ways in which interests were articulated and placed before the Bagirmi court. One was what I have chosen to call the "door" system and the other was through audiences. We begin with the former. The *mbang* and his court officials would marry as many wives as possible. These wives were described by one imaginative Barma as being like doors, because kin and friends would pour out to them their worries, hopes, and fears, in effect stating their demands. Then the wives would spring open, like doors, communicating these concerns to their husbands. Husbands, however, were also officials, which meant that demands had been articulated to the court once a wife reported a concern of one of her relatives or friends.

There was a rough political reciprocity in this door system, because kin and friends of an official's wife were supposed to support that official. So, in a sense, a wife's kin and friends became an official's constituents, and he was their representative. This motivated enterprising men to marry their daughters or sisters to the *mbang* or other court officials so that they could have their own doors. Conversely, astute *mbangs* sought wives from men and regions whose interests they needed to be informed about. Thus, by the time of *mbang* Ab Sakin, southern tributaries were important to state revenues, and the *mbangs* had begun to take certain of their four primary wives, who had originally come from *malanange* groups, from the Sara, to whom they were allied at Kumra (Pacques 1977, 44).

There were as many doors as there were wives of officials. This meant that, if the *mbang* and another court member both had wives from Bousso, there would be two different doors and sources of information about the interests of those in Bousso. Hence demands bearing upon an affair might come from multiple sources. The most extensive door system, of course, belonged to the *mbang*. Gaurang II, who ruled at the onset of the colonial period, complained to a French administrator that his father, *mbang* Abd el Kader, and his father's brother, *mbang* Ab Sakin, each possessed 1,500 wives during their reigns. At the time of his complaint, French administrators estimated that Gaurang still had 150 wives. A descendant of Ab Sakin's said that Gaurang may have exaggerated, but he still insisted that Ab Sakin had 700 wives.

The geographic origins of court officials' wives tended to reflect their husbands' official history. A court member's first wife often came from his social milieu. If, for example, a man was normally part of the Massenya elite from which officials were chosen, his first wife might normally be expected to have come from the same background. A royal man would marry a royal woman, and so forth. However, once this person "ate" an office, additional marriages would be contracted. These wives often came from his estate, because enterprising men married off their daughters so that they might have their own doors to the Sun King's court.

Thus the *mbang* possessed a door system that tended to be diffused throughout the state, while the court officials had doors that tended to be localized within the estates. This meant that often demands and information relevant to acting upon demands could flow into the palace through multiple, independent doors. For example, in the late nineteenth century the *katourlil* possessed estates in the new southern tributaries (Fortier 1982, 40). There were thus the *mbang*'s and the *katourlil*'s doors to provide a perspective on affairs in this new tributary zone.

How easy was it to express a demand through the door system? Barma usually came up with a list of a hundred or so places when I asked for names of villages and cities that had been in the core during Gaurang II's reign. Remember that the *mbang* was reported to have 150 wives at the time. There were, thus, 50 percent more wives than there were villages and cities, which suggests that all somebody had to do to express a demand was to walk a brief distance to a household with kin of the *mbang*'s wife and gossip on a matter or interest. The juicier the item, the more quickly it would go from the wife's relatives to the wife herself and from her to her official husband. Interest articulation appears to have been as simple as having a good gossip with some close neighbors. Thus the fact that the *mbang* and his court amassed so many wives did not indicate a pandering to their testosterone levels. Rather, it suggested that the *mbang*'s sought as many doors as possible on the world they governed so that the varied interests of different groups could be effectively articulated.[10]

A second way in which demands could be articulated was through audiences. Audiences with the *mbang* might occur at any time in a building reserved for the *mange* called the *dab mange*. Barth describes the audience he was granted with Abd el Kader as follows: "I was led into an inner court-yard . . . where the courtiers were sitting on either side of a door which led to an inner apartment. . . . In front of the door, between the two lines of the courtiers, I was desired to sit down, together with my companions" (1965, 535). An important observation regarding audiences is that, though the *mbang* was the formal center of attention, he was always attended by "courtiers." These were, of course, court officials and perhaps some of their staff. Exactly which court officials attended what audiences is unclear. Informants said that it varied but that they generally involved two sorts of officials. Those who might have some especial expertise in the affair at hand, and those who constituted a sort of council of senior advisors.

Audiences varied from the door system in that they were a way of explicitly and publicly making demands upon the state. Thus audiences were often requested by officials, frequently from opposing states, on matters of major import. In the door system kin were in communication with other kin on matters in which there might be common interest, while in audiences officials made requests of other officials often on matters in which there was a conflict of interest.

Audiences were held in the style of a "divine" king. The *mbang* "remained invisible and gave audiences from a high dais enclosed by mats" (Lanier 1925, 472). Such a style piqued Europeans. When Barth arrived for his meeting described earlier with Abd el Kader, he could not spot him, and "being rather puzzled [as] to whom to address . . . I asked aloud, before beginning my address, whether the Sultan Abd el Kader was present, an audible voice answered from behind the screen that he was present" (1965, 535). There are a number of cultural reasons for the insulation of the *mbang* during audiences. A political one, however, appears to have been that audiences often dealt with charged situations where conflict was possible. By keeping the *mbang* aloof, the proceedings could be kept calmer.

Court officials also gave audiences. These were often held under the shade of trees in the courtyards of officials' residences, though the *ngarman* held his in a building in the *mbang*'s palace called the *uduma*. These audiences tended to include members of the court official's staff as well as the person seeking the audience. Affairs discussed appear to have pertained to specific areas of the court official's authority or to his or her estate. Thus there was a dual audience system in operation involving both the *mbang* and his court.

Finally, and this is a significant point, audiences were in principle easy to secure, for there was an ethic that the *mbang* and the court should be available to petitioners. This was because audiences were conceived of not as a privilege restricted to a few but as a right open to all. One reason for allowing easy access to audiences appears to have been that this was a way of communicating to ordinary folk and foreigners something of the supernatural luster of the Sun King and his planets. Whatever the reason, anybody seeking an audience at court, provided he or she followed the appropriate etiquette, was entitled to one. It was literally a case of "seek and ye shall find."

In sum, there were at least four channels through which demands could be articulated to the court: through the *mbang*'s and court officials' door systems and audiences. The effectiveness of this manner of articulating interest is unknown. However, it would certainly seem that the double avenues of the *mbang*'s and his court's wives in the door system in conjunction with the ease of securing audiences would have made it possible for individuals and groups to get their weighty interests across. The *mbang* does not appear to have been a despot in the sense that he was haughtily insulated from the interests of others.

It is time to consider the making of decisions in the Sun Kings' court. What appears to set nineteenth-century Bagirmi decision making apart from that in neighboring central Sudanic states was the absence of councils or assemblies. Barth, Nachtigal, Palmer, and Urvoy all suggest that decisions were taken by the *mai* and twelve important officials who constituted a council in Bornu (Brenner 1973, 12). The Hausa kingdom of Daura circa 1800 had a "lesser council" composed of junior officials that was concerned with routine matters of daily administration and a "senior council" of major officials vested with authority over affairs of war, taxation, and capital punishment (M. G. Smith 1978, 105–8). Information presented below, however, suggests that Bagirmi decision making was probably not so very different from that in the neighboring states and that there were both informal and formal assemblies.

It should be remembered that the term for a court official's staff was *aljema*. Barma understood this term to mean "council" and thus thought of staff members as counselors. Barma believed staffs should give advice because they believed a political office was like a household. Just as the *ngolbe* provided married men with fields and a place to stay, so court officials, including the *mbang*, informants said, gave their staff food, residences, weapons, and other goods needed to be a staff person. Associated with this belief was the notion that those who worked together should consult together, which included advising each other about their common concerns. It was in this sense that the staffs of court officials, as well as the entire court, were de facto councils.

These councils tended to be informal. There were no rules as to who had to attend. Nor were there rules about how proceedings were to be conducted. However, on most days of the year, a number of court officials would sit down with their *mbang* and, as one informant put it, "gossip" (*waya*). Sometimes such gossip was about frivolous matters of the heart; at other times it was about great affairs of state. In this light it is interesting to consider Brenner's conclusion about the council that advised the Bornuan *mais*. It was, he said, "probably amorphously defined, perhaps synonymous with the court itself" (Brenner 1973, 18). This could just as well apply to the *mbang*'s *aljema*.

When the *mbang* and his court made a decision, it was usually not the result of a scheduled meeting formally set for a specific time. Rather, matters were first brought to the attention of the *mbang* and the court either through the door system or through audiences or both. Then a matter was likely to be mulled over by the *mbang* and the court officials. This might include discussing its ramifications over meals and after meals. Anyone could participate in these discussions, though staff would be expected to show deference to their superiors. Gradually, a sensible course of action would emerge from these discussions. When this had occurred, the *mbang* was expected to state the agreed-upon course.

Certain court officials were explicitly designated as the *mbang*'s counselors. These were the four masters-of-the-earth officials, the *galadima, ngar mweymanga, ngar birkete,* and *mbarakudu,* as well as the *magira.* Pacques speaks of these officials as occupying "a preponderant place in everything concerning hierarchy and ceremony, but not always in that which concerns effective command" (1977, 43). This suggests that these officials might not have been influential counselors. Barma familiar with the workings of the late-nineteenth-century court said that this was simply not the case. Masters-of-the-earth officials were never military leaders. Rather, as Pacques indicates, they were participants in state ceremonial, which, among other things, was believed to insure the normal operations of society and nature. Thus, when they offered advice, they were respected because their ritual actions contributed to the general well-being. Conversely, to toy with a master-of-the-earth's judgment was to trifle with the state of nature and people. The masters-of-the-earth officials and the *mbang*'s mother (*magira*), then, might be said to have been a group of senior counselors whose judgments were weighty.[11]

Two affairs of the court were primary, the election of a new *mbang* and the decision to undertake military campaigns. Formal councils, composed largely of senior counselors, made each of these decisions. The Council of Succession was headed by the *ngarman* and included the *ngar mweymanga, ngar birkete, galadima, mbarakudu, milma, patcha,* and *mbarma.* There were formal rules specifying when and where this council met and through what procedures it arrived at its decisions (Pacques 1977, 26–27). The Council of War was a smaller group that, interestingly enough, included no military commanders. It consisted of the *ngar mweymanga, ngar birkete, galadima,* and *magira.* It too was guided by formal rules defining when and where it met as well as how it made its decisions (ibid., 45).

Thus, as was the case in the Hausa kingdom of Daura, there seem to have been two levels of counselors. First, the *mbang*'s court taken in its entirety was an informal council that acted on all sorts of demands. Then, there were the senior counselors to whom special deference might be shown because of their prominent roles in state rituals, who were also members of the formal councils of War or Succession.

Was this system of decision making despotic, as suggested by Fisher? Despotism exists where the sovereign alone makes decisions, no matter how capricious he or she might be. This is very far from what appears to have happened in Bagirmi, because once demands had been articulated, their merits could be pondered in the more junior council composed of the entire court, or by the more senior council composed of the senior counselors, or finally by the formal councils of Succession or War. This meant that the *mbang* lacked the personal authority either to make war, to name his successor, or to do a great many other things. In short, Bagirmi decision making does not appear to have been the capricious product of the *mbang*'s personal proclivities.[12] Thus neither the interest articulation nor the decision-making phase of the formation of Bagirmi policy appears especially despotic.

The Sovereign and His Court

Barth complained that "the duties of the chief offices are . . . by no means distinctly defined" (1956, 562). This complaint was in a sense correct. There were eight major authorities that might be attributed to a court member. These were: first, the right to contribute to policy formation by either communicating demands that had been articulated or taking decisions; second, the right to participate in the administration of policy; third, the right to conduct state rituals; fourth, the right to direct an estate; fifth, the right to direct military operations; sixth, the right to conduct judicial proceedings at the level of either the estate or the court; seventh, the right to supervise the activities of certain court officials; and eighth, the right to interpret Islamic ritual and law. Each court office, including that of the *mbang*, had some authority in the first six domains. Each office thus was broadly like other offices in these areas, and it is in this sense that Barth was perceptive in suggesting that court offices were undifferentiated.

There were, however, important differences between offices based upon the powers available to them and upon the specific authorities within the eight general domains of authority that were attributed to them. There were three major types of power in Bagirmi. The first was military strength, which could force people to accept an official's intentions. Military strength was in large measure dependent upon the number of troops one commanded.

The second power was ideological strength, which made people believe that they wanted to accept an official's intentions. Such strength was dependent upon whether or not there were ideological notions that gave an office divine attributes, because a person really wanted to stay on the right side of an official who was a divinity. The way offices were linked to the supernatural was through traditions of what the original occupant of the office was like, or did, during or subsequent to the founding of the second kingdom. For example, these traditions recall that the original *mbang* traveled to earth in a pirogue incarnating certain supernatural forces, met and married a woman named Nyonnyon, performed a sacrifice to become master-of-the-earth, and consequently founded the second kingdom based on an alliance with the eight tribes who were previously masters-of-the-earth. The original *mbang*, then, is remembered as a divinity. These same traditions remember the original *mbarma* as an ordinary slave of one of the original masters-of-the-earth groups, a memory that does not allow one to classify him as in any way supernatural. Such remembrances, then, might be said to be the means by which ideological strength was culturally constructed.

The third power was informational strength, which made people accept an official's intentions because he or she actually knew what was a superior course of action. Informational strength depended considerably upon one's position in the interest articulation system. Certain power resources and authorities associated with each of the different court offices are presented below.

Royal Offices

The most important of the royal offices was, of course, that of the *mbang*. He considerably exceeded all other court officials in power and authority. An official's military strength did not so much depend on the maximum number of troops commanded. This level of command only occurred after a long mobilization during warfare and was irrelevant to the day-to-day confrontations in which force might be decisive. Rather, one's strength depended on the number of soldiers one had in normal times. This was a function of staff size, because one's staff was one's permanent fighting corps.

The *mbang*'s staff included those who resided in the palace.[13] Aside from wives, these were largely slaves, many of whom were eunuchs. The latter formed a *corps d'élite* of the *mbang*'s soldiers (Gaden 1907, 441). The number of eunuchs who were also soldiers is not clear, but the estimates of a number of informants were in excess of five hundred horsemen.[14] There are reports that *mbang* Burkumanda III, who ruled in the first half of the nineteenth century, had a thousand or so eunuchs, many of whom would have been soldiers (ibid., 441). The corresponding estimates for the size of court official staffs ranged between fifteen and one hundred horsemen. Thus the *mbang* was normally championed by substantially more cavalry than any other official.

It was, however, in the realm of ideological strength that he truly shone, because the *mbang* was the sun, and all other officials were the planets. It was he who was

Table 6.1. The *Mbang* and His Court.

ROYAL OFFICIALS		NON ROYAL OFFICIALS	
Men	*Women*	*Originally Free*	*Originally Slave*
Sovereign	Royal Mother	Masters-of-the-earth	Ngarman
Mbang	Magira	Ngar birkete	Patcha
Sons	Wives	Galadima	Mbarma
Chiroma	Gumsu	Ngar mweymanga	Kirema
Ngar murba	Bedangul	Mbarakudu	Katurlil
Ngar daba	Lel murba	*Other*	
Ngar keleo	Lel daba	Milma	
	Daughters	Mange	
	Chikotima	Naib	
		Alifa ba	
		Alifa moyto	
		Alifa korbol	
		Alifa miltu	
		Imam ngolo	
		Arkali	

the incarnation of the forces that animated events, *mao* and *k̩ark̩ata*. When he traveled, his dancers went with him and performed a dance called the *dabrus*, in which they moved fans aloft over their heads in intricate patterns that symbolized the movements of *mao* and *k̩ark̩ata* (Pacques 1977, 41). Other rituals of state and insignia of office also symbolized his supernatural being.[15] The *mbang* thus was a potent divinity.

Barma thought that the sun was a thousand times brighter than the planets and that planets seemed to follow the sun. Such reasoning meant that it was utterly unthinkable that court officials would issue orders to the *mbang* and entirely normal that the reverse should be the case. After all, if the *mbang* spits in the face of a court member, the spit partakes of his force, and the official "should collect the saliva with care and rub it over the body as if he had received a special benediction" (Pacques 1977, 63). The *mbang*, then, had the authority to direct all officials in his realm.

Our attention now fixes upon his planets. The first sons of the first four wives were called respectively *chiroma*, *ngar murba*, *ngar daba*, and *ngar k̩eleo*. They were believed to have inherited some of the *mbang*'s force, but it appears that this was not thought to be activated until and unless they mounted the throne. So royal sons tended to be much like other court officials. They were given estates in the old inner core and had small staffs.

The *chiroma* was supposed to inherit the throne. He was the only son allowed to reside within the palace, not only to protect him from sibling rivalry but to permit him to observe the workings of government. He was supposed to head one of the original masters-of-the-earth groups, named the *Chilomari*, and so was given their area as an estate. This appears to have been near the village of Bougal on the Bahr Erguig (Pacques 1977, 42). Ngar Murba appears to have headed a masters-of-the-earth group, the Murba, and so appears to have had their territory as his estate. This may have been to the east of Massenya along the Bahr Erguig near Bodoro. Pacques reports that the *ngar daba* had the right to supervise a staff person of the *mbang* called the *k̩adamasinda*, who was in charge of the royal stable (ibid., 38). It is not known whether the *ngar daba* or other royal sons had this authority in the past. The *ngar daba* appears to have headed another masters-of-the-earth group, the Dabara, which may have placed his estate on the Shari river north of Bugoman (Pacques 1977, 42). Finally, the *ngar k̩eleo* seems to have directed a fourth masters-of-the-earth group, the Keleo. This would have placed his estate east of that of the Murba along the Bahr Erguig near the village of Kedede. On the death of a *mbang*, these sons appear to have lost the estates that had been assigned to them (Lanier 1925, 470).

Sons of the *mbang* have been described as "destined to become fraternal enemies" (Lanier 1925, 470). This is because, even though the *chiroma* was supposed to succeed, other sons were suitable as *mbangs* and could be so named by the Council of Succession. Thus civil war in Bagirmi normally involved conflict between royal offspring. The custom of blinding the brothers of new *mbangs* appears to have been instituted to dampen such divisive tendencies.

No mention is made of a formal role for royal brothers. There was certainly no office of "king's brother." Once the sovereign's brothers had been blinded, they seem to have been tolerated as informal advisors. If they escaped blinding, because they were of the same essence as the *mbang*, they were thinkable alternatives to the throne. This made them of interest to opposing states, for the state that harbored a *mbang*'s brother could legitimately propose him as a candidate for the throne. Thus royal brothers enjoyed some ideological luster but no authority within Bagirmi. This was not the case with royal women, who enjoyed real powers and authority.

The *magira* was the *mbang*'s mother, though it should be realized that on occasion mother was a man. The reason was that when the *mbang*'s real mother died, her replacement was often a male, frequently, according to Nachtigal, a eunuch (1889, 610). Lanier describes the *magira*'s office as honorific (1925, 468). Nachtigal, on the other hand, believed that the *magira* followed "the king in power and respect" (1889, 610). The *magira* had a staff, which is not remembered to have been especially large. The office had no special military responsibilities. It did, however, have some ideological strength because the *magira* was believed to be descended from Nyonnyon. Nyonnyon is mentioned in certain traditions of the kingdom's founding as a supernatural woman who was thought of as incarnating the land, the moon, and *mao* (Pacques 1977, 58). In certain traditions the *mbang* married Nyonnyon, who thus became the first wife and mother.[16] This mother consequently had considerable ideological strength.

The *magira* was supposed to have "moral authority" over all the young women in the state (Pacques 1977, 58). The degree to which the *magira* actually dealt with women's affairs is unknown. Perhaps some sort of door system operated, with women who wished their concerns dealt with at court making their wishes known to the *magira*. The office was also supposed to "command" all other court officials (ibid., 227). *Command* is perhaps too strong a word. One of my informants said that the *magira* should "act like a lawyer" toward these officials, because she was their "protector." The *magira* could not order other court officials; neither could she remove them from office; but she could, and indeed was authorized to, represent them. This meant that the *magira* should know what other court members were doing and then should give advice as to what was good and what was bad. Other court members enjoyed the right to "command" different court officials. None, however, could represent as many officials as did the *magira*. Thus the *magira* was militarily undistinguished, ideologically strong—and authorized to protect.

The wives of the *mbang* were called *lelge*. The first four wives were the most important and were called by a single term. They were the *gabdel* and were, in order of marriage, *gumsu*, *bedangul*, *lel daba*, and *lel murba*. Wives not in the *gabdel*, because the total exceeded the four permitted by Islam, were technically classified as concubines. Only the first two wives in the *gabdel* may be considered to have held political office, and of these that of the *gumsu* was the most important.

Wives had no military functions. They did, however, enjoy some ideological strength, because both the *gumsu* and the *bedangul*, like the *magira*, were associated with Nyonnyon, the earth, the moon, and *mao*. The other wives were each assigned to the *gumsu* or the *bedangul*, and each directed the activities of the wives assigned to her. In addition, the *gumsu* could tell the *bedangul* what to do. It appears that all the *gabdel* wives were given estates. There is no record of how large these were, which suggests that they may have been relatively small.

A daughter of the *mbang* was called a *mairam*. Nachtigal said of these "princesses" that "only one who has the title *chikotima* . . . has an official position" (1889, 611). She was the *mbang*'s first daughter by the *gumsu* and appears to have been to the *gumsu* as the *chiroma* was to the *mbang*. Descent from the *gumsu* meant that the *chikotima* was descended from Nyonnyon and thus had the same supernatural associations as the *gumsu* and the *magira* did. She appears to have had no role in military operations, though she possessed an honor guard of women who clapped and sang as she traveled. *Chikotima* thus had some ideological but no military strength.

Barma women, as we learned earlier, were expected to show deference to their men. They stayed in the domestic sphere, walked behind their men, carried loads while their menfolk strolled empty-handed, and approached important males with heads lowered in respect. A woman behaving in this way was said to show the appropriate deference. The *chikotima*, on the other hand, was the sole woman in Bagirmi allowed to ride a horse, the crucial instrument of war (Lanier 1925, 468). She married a court official, the *milma*, who alone of all men in the state was expected to remain monogamous. She, however, was allowed as many lovers as she wished. Even the normal rule of patrilocal residence was reversed, because she was supposed to bring her groom home to the palace after marriage. The *magira* might be a male female. The *chikotima* on the other hand was a sort of female male.

The *chikotima* had an estate. Where this was is unknown for the late nineteenth century, though the market in Massenya was included in it. She was also authorized to direct the palace women. How her administration of these women was integrated with that of the *gumsu*'s direction of the *mbang*'s wives is unclear.

Other royal daughters seem to have been important to the state not as officials but as principals in the forging of matrimonial alliances. Royal daughters were given in marriage to the heads of tributaries and non-Barma ethnic groups to help insure their loyalty.

Free Officials

Two categories of free court members can be distinguished: first, those officials believed to be descended from the leaders of the groups that possessed the land in the original core, and second, those lacking such descent. The former, even though their ancestors had ceded the land to the *mbang*, were still thought of as masters-of-the-earth officials. There were four such officials, whose offices are discussed below.

The first master-of-the-earth official was the *galadima*, who was supposed to come from the group called the Guledimari. The *galadima* had no specialized military functions, which does not mean that he had no military responsibilities. He would be expected to lead his staff as a military body, and to have his staff mobilize soldiers from his estate. The *galadima* shared this military role with all the other male court officials.

The Gudedimari were believed to have given a woman to the first *mbang*, Dala Birni, at the foundation of the state. In return, the *galadima* received a wife from Dala Birni. Further, the *galadima*'s Guledimari ancestors were believed to have participated in the ritual in which they transferred their master-of-the-earth status to Dala Birni. Such memories give the *galadima* some ideological strength, but they equally clearly establish that he is inferior to the *mbang*. The *galadima* clearly enjoyed some power resources, but at a level far below that of the *mbang*.

Nevertheless, the *galadima* enjoyed extensive authority. Perhaps the most important was in policy formation, because he was described as the "first counselor" of the *mbang* and was a member of both the councils of War and Succession. He had a role in a number of state rituals, of which that of the *mbang*'s investiture was perhaps the most important. He directed his estate, which appears to have been in the Bugoman region, among the most populous in nineteenth-century Bagirmi. He constructed and maintained certain of the palace buildings and oversaw the affairs of the first four sons of the *mbang*.

The second of the master-of-the-earth officials was the *ngar mweymanga*.[17] He was supposed to have come from the Mweymangas. He had no special military role and appears to have had a smaller staff than the *galadima*. However, like the *galadima*, his ancestors were remembered to have given a wife to the first *mbang*, to have received one in return, and to have taken part in the ritual that ceded the land to the *mbang*. The *ngar mweymanga*'s office, thus, had some military and ideological strength.

The *ngar mweymanga* had authority in policy formation because he was a senior counselor as well as a member of the councils of War and Succession. He exercised authority in state ritual, being, among other things, a participant in the investiture ceremonies. He had an estate, although where it was is unclear. Barth says that he was "the governor of the open pasture grounds and forests" (1965, 562). Pastures are where pastoralists resided, so that it may have been that in Barth's time his estate included a number of pastoral groups. The Mweymanga are remembered to have lived around the contemporary villages of Er, Arkoua, and Tchoe (A. A. -D. Lebeuf 1967, 237). These were ten to twelve kilometers east of the old capital of Massenya, near Bideri, and so might have been places of both Fulani and Arab habitation. Nothing else is known about the *ngar mweymanga*'s authority. He appears to have had no special role in palace administration or the supervision of court officials.

The third of the masters-of-the-earth officials was the *ngar birkete*. Less is reported of him than of any other such official. He is not mentioned in Barth, and, while he is noted in Nachtigal, nothing is said of him (1889, 611). Like the *ngar mweymanga* he had no special military role. Further, he had the same traditional role in the founding of the state as did the *galadima* and the *ngar mweymanga*. He had authority in policy formation, being a senior counselor and a member of the councils of War and Succession. He played a role in certain state rituals, and he directed an estate. If this estate was where the Birkete were supposed to have been located, it would have been to the immediate west of the Mweymanga, between the present villages of Daday and Er. He does not appear to have had special authority in other domains.

The *mbarakudu* was the last of the four masters-of-the-earth officials. Like the others, he had no especial military role, and like them, he was associated with the traditional notions of the state's founding, for his ancestors were believed to have come from the Kutu, who were believed also to have given and received wives from the first *mbang* and to have taken part in the ritual that ceded their master-of-the-earth status. However, Lanier reported that the *mbarakutu* was of a "less elevated rank" than the other such officials (1925, 468). Nachtigal reported one tradition of the origin of the office that may explain why this was the case. He said that the office "was given as a favor to an especially eager servant of the king," who, as "the latter one day coughed and spat," strove "each time to catch the royal expectoration with his clothes, and as a reward was given the above title" (1889, 614). Thus the office does not appear to have been powerful in either ideological or military terms.

The *mbarakutu*, however, exercised considerable authority. He was a senior counselor and member of the Council of Succession and had a hand in a number of state rituals, including the investiture. He directed an estate that, if it were on lands that were supposed to be Kutu, would have been located around Weske and Guangala on the Bahr Erguig river. Nachtigal suggested that this estate was small (1889, 614).

The *mbarakutu*'s most distinctive role was in policy implementation. This was because he was "an immediate satellite of the sultan from whom he carried orders and utterances. He is named to take the place of the *ngarman* outside the palace" (Lanier 1925, 468). The *mbarakutu* seems to have had the authority to make policy decisions, which he was supposed to be informed about by the *ngarman*, and communicate them to other court officials. For example, if the Council of War decided upon a military action, this decision would be communicated to the *ngarman* and thence to the *mbarakutu*, who would see to informing the other court members about their roles in the affair. The *mbarakutu* thus had authority to begin policy implementation outside the palace. Aside from this role, he appears to have had no other special authority in the governance of Bagirmi.

It is time to consider certain other free court officials, the *milma*, *mange*, *naib*, *alifa ba*, *alifa moyto*, *iman ngollo*, and *arkali*. The *milma* may well have been the most important of these in the late nineteenth century. The first *milma* was thought to have come from either the Guledimari or the Kutu (Pacques 1977, 49). However, he was not considered a master-of-the-earth official for reasons that are unclear. He had no special military responsibilities. Yet he did have some strength deriving from his position in the state ideology. The word *milma* in Tar Barma means "blacksmith," and the official who was the *milma* was believed to be an incarnation of a supernatural Great Blacksmith who performed a sacrifice that created a world prior to that of the *mbangs*. As Pacques expressed it, the *milma* "somehow represents a state anterior to the sovereign" (1977, 51). When black clouds hide the sun, these are thought to be the *milma* before the *mbang*. Thus the *milma* is ideologically significant but less so than the *mbang*, for he incarnates the force that created the world that the *mbang* took over.

With this ideological strength came considerable authority, especially in policy formation and state ritual. Devallée says that, after the *galadima*, the *milma* was the "second counselor" of the sovereign (1925, 24). He was a member of the Council of Succession, and he played a rich and varied role in state rituals, especially in the burial of old and the investiture of new *mbangs*. He directed an estate. Nachtigal said that the *milma*'s title was "derived from the Kanuri division BioMilma that he commands" (1889, 611). Exactly where this division was is unclear, but the association of the *milma* with the Kanuri suggests that members of this ethnic group who lived in Bagirmi may have been part of his estate. Pacques thought that part of his estate included the villages of Onoko and Odumfi, which are in the secondary core along the Shari river. Onoko is today inhabited by a large number of Kanuri. Pacques also said that the towns of Chama to the northeast of Massenya and Bouke, in an unknown location, together with the Assale Arabs belonged to the *milma* (1977, 51).

The *milma* had one final authority, which was to "command" the four master-of-the-earth officials (Pacques 1977, 49). This right was like that of the *magira*. There was no other special authority attached to the *milma*. His office was strong in ideological meaning and significant in policy formation, state ritual, and the guidance of the masters-of-the-earth.

Little is known about the *mange*. The office is mentioned in neither Devallée or Lanier. Barth mentions no *mange*, though he does speak of a *kadamange*, who he suggests was an important official with originally the responsibility of "the tutorship of the sons of the king" (1965, 562). I surmise that Barth's *kadamange* is the same official that Nachtigal, Pacques, and my informants called the *mange*.

In Barth's time (c. 1850) the *mange* was important enough to assume the *mbang*'s functions when he was away on campaign (Barth 1965, 562). However, sixty years or so later he was so insignificant that neither Lanier or Devallée thought to refer to him. This suggests that the *mange* was demoted in authority in the nineteenth century. Perhaps his significance decreased because of the nature of his authority. Nachtigal said that he "introduces *alifa moyto* and the *ngar murba* at court" and is sent "as a royal messenger . . . to the Arab *sheikhs*" (1889, 613). The *alifa moyto* and the Arab *sheikhs* were largely involved with northern tributary affairs. This suggests that the *mange*'s chief responsibilities were in northern tributaries. These, however, were increasingly lost to Wadai throughout the course of the nineteenth century, which would have meant that the *mange* lost authority in these regions.

What follows is my informants' account of the office circa 1900. The *mange* appears to have been a free official and to have occupied a position analogous to that of the *ngarman*. He was always to be found in the *dab mange*, a shelter like the *udema*, where the *ngarman* was found. On Fridays after prayers, the *mange* went to the *dab mange* to hold a weekly audience. The Council of War was also held in the *dab mange* (Pacques 1977, 45). Clearly, the *mange* had considerable authority in the articulation of different interests, but exactly how this authority was exercised is unknown.

We now move on to a less important official, the *naib*, who is described as "always at the disposition of the *mbang* to execute his orders" (Lanier 1925, 468). When doing so, his primary role appears to have been as a messenger between the sovereign and the *ngarman*, and perhaps the *mbarakutu* and the *mange* as well.

There were a number of officials in the state who were called *alifas*. Lanier says that they were: "the governors of distant provinces who didn't live at Massenya. They were veritable viceroys passing after the great dignitaries. They come in grand pomp to the capital at certain times and obligatorily at the *fête de mouton* to deliver their annual tribute and taxes. They have their retinues, their soldiers, their musicians" (1925, 465). Most *alifas* were, as Lanier suggests, estate officials. They were the leaders of tributary communities. Two of these, the *alifa ba* and the *alifa moyto*, however, appear to have been promoted to the court at Massenya.[18]

The *alifa ba* was the more important of the court *alifas* at the end of the nineteenth century. He appears to have had no specialized military functions. He was associated with neither royalty nor the masters-of-the-earth groups and goes unmentioned in the traditions of the state's founding. Nor does he appear, like the *milma*, to be associated with supernatural forces that were believed to be anterior to the *mbang*. The term *ba* means "river" in Tar Barma, and the river this *alifa* was associated with was the Shari. I suspect that the original *alifa ba* may have been a person from the Massenya political elite who was given responsibility over the area along the Shari that was to become the secondary core at the time when this was a tributary area. The preceding suggests that the *alifa ba* may have possessed military strength similar to that of other court officials but that his ideological strength was less than that of royal and masters-of-the-earth officials.

Barth, however, said that the *alifa ba* exercised "a great deal of authority" (1965, 499). This authority was neither in policy formation, administration, state rituals, or judicial or Islamic affairs. Rather, it was derived from his estate. Nachtigal called him "the governor of the river" (1889, 612). Barth described him as the "officer for the river communications" (1965, 499). It is not exactly clear over what part of the Shari the *alifa ba* had authority whether he shared this authority with other court members. Nachtigal said that the *alifa ba* resided in Bugoman and that his estate was from Bugoman northward toward the area around contemporary N'Djamena (1889, 614). It should be noted that both the *galadima* and the *mbarma* had at least part of their estates along the Shari, with the former's apparently centered at Bugoman and the latter's located around Mandjaffa.

This suggests that there may have been a geographic co-mingling of estates. There are two explanations for this. First, the estates did not actually overlap because the riverine area was enjoyed by different officials at different times. Second, different officials had different kinds of authority in the same area. Pacques suggested the latter possibility when she reported that "the *mbarma* was responsible for collecting all the fees that people crossing the river had to give to him" and which "he then transferred to the *alifa ba*" (1977, 46). The *alifa ba*'s great authority, then, appears to derive from two responsibilities he had along the Shari, that of overseeing the entire region with his agents and that of collecting taxes.

The *alifa moyto* was an official who may well have been raised to court status at a time when his authority and power were being reduced.[19] Barth, writing in the 1850s, said that he had "considerable power" (1965, 562). Twenty years later, Nachtigal says he had "lost a lot of importance and his prestige was based solely on his historical significance" (1889, 612). In the 1870s the *alifa moyto* lacked special military responsibilities, nor was there any ideology surrounding the office (Pacques 1977, 45). Similarly, he had no unusual authority in any other domain.

His greatest authority, like that of the *alifa ba*, may have originally been over his estate. Prior to the nineteenth century, Bagirmi centered the administration of its northern tributaries at the town of Moyto, much as in the latter part of the nineteenth century it centered its administration of the southern tributaries at Goundi. The *alifa moyto*'s estate was these northern tributaries. Prior to 1800 this may well have been the largest estate in Bagirmi. However, by the 1870s the entire Lake Fitri region was a

tributary of Wadai. Thus for the *alifa moyto* to try and administer his estate was an act
of war with Wadai, so, for the most part, this *alifa* was an anachronism by the 1870s.
His "promotion" to court may have occurred because he had no other place to go.

Finally, there were two free officials about whom almost nothing is reported. These
were the *imam ngollo* and the *arkali*. The former was the chief Islamic specialist in the
state who may well have frequently been a Fulani from Bidiri. The *arkali* was the chief
judge. The *ngarman* was also involved in judicial administration, and it is unclear what
the relations were between these two. One possibility, however, is that the *ngarman*
tended to select the cases tried by the *arkali* and that he tried to send to him those
involving important aspects of Islamic law.

"Slave" Officials

There were five court officials of slave origin. Four of these were called "posts of the
royal shelter" (Pacques 1977, 47). They were the *ngarman, patcha, mbarma,* and
kirema. A fifth office was that of the *katourlil*, who appears to have been promoted
during the second half of the nineteenth century. The holders of these offices, with the
exception of the *katourlil*, originally appear to have been slaves of masters-of-the-earth
leaders. However, by the late 1800s their occupants might be of either slave or free
status. They were, after the *mbang*, the most powerful officials in the realm.

The *ngarman* may have had the greatest authority, if not power, of the slave officials.
He had no military leadership responsibilities. Further, according to tradition he was
originally a slave recruited from among the Guledimari. He was also often a eunuch,
a choice that was supposed to have begun under the third *mbang* Malo. [20] As a slave
the *ngarman* could never aspire to the throne; as a eunuch he could never take a wife
or create descendants. He was consequently, as one Barma put it, "safe," and perhaps
for this reason he exercised extensive authority.

Barth described the *ngarman* as the "minister of the royal household" (1965, 562).
He was, according to Nachtigal, in "constant and direct contact with the king" (1889,
612). He was authorized to administer affairs pertaining to the *mbang*'s private property,
the *mbang*'s wives, and the maintenance of the palace. He appears to have overseen
the administration of criminal law, reserving for himself one-half of the fines imposed
and passing the rest on to the sovereign. He was prominent in a number of state rituals
and had directed an estate that appears to have originally been in the old core near
Massenya.

Each and every day the *ngarman* would sit in a building in the palace called the
udema with the *naib* and receive those who had business with the *mbang*. Routine matters
were settled on the spot; important ones, requiring some decision, were passed on to
the *mbang*. Once a decision had been made, the *ngarman* transmitted the sovereign's
orders to other court members through the *mbarakutu*. The *ngarman* thus might be seen
as the state's central administrative officer. He alone was authorized to start the process
of deciding upon and then implementing the Sun King's affairs.

The *ngarman* probably had considerable power over decision making because of his
informational resources. These were threefold. Every morning, because he was in charge

of the *mbang*'s wives, he would greet them in their quarters in the palace. This was the time when the doors opened in the door system. The *ngarman* was the only official in the state who on a systematic, daily basis collected information from this source, and this was the single broadest source of information available to the state, with "gossip" coming from core, tributary, and even predation zones.

The *ngarman* received information from two additional sources. These were his daily audiences in the *udema* and the meetings involving the adjudication of officials' squabbles. The former usually involved foreign or court officials bringing to the palace matters that might or might not be weighty enough to require royal audiences and court action, and the point to grasp is that the *ngarman* knew about these affairs well before either the *mbang* or the other court members. The adjudication of squabbles among officials usually gave the *ngarman* rich details of other court members' intrigues.

The fact that the *ngarman* received news from the *udema* meetings, court officials, and the *mbang*'s wives meant that he often acquired information about the same topic from multiple sources. For example, the *ƙirema* during the 1870s appears to have supervised the allied territory of Koumra. This town provided at this time at least one wife to the *mbang*. If a decision had to be made about Koumra, the *ngarman* had information about the issue from the *mbang*'s wife from the area, his daily *udema* meetings concerning the subject, and from the *ƙirema* himself. The *ƙirema* was not privy to the first two information sources. Examples like this lead us to speculate that the *ngarman* may have enjoyed considerable power over decision making simply because he knew more than others did about what to do.

If the *ngarman*'s role in the governance of Bagirmi depended on his ideological safeness, that of the *patcha* depended on his military dangerousness. According to Nachtigal, the *patcha* was the "highest commander in war," who had "been for quite some time the most important person in the land" (1889, 612). Associated with this military power was an ideological strength.

The *patcha* seems to have been conceived of as a surrogate *mbang*. The *mbang* was the sun. The *patcha* was believed to be the "sun of the night," that is, the moon. The *patcha* dressed in his sovereign's clothes in battle. But this royal alter ego was carefully put in his ideological place. During the rituals of the *patcha*'s investiture he slept in the chamber of the *mbang* and the *gumsu*. The king and queen slept parallel to each other, while the *patcha* slept perpendicular to them at their feet. The original *patcha* was supposed to have been donated to the *mbang* by the Birkete and was remembered as one of their slaves. The position that the *patcha* was supposed to assume during his investiture evokes this servile origin. The *mbang* and the *gumsu* were incarnations of supernatural forces that control events. The *patcha*, in his own way, was also an incarnation, but of something quite different, that of royal servitude.

Bagirmi was a state that lived by war, and the *patcha* was the finest "master of war" (*malawaya*) in the land. He normally commanded more soldiers than any other court official. When he did so, he directed the troops of his staff and estate, together with those of other court members.[21] *Patcha*s were members of the Council of Succession, though significantly not of the Council of War. They performed in certain state rituals. They directed their estates, which were supposed to be large and tended to be as far from Massenya as possible. There is some suggestion that they were located in the 1870s north of Massenya, which would have placed the *patcha* between Bagirmi's heartland and the forces of Wadai. The *patcha* was also authorized to construct and maintain a number of palace buildings. Finally, he administered the affairs of the previous *mbang*'s wives and sons.

The *mbarma* was the second court official who was primarily a military leader. There was not a great deal of ideology defining his position. He was remembered to have been originally a slave who came from the Mweymanga, and no supernatural qualities are remembered about him. He participated in policy formation, was a member of the Council of Succession, but did not have a specially prominent role in state ritual, administration, or judicial and Islamic affairs. He was authorized to construct certain buildings in the palace and to direct the affairs of the *alifa moyto*. He had an estate that was remembered as located around Mandjaffa.

The *mbarma*'s greatest authority, however, was as a general. According to Nachtigal, he originally had been "the highest leader in war. Now, he . . . has to be satisfied with historical prestige because for a long time his power has been pushed into the background by the power of the *patcha*" (1889, 612). My informants had a somewhat different version of *mbarma-patcha* relations. For them, the *mbarma* was still an important general at the end of the nineteenth century. However, they said that he always resided within Massenya, while the *patcha* was only allowed there once a year at *eid el ḳabir*. It should be noted that Bagirmi underwent at least one attempt by a *patcha*, Araueli, to seize the throne. Further, it appears that there was a general policy of not committing both the *patcha* and the *mbarma* to military action at the same time. It would seem, thus, that the *mbarma*'s military role was partly as counterweight to that of the *patcha* and partly as an element in a military strategy that kept one general home in a defensive posture while another assumed the offense.

The *ḳirema* was the third slave official who served as a military commander. There is a tradition, like that for the *ngarman* and the *patcha*, that traces the origin of the office back to the founding of Bagirmi. The first *ḳirema* appears to have come from among palace slaves who showed an aptitude for combat. No other ideological notions define the office. The *ḳirema* appears to have been less crucial than the other slave officials in policy formation. He was not especially prominent in state ritual. He possessed an estate that, in the latter part of the nineteenth century, included the Kotoko polity at Kousseri, some Arab pastoralists, blacksmiths, and certain Sara areas. He was busy in palace administration, for he was considered to be the "husband" of the *mbang*'s daughters and appears to have looked after their affairs. Equally, he was the intermediary between the *gabdel* and the *mbang* and, as such, appears to have represented their interests before the sovereign. He was also responsible for maintaining certain structures in the palace.

Above all, as Nachtigal notes, his duties were "fairly war oriented and his post is the stepping-stone to that of the *patcha*" (1889, 613). The *ḳirema* is not mentioned at all in Barth's account of Bagirmi's government, yet by 1870 he was aggressively leading attacks in southern tributary and predation zones. I surmise that the *ḳirema*'s office changed in the course of the nineteenth century. It may well have been almost exclusively involved in the administration of palace affairs at the beginning of the century. Then, as Bagirmi began its southern expansion, thereby experiencing a demand for military leaders in this region, the *kirema*'s office expanded to fill the role.

Attention now turns to the final slave official, the *katourlil*, who also appears to have been promoted during the second half of the nineteenth century. He was not important enough to have been mentioned by Barth at mid century, but twenty years later his office was significant enough to be discussed by Nachtigal. He was a eunuch, and his original duties seem to have been as a "guard of the *mbang*'s wives" (Devallée 1925, 26). However, by the time of Nachtigal he is described as having "the supervision of many heathen districts and tribes, and his familiarity with these pieces of land and their political conditions makes him a successful raid leader and tax collector" (1889, 614). The *katourlil* seems to have worked as a subaltern of the *kirema*. Then as Bagirmi expanded in the south, first the *kirema* and next the *katourlil* became involved in the administration of these new tributaries. The *katourlil* appears to have been the Bagirmi official who was on the spot in the south, probably communicating to his superior, the *kirema*. Nothing further is currently known about the *katourlil*'s office. Although there were still other offices in Bagirmi, we have described those that were important to an understanding of the workings of the *mbang* and his court.

Finally, it should be understood that Bagirmi's polity was not a great deal different from those of its neighboring states (Khayar 1984, 45). This is only to be expected, because about 24 percent of Bagirmi court offices derive from Bornuan and, perhaps, even earlier Kanemi offices.[22] Similarly, the founder of Wadai was said in certain traditions to have been educated in Bagirmi and presumably to have brought political notions with him (Gaden 1908). The Sun King and his court, after all, performed their stately theater before an audience of other kings and their courts, and this professional audience felt entirely free to borrow parts of the script with which they were particularly impressed for their own works.

The domestic mode of production was presented in chapter 5 and the state in the present one. Now the two must be articulated. This is done in chapter 7, where attention turns to the material reproduction of the Sun King's realm.

Revenue Collection
and Allocation

An ancient central Sudanese song has it that "the poor are grass." This chapter suggests why. First it presents a model of the state. Then it examines the processes of revenue collection and allocation through which the state resupplied itself with the means it required to govern. It performs this analysis by first discussing the collection of different revenues and their amounts, showing how revenue collection could mitigate some of the consequences of environmental uncertainty. Next it shows how these revenues became private incomes that were allocated to public purposes. Finally, it argues that this system of revenue collection and allocation drew products and labor from food producers' households and thereby hindered the reproduction of the domestic mode of production. An understanding that the reproduction of the state was at the expense of the domestic mode of production suggests why poor food producers were "grass."

A Household State

O'Fahey says, speaking of Darfur, that "the creation of hierarchies was an ongoing process; (and) the titled hierarchy was in fact a palimpsest of titles" (1980, 30). This notion of the central Sudanic state as an erasable parchment, a palimpsest, implies that its structure was evanescent. Certainly the state of Bagirmi at the end of the nineteenth century was an odd concantenation of officials and their responsibilities, with *katourlils* rising and *alifa moytos* falling. But behind this appearance of flux was order.

　　Viewed functionally, free court officials, in conjunction with the *ngarman*, appear to have had a preponderant role in assisting the *mbang* in the formulation of policy. Slave court officials seemed to have had a leading role in administration, especially that of force, and a mixed group of slave and free officials, the *ngarman, mange, naib,* and *mbarakutu*, did the jobs of first articulating demands and then translating the resulting policy decisions into administrative action. All court officials seem to have shared the task of administering the various villages, towns, and ethnic groups that comprised the portfolio of their estates, which, taken in their ensemble, were the territory of Bagirmi.

　　This functional division of political labor operated in a structural hierarchy. The building block in this hierarchy was an office, but an office consisted of the official and his or her staff, who were thought of as being like households. So the building blocks of the state might be thought of as household units, with an official elder at the center surrounded by the different juniors on the staff. These households were linked to each other in a hierachy composed of three levels of power and authority: the *mbang's* office exercised power and authority over the offices of the court, which in turn wielded power and authority over those in the estates, which, in turn, did the same over food producers in their households.

This meant, for example, that if a policy was to be administered, the *mbang* would so instruct the *naib*, who would tell the *ngarman*. The *ngarman* would then inform the *mbarakutu*, who would advise the relevant court officials, perhaps the *galadima* and the *katourlil*. At this point the affair had passed from the level of the *mbang* to that of the court. If the matter had to do with Bugoman or the Sara, the *galadima* and the *katourlil* would each summon the members of their staffs responsible for these areas. The *galadima* would call his *agid* Bugoman and the *katourlil* would call his *agid* Koumra. The *agids* would in their turn travel to Bugoman and Koumra and deliver their instructions to the chief officers there, who would be the *ngar* Bugoman and the *ngar* Koumra. At this point the matter had passed from the level of the court to that of the estate. Finally, at the bottom of the hierarchy, the *ngars* of Bugoman and Koumra would summon their subordinates, who would transmit the matter on down to the level of individuals in hamlets and villages.

This hierarchy strung its threads of power and authority from the household of the *mbang* at the center to those of his court officials administering their estates, and thence from the households of estate officials on to all the food producer households in the tiniest hamlets and villages. This, then, was the Sun Kings' realm. Officials, and their responsibilities, could change rapidly, but beneath the evanescent bustle of institutional activity lay the abstract, three-tiered model of power and authority. When Bagirmi thought of this state, they tended to do so in the familiar discourse of households. We might continue this comfortable metaphor by calling the Bagirmi hierarchy of power and authority a household state.[1]

Two types of processes reproduced this state. One enculturated individuals to have the knowledge and the will to occupy the structural positions available in the state. The other provided individuals with the material means of occupying these positions. The first type of process appears to have largely involved the performance of a theater of state ideology at various social occasions. Royal sons, for example, by attending the round of official funerals and investitures, came to understand and appreciate something of the nature of the office of the *mbang*. Our concern in this chapter is not with this first type of reproduction but rather with the second.

A vignette may help the reader understand the processes by which the material requirements of officials were satisfied. I lived in 1969–70 with Ahmet Ngollo, who was simultaneously an official in the newly independent Chadian and the old Bagirmi state. This was because the official hierarchy of the precolonial Bagirmi state continues in postcolonial times, though its offices have been stripped of most of their nineteenth-century functions. In fact, Ahmet was an important court official who was, as much as was possible, governing according to custom (*hada*).

Consequently he had gathered around him a staff. Ahmet Mbassa was one of these. He had decided to marry, which immensely amused everybody, for Ahmet Mbassa was judged too old to need a wife. He was after all a ripe old sixty-five. Ahmet Mbassa, however, was not amused and requested that Ahmet Ngollo provide him with bridewealth. Such payment could be most expensive, and Ahmet Ngollo said, "Maybe." On every occasion that Ahmet Mbassa renewed his request, he was met again with "maybe." After six months of this Ahmet Mbassa was threatening to leave, and a year later, still wifeless, he left.

Ahmet Ngollo was upset by this turn of events, which seemed surprising to me, for it was not clear why he should fret over the loss of an old man who was too frail to work and who made exorbitant demands. Ahmet Ngollo was saddened because he had violated what was perhaps the major imperative guiding court officials, namely that they look after their staff. This principle was the basis of the material reproduction of the state, for court officials, including the *mbang*, had to satisfy their staffs' material needs as well as their own. Just as a household head was responsible for his junior kin, so a court official was responsible for his staff, which is another reason for thinking of Bagirmi as a household state.

Exactly what the material requirements of Bagirmi officials were is at present unknown. Theoretically, the magnitude of their needs depended upon the number of officials and their dependents as well as the amounts of material goods they consumed. I roughly estimated that there were at least 3,500 male officials at the end of the nineteenth century. This figure, however, underreports the total number of officials in Bagirmi because it excludes female and child dependents and in addition probably underestimates the number of estate officials. All officials and their families would have required food and clothing. Males would have required, in addition, weapons — including cavalry mounts — which were extremely costly. If it is assumed that men required about 1 kilo of grain a day for minimal adequate nutrition (Chevalier 1907), then the *mbang* required about 1,100,000 kilos of cereals annually simply to keep his men alive. Equally, he required millions upon millions of kilos of fodder to keep his officials' horses galloping. It can thus be appreciated that the state had considerable requirements that had to be met if it was to satisfy its official households' needs, that is, materially to reproduce themselves. These requirements were satisfied through its revenue system.

Revenues and Regions

State revenues are the "compulsory transfer" of products, money, or labor from "private individuals, institutions or groups to the government" (Bannock et al. 1972, 432).[2] Barth was the first person to discuss Bagirmi's fiscal system, and he lumped all the different revenues together as *haden-banga* (1965, 563). *Hada*, as we noted earlier, was the term for "custom." *Haden-banga* or, as we might transcribe it, *hada mbang* thus literally meant "that which was traditionally the *mbang*'s." However, when Barma spoke about the collection of taxes, they would say that such-and-such an official went to such-and-such a place and "pulled" (*tirga*) from it. The verb *to pull* (*tiru*) was used to describe the collection of any sort of state revenue. A characteristic of the Bagirmi fiscal system was that each region of the realm specialized in different types of "pulling": from the core came taxes, from tributary areas came tribute, and from predation zones came booty. The different revenues from the different regions are discussed more fully below.

Non-Islamic religious and ontological Barma notions, as well as Islamic law, authorized officials to "pull" products from food producers. When I asked food producers who owned the land before the French arrived, their response was that it had been the *mbang*. He, however, did not own the land in any Western, legal sense. Rather, he was, as we saw in chapter 6, a divine king, a part of the supernatural order that caused events to occur. Lands were the *mbang*'s not because he owned them but because he incarnated the forces that allowed them to bear fruit. Just as the rains fell, or plants grew, so the *mbang* and his officials "pulled" their fruits. Such notions justified two obligations, the *gugari* and the *hadjar*.

Gugari means "whirlwind," and it will be remembered that the *mbang* was supposed in certain traditions to have descended to earth in such a storm. Each year during the cold season, from approximately December through February, the *mbang*, together with a number of his court, would journey through parts of his domain, stopping at villages along the way, where he would be presented with gifts. The procession was called a *gugari*, and the gift giving appears to have been an acknowledgment of the *mbang*'s supernatural nature. Villages visited in the *gugari* would not be visited each year. Nor were all villages in the core liable to participate. In fact, according to Pacques, the only villages involved were those in the *kubar* areas of the original core (1977). Further, there were no exact amounts that had to be given in the *gugari*.

The *hadjar*, called by Devallee *bourma* and *marassouba* (1925, 64), was collected annually and appears to have been the major burden on food producers. It was a duty required of each household within the core and was calculated as a percentage of the household's output. I think that the *gugari* was probably an earlier tax collected when the *mbang* and his retinue "showed the flag" through new, still insecure possessions as the state formed during the sixteenth century. The *hadjar* was probably instituted at a later date when the state was firmly established and there was need for more predictable and larger revenues.

Muslim *sharia* (law) sanctions the collection of certain religious dues. The *zakhat*, called *zaka* by the Barma, was in theory used to provide nourishment for pilgrims undertaking the *hadj*. It was supposed to consist of one-tenth of a farmer's harvest. My informants said that only the court officials paid a regular annual *zaka* to the *mbang* and that the food producers paid only rarely, and then only when their harvests had been especially abundant. Barma equally insisted that the *mbang* pretty much used the *zaka* as he saw fit. A second Islamic duty was the *futra*, an alms that according to *sharia* was supposed to aid the poor. It was annually collected by officials and used by the state. There were thus four taxes—*gugari, hadjar, zaka,* and *futra*—that provided the bulk of core revenues, and because these were derived from religious beliefs, they may be called religious exactions.[3]

Attention turns now to understanding what these religious duties were paid in and what one implication of such payments was. Barth said that "the inhabitants of Bagirmi proper," that is, what we would call the core, paid duties of: "two different kinds, viz., in corn and cotton strips. The tribute in corn, . . . the *tsidiram maibe* in Bornu and the *kurdi-n-kaissa* in Hausa, is here called . . . *motten-banki*, while the tribute in cotton-strips bears the name *farda-a-banga*'. But many places have to deliver also a tribute in butter, although the Shuwa . . . are the principle purveyors of this article to the court" (1965, 563). This quotation suggests that religious duties were paid in two main forms: "corn," meaning sorghums and millets, and money, because cloth was a major currency throughout the nineteenth century. The quotation also suggests that the form in which a community or ethnic group's religious duties were paid depended upon its production specialities. Since Arabs specialized in dairy products, butter was "pulled" from them. This assured, according to Nachtigal, the "periodic delivery of livestock, honey, pieces of cotton, land taxes in kind, (and) fish from the Shari" (1880, 388). Thus religious duties appear to have been something of a catering service, satisfying official nutritional and other subsistence needs.

This direct provisioning of officials reduced their need to go out and purchase products in the marketplace. They still had to buy a considerable quantity of goods, but these were often sumptuary or military goods that were frequently imports brought by the trans-Saharan trade. Thus religious exactions, because they were only partly in money, did not stimulate the growth of the market as fully as they might have if they had been entirely in currency.

There was one form of tax payment that does not appear to have been especially significant in the core. Archaic states frequently exact taxes in the form of labor. Such taxes, for example, seem to have been important in Dar al-Kuti, whose founding was influenced by Bagirmi. Here officials set up large fields upon which food producers were required to work for certain periods, thereby paying a labor tax (Cordell 1985, 127–28). However, neither the *mbang* nor his court officials seem to have had such fields cultivated for them during the latter years of the nineteenth century. This is not to say that they may not have exacted such taxes at other times. Certain estate officials, on the other hand, are known to have "pulled" labor taxes. *Mbang* Bousso, for example, possessed a field that was believed to be "the primordial field," and which was the "vastest" in Bousso (Pacques 1977, 177). This was worked by inhabitants of Bousso and neighboring towns. Other officials in Bousso had fields that appear to have been cultivated in the same manner.

Slave hamlets were subject to a form of taxation. Little is known about such places, but we do know that most slaves were owned by officials and that they were kept in the core, preferably close to Massenya or in the community from which their owner came. This made them easier to supervise and reduced the difficulty of transporting their products to their owners. Such hamlets tended to be small in size, less than one hundred persons, and located in favorable farming spots on the outskirts of villages. Most occupants of such villages were Sara. Slaves were supposed to cultivate two sets of fields, on one of which they were expected to work two days, on the other, five days. The products of the latter fields belonged to their owner. Thus slave hamlets provided labor to their owners, and because these were usually officials, in so doing they paid in

effect a labor tax to the state. However, as was earlier noted in chapter 4, there were relatively few slave villages, so it does not seem that labor from slaves was a major core tax.[4]

There were other, more minor taxes demanded of core residents. These included
market and judicial taxes. Both were said to have been less important than the previous
revenues. It may seem curious that a state that was as keenly involved in the trans-
Saharan trade as Bagirmi would not tax the sale of slaves in its markets. However,
and this is crucial, the state participated in the trans-Saharan trade as a supplier of
slaves. Its officials sold slaves, and from these sales they derived considerable income.
This meant that taxes on the sale of slaves would have been taxes upon income that was
already the state's, which would have made little sense.

Further, if officials were to be effective sellers of slaves, there had to be buyers.
This meant that the state had to compete with other central Sudanic states to make
it attractive for trans-Saharan merchants to purchase Bagirmi's wares. To further this
goal, Gaurang II was said by Dubois to "receive (merchants) with open arms." When
they arrived they "presented themselves to the Sultan, who visited their merchandise,
and chose from it what he estimated was necessary for his need and nearly always paid
without discussion. This formality fulfilled: the market is *freely* open to them" (1968,
39–40; emphasis added). In short, during Gaurang II's reign there appears to have
been a policy of not taxing the trans-Saharan merchants. Such coddling clearly worked.
Dubois described the market at Chekna, the new capital of Bagirmi, as having attained
prosperity, for it had become a "veritable entrepot of transaction between, on the one
hand, Tripolitania and, on the other, Sokoto and the Hausa" (1968, 39). Such a
policy, however, depended upon low market taxes. In fact, most market taxes were
upon food producers, who paid small fees when they entered the marketplace. The
core thus contributed three taxes to the state: most importantly religious exactions, then
market taxes, and judicial fines.

It is time now to consider revenues from tributary and predation zones. The exacting
of tribute was often sanctioned in the central Sudan by documents called king lists. These
were written or verbal chronicles of a Sudanic state's sovereigns and their doings and
were almost exclusively laundry lists of kings and battles (Urvoy 1949, 7). Bornu's
diwan is the longest and most famous of such king lists. Written Bagirmi king lists,
called the *dabcar*, have never surfaced, but they appear to have existed.[5]

When I listened to Barma explain the *dabcar*, it became clear it did not exist for
them as a means of giving Bagirmi a history. Rather, when they described how they
used it, it seemed to me that their king list functioned much as do genealogies in societies
organized on the basis of descent. In the latter case genealogies explain relationships
within or between descent groups in terms of shared apical ancestors. The *dabcar*
established relationships between Bagirmi and other groups in terms of shared wars.
A genealogy carefully preserves the memory of parent-child links to establish a descent
relationship and thus justify membership in descent groups. The *dabcar* preserved the
memory of wins and losses to establish a tributary relationship, and thus justify payment
of tribute. It Bagirmi won a war, then the defeated group paid tribute to Bagirmi. If
they lost, a tributary relationship might still be established, but in this instance it was
Bagirmi who would have to pay the tribute. A king list, by recording wins and losses,

remembered who was payer and payee. Thus Bagirmi remembered kings and battles for the same reason that societies with descent groups remembered ancestors. If they did not, they forgot an important part of how they were organized.

There was a considerable difference between religious exactions in the core and tribute from allied areas. There was a moral correctness in paying *hada-mbang* that was absent from tribute. Religious obligations were largely justified on the basis of notions that the *mbang* was their legitimate receiver, so that the person who paid them thought of himself or herself as morally "straight" (*tal*). Tribute, on the other hand, was given because the tributary had been militarily crushed and would be subjected to more of the same if it should be omitted; or, to make the matter brutally clear, tribute was justified by the fact that the *mbang* would try to kill you if you did not pay.

The core paid its taxes largely in the form of foodstuffs, but while the *mbang* was always interested in these, he was especially concerned with other products from tributary areas. In fact, according to Barth: "the most considerable tribute . . . which the Sultan levies consists of slaves, which the tributary pagan provinces have to pay him, . . . and all others of whose territories and power we obtain some information. . . . This tribute of slaves constitutes the strength and the riches of the king"(1965, 563). Other goods, however, were also accepted as tribute: those that were either part of the trans-Saharan trade, such as ostrich feathers, or were militarily useful, such as horses.

The actual collection of taxes and tribute was an administrative action of the state hierarchy. In the core, the head of a village (*ngolbe*) or an ethnic group collected the *hadjar* and other taxes and gave them to an *agid* who was on the staff of the court official in whose estate the village or ethnic group belonged. The *agid* then transported them to the court official. Next, an *agid* came from the *mbang* and collected a portion of these taxes and passed them on to his master. Staff were paid a portion of the court official's and the *mbang*'s revenues. One informant said that of twenty or thirty bowls given to the village head, twelve might eventually reach the *mbang*, suggesting that in the order of one-half to one-third of the core revenues remained with different court and estate officials. Tribute was handled slightly differently. It was collected by whatever state official was responsible for the tributary, using whatever system of collection was employed by the tributary's polity. Then it might be given directly to the *mbang*, usually at an impressive ceremonial during *eid el kabir;* or it might be given to the court official in whose estate the tributary belonged, who in turn would give a portion of it to the *mbang*.

At first blush it might seem dubious that the Bagirmi fiscal system would extend into its predatory zone, for polities do not generally extract revenues from areas over which they do not exercise sovereignty. However, Bagirmi and other central Sudanic states did so for reasons we now explore. We begin with Bagirmi conceptions of non-Muslims (*kirdi*) in predatory zones. Bagirmi notions about them in the 1970s were strong. They were viewed as people who went naked, got drunk, and were ignorant of Allah. Such notions were held even more strongly in the past, when certain religious leaders encouraged the pillaging of such infidels as a sign of piety and as a preparation for paradise. In short, it was good works to do bad works by taking booty from the *kirdi*.[6]

Raiding was called by Barma *kab kirdi* (literally to "go (after) pagans"). It was an annual effort conducted as regularily as planting. Perhaps this was because not all plantings led to harvest, while most raids harvested considerable booty and motivated raiders to try again next year. Raiding was conceived of as a privilege that was restricted to officials. It occurred at roughly the same time of the year as the *gugari*, and might be thought of as a martial extension of the latter institution into predation zones.

However, raiding and the concomitant amassing of booty were often closely associated with the collection of tribute, as the following quotation from Chevalier makes clear:

> Employing the excuse of raising taxes in a country, Gaurang unexpectedly comes with a large following of courtisans, soldiers, and children, who march at the end of troops to pick up the crumbs of booty. There are often several thousand of them. Under the pretext of awaiting complete payment of tribute, the Bagirmi live off the country, depending on the harvests amassed by the *kirdis* until these are exhausted. As for the tribute, it consists of slaves, herds, poultry, millet, honey and other agricultural products. (Chevalier 1907, 356)

Chevalier seems to be indicating that Bagirmi perceived of its raids as exercises in tribute collection—from populations who had not yet made this perception.

Bagirmi and its tributaries frequently raided together. There appear to have been at least two reasons for joint expeditions. First, integrated raids assured that Bagirmi's tributaries would have the wherewithal to satisfy their obligations to Massenya. This was in Bagirmi's interest. Second, those raided were often neighbors of the tributary who, for some reason, had fallen into its bad graces and had to be taught a lesson, or made the tributary's tributary.

The massacre at Kimre, which began this book, may have been an example of just this sort of a raid. The *mbang* Ab Sakin, with the assistance of Somrai tributaries, had camped in the Gaberi town of Broto. From there Ab Sakin "sent his emissaries in all directions to persuade communities to submit without combat, or to discover favorable occasions for attacks" (Nachtigal 1880, 388). Kimre, for unknown reasons, was a "refractory" village (ibid., 391), and so the *patcha*, apparently acting in collaboration with Somrai tributaries, attacked it. Somrai motives for participation in this particular raid are unknown, but my informants said that they were in the process of creating their own tributaries at this time.[7] What is unclear about the incident is whether *mbang* Ab Sakin was simply raiding, or helping the Somrai to settle a score amongst their Gaberi neighbors, or perhaps helping them expand their tributary zone. Whatever the reason, some of the booty at Kimre probably went to the Somrai to help them to acquit their own tributary responsibilities. Further, the raid's carnage suggests why predation zones would eventually consent to become tributaries, for it was better to submit than to be disemboweled at dawn.

Accounts of raiding often emphasize slaving, and indeed, slaves were important. However, anything and everything of value was taken, including foodstuffs. Denham, describing a Bornuan raid in the Mandara, reported that "with the assistance of a good telescope" he was able to see *kirdis* pouring off a mountain "bearing leopard skins, honey and slaves . . . also asses and goats" (1826, 117–18). Slaves were but one item among four in this raid. Similiarly, Denham described some of the loot that had been seized during the Bornuan expeditions into Bagirmi as including "thousands of cattle" (ibid., 86).

Raiding parties usually lived off the land, which meant that they seized foodstuffs as they foraged (Chevalier 1907, 356). This was a quickly invisible revenue, because they literally ate the evidence. However, raiding expeditions were normally conducted for all, or a signficant portion, of the dry season; and many officials participated in these parties. Thus, the invisible booty was nutritionally crucial for many officials for much of the year, and raiding that produced it might be thought of as an official form of foraging.

We now enter a treacherous domain, that of estimating the size of certain Bagirmi revenues at the end of the nineteenth century in comparison to those of Wadai during the same period. Barth said that "the circumstances connected with my stay in the country did not allow me to arrive at a definite conclusion in regard to its (the *hada-mbang's*) amount" (1965, 563). No other source that discussed Bagirmi's taxes clearly mentions their amounts (Nachtigal 1872, 388; Lanier 1925, 468; Devallee 1925, 64; Pacques 1977, 59). My discussions with different Barma sought to establish, first and foremost, the rates at which products had been taxed. For example, I would ask what percentage of the harvest had to be paid to officials. This could be answered because harvests were counted in terms of bowls, and people would remember that so many bowls were eaten and so many were given to officials. Such inquiries uniformily resulted in conflicting statements concerning the amounts of religious exactions, especially the *hadjar*. At first this imprecision exasperated me, and I thought that informants didn't know or, worse, that they were concealing the correct information. Then it became clear that neither was the case.

They reported various tax rates because there *were* various tax rates — that is, the rates kept fluctuating. One informant said that a normal *hadjar* might be: "eat thirty bowls, give one." Others said that though this could be true, it could equally be untrue. Finally, someone noted that the *maladonoge* might "pull" less in a growing season that had been poor than they might "pull" if it had been generous. Others concurred with this judgment. So what Barma were explaining was that the availability of food, which was in good measure controlled by prevailing climatic conditions, appears to have at least partially influenced how much officials chose to "pull." This was especially true of the *hadjar* and *zaka*. Volatile tax rates, then, appear to have been one response to environmental uncertainty.[8]

However, it is possible to make rough estimates of the magnitude of certain revenues. We begin with religious exactions, the most important of which was the *hadjar*. The level of the *hadjar* can be estimated by multiplying the amount produced per household by the tax rate and by the number of households responsible for paying the tax. Estimates are provided below of a high and low *hadjar* based upon different estimates of amounts produced per household and the number of households that were taxable.

In 1969–70 I suggested that the average Barma household cultivated approximately 7.5 acres from which it produced a mean of 1,211 kilograms of grains per year (Reyna 1972). Bagirmi is in an area where population density has decreased, so that the types of farming practices that appear under conditions of high population density, and which compromise yields, have not occurred. Thus there is no reason to posit a deterioration in yield levels since the onset of colonial rule. The rate at which the harvest was taxed seems, as indicated earlier, to have been at certain times about one-thirtieth of the harvest. This meant that a household's *hadjar* would be in average years on the order of 40 kilograms.

The number of households from which the *hadjar* was extracted may be estimated by dividing the population liable to taxation by the average household size in the core. Barma average household size, among a sample of riverine villages, was 5.1 persons in 1969–70 (Reyna 1972). It is strongly suspected that Barma household size has declined since precolonial times, though by how much is not known. However, the French Institute National de la Statistique et des Etudes Economiques (INSEE) conducted a major study of Chadian agriculture in the late 1970s in southern regions of Chad. In this study the largest mean household size of any ethnic group was 6.5 persons (INSEE 1967, 21). It would thus seem that mean households of 5.1 and 6.5 persons would be fair low and high estimates of household size. There are two early twentieth-century estimates of core population size. The first is from circa 1900 and is of 60,000 persons (Chevalier 1907), which is acknowledged to be a rough administrative guess. If anything, it is high, because administrators would be given to exaggerating their figures to enhance their own importance. There is a 1930 figure of approximately 41,000 persons (NA: W, 33, 13). This figure was collected during a time of high emigration from Bagirmi. It seems plausible to take the 1900 figure as a high and the 1930 figure as a low estimate of core population size. Subtracting the 3,500 or so persons, the earlier estimated size of the *maladonoge*, we get a core *tashkipage* population of from 37,500–56,500 persons. A low estimate of the number of households in the core can be calculated by dividing the smallest population size by the largest household size. This suggests there were about 5,770 households in the core. A high estimate of the number of households would reverse the calculation and divide the smallest household size into the largest population size. This would have meant that there were about 11,078 households in the core.

The preceding estimates indicate that a low *hadjar* would have extracted about 232,915 kilograms of cereals, which would have had a value, at the prices prevailing around 1900, of 23,291 francs. A high *hadjar* would have take almost 100 percent more cereals or about 446,443 kilograms valued at about 44,644 francs

There is no information concerning the amounts taken in the *gugari*, *zaka*, judicial fines, and market taxes. As was indicated earlier, the *gugari* did not happen to every village each year. Rather, it appears, at least by the end of the nineteenth century, to have become a rather rare event, more of a survival than a revenue. The situation with the *zaka* is less clear. My informants regarded it as a tax that wealthy people paid in good times. Under such conditions it might have yielded substantial revenues. However, if it did, we simply do not know; but we do not suspect that it was very important, because Barma vividly remembered the most burdensome taxes.

Nothing is reported about the level of judicial fines in Bagirmi. However, such fines were reported to have been only a very small percentage of the total revenues of Wadai (Bjorkelo 1976, 184). There is no reason to believe that such fines were any more important as a revenue in Bagirmi than in Wadai. Similarly, nothing is known about the levels of market taxes in Bagirmi. However, they are also stated to have been a very small percentage of Wadai's total taxes (ibid.). It is known that trade was considerably livelier in Wadai than Bagirmi throughout much of the nineteenth century. This suggests that market fees in Bagirmi may have been somewhat less important than they had been in Wadai.

It is possible to estimate the *futra*. Devallee said that about 3 kilograms were collected from each adult (1925, 64). Barma said that Devallee had been inaccurate when he said that it was required of all adults, they reported that only able-bodied adults would have been responsible for its payment. Roughly 54 percent of the people in Bagirmi fell into the age group 15–59 in 1969–70 (Reyna 1972). Assuming that this age group contained the vast majority of able-bodied adults and that the proportion of 15–59-year-olds to the total population was roughly the same circa 1900 as it was circa 1970, then the number of persons who should have paid the *futra* would have been roughly 54 percent of the food producer population of the core. This would have been 25,990 individuals if we use the high core population figure, or 17,191 if we use the low figure. These individuals might have paid a high of 77,970 kilograms of cereals, worth about 7,797 francs (in 1900 francs), or a low of 51,573 kilograms of cereals worth about 5,157 francs (in 1900 francs).

Three points must be emphasized concerning table 7.1 which includes low and high estimates of Bagirmi's core tax revenues.

First, the estimated taxes are just that, estimated. Second, it is known that some market taxes, judicial fines, *zaka*, and *gugari* would have been collected but were not included in the calculations, because there was no way of estimating their amounts. Had these been included, both the low and the high estimates of core revenues would have been higher. Third, the most crucially, even if the estimates in table 7.1 turned out to be correct, they should not be considered typical. There is simply not enough information at present to decide whether a particular estimate of taxation did or did not approach a mean.

As for tribute, it should be recalled that much tribute was in the form of slaves. Le Cornec said that around 1900, Bagirmi received about one thousand slaves annually as tribute (1963, 19). Le Cornec's source was Bruel (1905), whose figures were probably fairly accurate but were restricted to southern tributaries. He tells us nothing about what Bagirmi was acquiring from tributaries in the east, especially from the Bua and

Table 7.1. Estimated Bagirmi Taxes during the Late Nineteenth Century.

	LEVEL OF ESTIMATE	
Type of Tax	Low	High
Hadjar	Fr 23,291	Fr 44,644
Futra	Fr 5,157	Fr 7,797
Total	Fr 28,448	Fr 52,441

the Sokoro. Nor does he say what Bagirmi was receiving from the Kotoko. Thus the figure of one-thousand slaves, if anything, may have been an underestimate of slave tribute.

The price of slaves in the Massenya market circa 1900 ranged between 15 and 75 francs depending upon the age and sex of the person (Chevalier 1907, 359). The sex and the age of slaves sold is unknown. However, high and low estimates of the value of tribute can be made by multiplying the number of tributary slaves by their highest and lowest prices. This gives a high estimate of 75,000 francs (in 1900 francs) and a low one of 15,000 francs (in 1900 francs). Both the low and high estimates probably undervalue the total tribute because there was tribute in other items besides slaves, and there was more tribute in slaves from eastern and perhaps western allies, neither of which were counted in the present estimate.

Finally, there were two types of booty: slaves and "other goods." Bagirmi appears to have captured considerable numbers of slaves during the early years of the twentieth century. Chevalier suggests that five-thousand were captured annually (1907, 357).[9] Mortality among captured slaves before they were brought to market was extremely high. One source, Jacquin, told Chevalier that it was as high as 60 percent (1907, 358), but French officials would presumably elevate mortality rates among newly captured slaves to make the slave trade appear more odious and justify the extension of their colonial rule. Barma acknowledged that many slaves died before reaching the market, but they also noted rather pragmatically that it was not in their interest for slaves to die: a dead slave, after all, could not be sold. They thought that perhaps two or three slaves out of a group of ten might die, which is still a shockingly high mortality rate of 20–30 percent.

Estimates of the value of booty in slaves can be made by multiplying the worth of a single slave by the number surviving for sale. A low estimate is that the value of slave booty was on the order of 52,500 francs, and a high estimate is that it was in the neighborhood of 262,500 francs.

Certain accounts of raiding suggest that the raiders returned loaded with considerable amounts of nonslave booty (cf. Nachtigal 1880, 408). Aged informants, whose kin had participated in raids, insisted that this was the case. However, neither informants nor historical records identify the quantities or the values of these goods, so it is not possible to assess the significance of this booty. Barma, however, said that slaves were the most sought-after booty at the end of the nineteenth century. Value and transportation considerations appear to have been decisive here. A male slave aged 20-25 was worth 750 kilograms of millet or sorghum, and even though he might weigh 40 kilograms, he could march himself to market. Forty kilograms of cereal, however, was worth just that, or 19 times less than the slave, and had to be carried to market. Thus, though an official might return with some ostrich feathers, honey, valuable cloth, or livestock, slaves were definitely the preferred form of booty.

Each of the court officials had slave hamlets. In the early 1920s the *galadima* had two of these in the region of Bugoman. It is not known how many others were possessed by the court. Nor is there any mention of the *mbang* having them. Undoubtedly he did, but the absence of mention in reports suggests that he may have had relatively few.

How many of these were settled in hamlets owned by court officials and how many were household slaves in ordinary households is unknown. Most, as was suggested earlier, were owned by the court officials, and how many of these were of working age is also unknown. Given the preceding unknowns it is difficult to speculate about the amount of revenue the state derived from its slaves. One conclusion, however, can be drawn. There were far fewer slaves than free food producers, and though they may have given more of their harvests to the owners, it would have been considerably less than the total amount derived from free households.

It is now time to compare Bagirmi with Wadaian taxes. Julien published a remarkable account of the annual taxes of Wadai circa 1900 (1904, 140–41). His information was collected before France had fully conquered Wadai, when he would have had neither the time nor the knowledgeable individuals to validate its accuracy. My belief is that Julien's informants may have been trying to enlarge upon Wadai's importance, so that his figures may be a bit high. Nevertheless it is possible to compare Bagirmi's revenues with those of Wadai at roughly the same time. This is done in Table 7.2. Wadai's revenues are estimated at circa 2,175,000 francs (in 1900 francs). The low and high estimates for Bagirmi are approximately 95,500 and 390,000 francs respectively (in 1900 francs). Such estimates place Bagirmi's revenues anywhere from about 23 times to 5.5 times less than those of Wadai. It should be remembered, however, that the estimates of Bagirmi's revenues are far less complete than those of Wadai and that those for Wadai may well be overestimates. This suggests that Wadai's revenues were on the order of 5–6 times rather than 20–25 times those of Bagirmi. But it is entirely reasonable that Wadai's revenues should have been greater than Bagirmi's. Not only was Wadai much larger, but Bagirmi was in fact a tributary of Wadai, so that a fairly large part of Wadai's revenues were possibly derived from tribute from Massenya. Since the defeat of Gaurang I, Bagirmi was supposed to pay to Wadai a tribute of one hundred male slaves, thirty female slaves, one hundred horses, and one thousand robes each year (Lanier 1925, 461).[10]

Comparison of Bagirmi's and Wadai's taxes yields an interesting observation. In

Table 7.2. Revenues of Bagirmi and Wadai during the Late Nineteenth Century.

	BAGIRMI		WADAI
Type of Revenue	Low	High	WADAI
Taxes	Fr 28,448	Fr 52,441	Fr 558,000
Tribute	Fr 15,000	Fr 75,000	Fr 1,512,000
Booty	Fr 52,500	Fr 262,500	Fr 105,000
Total	Fr 95,748	Fr 389,941	Fr 2,175,000

Note: The source of Wadaian revenues is Julien 1904 as presented in Bjorkelo 1976. Julien's revenue information is in amounts received by the sovereign from different sectors. Those amounts from sectors known to be tributary were classified as tribute, while those from Wadai's core, around Abeche, were classified as taxes. Julien reported the value of revenues in thalers. One thaler around 1900 equaled three francs.

both, roughly 75 percent of the revenues seem to have come from tributary or predation zones. This meant that if an ambitious official sought to increase his or her income, the best way to do so was to increase revenues from tributary and predation zones. Most tribute and booty, however, was in the form of slaves. Thus slaves were, as Barth had suggested, "the strength and riches" of the east-central Sudanic states.

Revenue Allocation

How were the revenues discussed in the previous sections allocated to reproduce the household state? An understanding of Bagirmi revenue allocation depends upon an understanding of how private incomes were expended for public purposes. There is a crucial difference between the way contemporary states and Bagirmi handled revenues after their collection. In the modern state revenues flow into a treasury and are then disbursed on the basis of a budget formulated as a result of legislative and/or executive action. The majority of such revenues are reserved for public accounts such as defense, social services, and transportation; however, a percentage goes to officials as their personal incomes. In contemporary states officials may dispose of their incomes as they wish, but it is a grave crime to administer public revenues in other than the authorized ways.

Bagirmi had no formal budget. All revenues became officials' private salaries, and as personal income they could be disposed of as the officials saw fit. Thus there was no institution that disbursed state funds, because these did not exist. There was only a multitude of officials with their private incomes. Officials, however, tended to expend their incomes on public enterprises because they were obliged to use their private incomes to implement policy once the *mbang* and the court had made a decision. In contrast to the contemporary state, where there are two discrete sectors, public and private, with public revenues expended for public purposes and private incomes for private ends, an important characteristic of Bagirmi's fiscal system was that public revenues became private incomes that were expended upon public goals.

Private incomes were paid in either products or slaves. Most taxes were religious exactions, and most religious exactions were cereal or animal foodstuffs. Products that are "necessary for the survival of the community" are necessary products, and those that are a "permanent surplus" above and beyond the necessary products are surplus products (Mandel 1968, 27). Clearly, taxes taken from communities formed a surplus above and beyond the communities' subsistence, hence most taxes were in the form of surplus products.

Slaves formed the bulk of tribute and booty. Some, perhaps most, slaves were sold for money by officials who had acquired them. Surplus value is "the difference between the value of the product and the value of elements consumed in the formation of the product, in other words, of the means of production and the labor power" (Marx 1906, 317). Thus, when slaves were sold, the value realized that exceeded the costs of capturing and nourishing them until sale was a surplus value.

Some slaves were not sold. A few worked in their owner's slave villages. Most, however, became members of a court official's staff, usually starting by performing the most menial domestic chores and occasionally rising to become trusted advisors, and even on rare occasions to become court officials such as *patcha*. Such slaves may be said to have become a form of labor.

However, they were a rather specific form of labor. Marx often spoke of productive labor, by which he meant labor that employed means of production to produce economic capital (1973, 305). One might distinguish this from violent labor, by which is meant labor that is combined with other means of destruction, such as weapons, to attain certain political goals. Slave officials, like all officials, were soldiers, and as soldiers they hefted weapons to make political hay. Hence they were a most violent form of labor.

Thus official incomes from public revenues were realized as either surplus products, surplus value, or labor. These, in their turn, were expended in ways that helped materially to reproduce the state. Surplus products, in the form of foods, fed existing officials; so they contributed to the state's reproduction by replacing the calories that officials had consumed in the performance of their duties. Surplus value, in the form of the money realized in the sale of slaves, was used to acquire the equipment necessary to outfit officials. Some of this money was spent to purchase replacement or additional clothing and other sumptuary goods. Most, however, went to purchase replacement or additional military supplies such as chain mail. Hence surplus value contributed to the state's reproduction by replacing the means of destruction that officials had used during official duties. Violent labor, in the form of new slaves, was attached to court officials' staffs to replace officials who had died of old age or perished in combat, or to add to a court official's staff when he or she assumed new, additional responsibilities. Labor used in this manner contributed to the state's reproduction by replenishing its supply of violent labor, which will be discussed in chapter 8. Thus, officials' incomes replaced or augmented the men and their weapons that had been exhausted in the governance of the Sun Kings' realm. It was in this sense that private incomes reproduced state structures.

Three attributes of Bagirmi's revenue collection and allocation system need to be emphasized in conclusion. First, it did not stimulate the growth of markets as much as might be expected, because a number of taxes in the core were paid in kind. Second, it was a system that could be responsive to the environmental uncertainties and production risks that dominated the domestic mode of production. This appears to be true for two reasons: the amounts taxed, especially for the *hadjar*, could be raised or lowered depending upon the success of agricultural production; and the revenues raised could be shifted from region to region. Thus, if the core had had a poor growing season, the rate at which the *hadjar* was extracted could be reduced, and revenue collection could be shifted to raiding in a predation zone. Third, officials did not produce food or any other economic product. This meant that states could not exist without food producers. The million or so kilograms of grain that the thirty-five hundred Bagirmi officials needed to survive was grain that food producers could not use to satisfy their own nutritional needs. Thus the third and most elemental attribute of Bagirmi's revenue system and those of other central Sudanic kingdoms was that they articulated states with food producers so that the former could reproduce at the expense of the latter.

One point should be obvious, as Barma of all walks of life were at pains to point it out: for Bagirmi and the other states, the more different revenues were "pulled," the bigger were officials' incomes. Officials thus were motivated to "pull" hard. Certain individuals must have grasped this situation, for the old Bornuan royal praise song had it that: "The poor are grass; they are fodder for horses. Work, poor man, so that we may eat" (Prietze 1914, 251). Just as grass reproduces horses, so food producers, through their taxes, reproduce officials; and then officials, through their incomes, reproduce the state. We have not, however, finished with the analysis of the material reproduction of the state. Chapter 8 considers the sickle that officials used to harvest their "grass." Attention turns to warfare.

Chapter 8

Warfare

Certain Sara say that a lazy man "cuts grass without a sickle" (Fortier and Villeon 1977, 107), the sickle standing for the tool one needs to accomplish something. The saying itself reminds people that they won't get anything done unless they use the proper tools. This chapter describes the military ethos that motivated men to war, the means they had at their disposal when fighting, and the different types of conflicts in which they actually wielded these means. Thus in a metaphorical sense the chapter describes the Sun Kings' sickle and shows the type of work it did.

The Military Ethos

Major Denham—a stalwart, if ever so slightly Victorian, officer—participated in a cavalry battle in the Mandara during the early part of the nineteenth century. The engagement pitted Bornu, supported by Arab and Mandaran allies, against the Fulani. Denham was with the Bornuans, who were beaten and fled in disarray. Denham describes his flight. "I felt that nothing could save me: however, there was not much time for reflection; we instantly became a flying mass." Denham galloped with "one of the Mandara eunuchs," who, he "observed, kept a good lookout, his head being constantly turned over his left shoulder, with a face expressive of the greatest dismay," perhaps because the Fulani pursuers were gaining. This motivated Denham to spur his horse, which: "had the effect of incapacitating my beast altogether, . . . and . . . he stumbled and fell. Almost before I was on my legs, the Fulani were upon me; I had, however, kept hold of the bridle, and seizing a pistol from the holster, I presented it at two of these ferocious savages: . . . they instantly went off." Immediately, Denham remounted, raced a hundred yards, when again his horse came down, throwing him against a tree. From this position he watched as "the eunuch and his four followers were butchered: . . . their cries were dreadful." Next the butchers turned on Denham. He was stripped of his clothes, and: "when my plunderers began to quarrel for the spoil, the idea of escape came like lightning across my mind, . . . and I started as fast as my legs would carry me, . . . and I seized the young branch issuing from the stump of a large tree, . . . as the branch yielded to the weight of my body, a large . . . serpent . . . rose from its coil, as if in the very act of striking. I was horror struck; . . . the shock, however, revived me, and . . . I reached the opposite bank; . . . then for the first time felt safe from my pursuers."

Thinking back on the incident, Denham reflected, "My hopes of life were too faint to deserve the name"(1823, 134–36).

The engagement that has just been described was standard of central Sudanic war. Bagirmi officials expected to enter such battles on an annual basis. If they won, they might be the butchers. If they lost, they might be the butchered. Such war was not for the fainthearted. Clearly something was needed to fortify the will to butcher.

To this end Bagirmi officials, as well as those in other east-central Sudanic states, underwent continual military socialization, with constant training and rewards as key elements in the process. The child-rearing practices of the official class, for example, emphasized activities in which "young people were trained very early to capture slaves without either wounding or mutilating them" (Pacques 1977, 63). Similarly, jousting was practiced (Temple 1912). Staff were given horses at the time that they joined a court official's retinue; then afterward, any ritual involving a court official included the performance of a cavalry charge (*n'ur sinda*), which gave them a chance to try out their new mounts. Such charges were practiced incessantly. This, in conjunction with the fact that young officials were encouraged to join military expeditions once a year, suggests that they rapidly became seasoned cavalry.

Good soldiering tended to be rewarded with, and by, women. For example, in certain areas young soldiers were not permitted to marry unless they had proved "their courage and skill" by "capturing slaves" (Pacques 1977, 63). Further, Barma from the Bousso area said that once a man was acknowledged to be a fine soldier, he would be followed on certain occasions by a woman who carried objects on a tray that symbolized his prowess. Following such training, officials became "masters of horse," or *malasinda*, bearing a demeanor that sharply contrasted with that of food producers.

O'Fahey speaks of there being a chivalric, or *furusiyya*, ethos among Darfur's professional soldiers (1980, 39).[1] Such an ethos seems to have been widespread among the officials of the central Sudan. Two incidents suggest how this ethos was expressed among the Bagirmi. The first occurred as a result of bringing two men to the apartment I used during my stays in the capital in 1970. One was an aged official, the other a food producer. Neither had visited a "modern" house before. Both became painfully sick with stomach disorders. The food producer moaned, complained, and demanded to use the toilet, of whose operation he was ignorant. Here he relieved himself in the shower and performed his ablutions in the toilet. The aged official sat cross-legged on a mat throughout the other's rather noisy ordeal, utterly uncomplaining. He did not say a word, and I knew he had been ill only after the fact, when the food producer told me. The food producer's ethos seemed to be that of a practical, matter-of-fact person. If there were urgent problems, they should be dealt with urgently. The official's ethos seemed to be that of a stoic. If there were urgent problems, one should endure, only endure.

The second occasion that revealed something of the ethos of officials was during preparations to thwart a rebel raid in a village where I was living on the Shari river. This place was the residence of a *chef de canton*, Ahmet Ngollo. At the time of the incident, it held most of the year's tax revenues. At the same time that Ahmet Ngollo was an official in the government of the Republic of Chad he was also a court official in traditional Bagirmi. He had surrounded himself with a staff of persons who were descendants of *maladonoge* and had, as was observed in chapter 8, recreated something of the old court official's office in that of the *chef de canton*. Warning of the impending raid came at 11 P.M. Most of Ahmet's fighting-age staff were away collecting taxes. It seemed that, given this weakness, it would be appropriate to slip away under the cover of darkness.

This was not to occur. The tax money was buried on the sandy beach close to the river. Ahmet's wives were also buried in the sand—up to their necks—between the taxes and the tree at the beach's edge where he normally held court. The chair that indicated his authority was placed under the tree facing the only road into town, and he seated himself facing the road, his chair flanked by the few old staff left in the village. These arrangements were made matter-of-factly, quietly, and quickly.

Though in fact no attack materialized, the preparations for its occurrence indicate Bagirmi notions of appropriate behavior in combat. The placing of Ahmet before his wives, and the wives before the taxes was, of course, a challenge to the rebels. If you fought through Ahmet you got the wives, and if you got the wives you got the taxes. But he was there, in his normal, public place, and before you got your prizes, he, and his men, would try to kill you. Throughout the evening they waited, sipping tea. Above all the ethic was one of *sang-froid*.

Ahmet Ngollo and his men seem to have acted as the Bagirmi military behaved in the past. Consider, for example, a battle at Ngala (1824), when Bagirmi attacked Bornu and Major Denham watched with some admiration as "the Bagirmi came on with great coolness, . . . five thousand strong, with two hundred chiefs at their head" (in Bovill 1968, 449). Barma think an official is like a force of nature, and his nature is to fight with "coolness."

Such an ethos appears different from that revealed in the *Iliad* or the Germanic sagas, and equally from those reported for the Tubu of Chad (Chapelle 1957) or the nineteenth-century Plains Indians (Lowie 1920). These peoples' warriors courted battle in order to perform extraordinary feats of combat and become, like Achilles, famous heroes. This has been described as a heroic ethos (Alcock 1971, 319–27). Such heroism seems to be found in societies that were more acephalous than Bagirmi and where warfare may have been less central to maintaining basic institutions. Achilles fought somebody else's battles to acquire his own personal fame. Plains Indians competed for glorious coups. But the Bagirmi warrior-official fought for his income, which provided his daily sustenance. Perhaps, with war so fundamental a business, heroic showboating got in the way of coolness and its fundamental purpose, butchering.

The Means of Destruction

A society's means of destruction may be thought of as the combination of resources, people, and instruments deployed to practice violence.[2] The chief means by which Bagirmi performed the grisly task of destruction were the institutions of police and army fighting as a cavalry. These are discussed below.

Police and Army

Certain authorities define the state in terms of the possession of a standing army (e.g., Fried 1967). Merely to note that Bagirmi had a permanently organized, paid military establishment might be technically correct, but quite misleading. Bagirmi's institutions of violence were quite flexible, with some more permanent than others. How this was the case is explained below.

No matter what the affair, a court official dispatched a portion of his or her staff when administrative responsibilities involved actually visiting some part of the estate. This retinue would be typically composed of a core of younger men led by an older man. Descendants of both officials and food producers remembered that such troops would ride into a village or hamlet at a brisk canter—robes flowing, weapons jangling—making directly for the compound of its head. There formal greetings would be exchanged between the troop and the head, and as these occurred, important villagers would move to surround their leader. The greetings served a communication function, for as villagers first gathered to discover what all the commotion was about, and then as they sought out acquaintances from among the troopers, they could not help but count the number of cavalry and see what weapons they displayed, thus acquiring information about the troop's potential for violence.

After the greetings, the staff official in charge of the troop would state its business— often the collecting of taxes or the removal of an accused person for judgment. Usually, following the execution of the troop's task, the village head would give a meal for the troopers and the village elders. If, perchance, force was required to execute the troops' responsibilities, they did not need to call the police: they were the police. Thus, insofar as a court official's staff operated to maintain law and authority in his or her estate, it operated as a police force.

This was the standing part of Bagirmi's military establishment. An important attribute of this organization was that permanent military units were for the most part relatively small and divided between separate commands. Each court official had, as was estimated in chapter 6, a staff of between fifteen and one hundred men, and these were not normally integrated into a military command hierarchy. Rather, they took orders only from their court official. Thus the standing part of Bagirmi's military was decentralized. Larger, hierarchically organized units, however, were possible, as we shall now explore.

Major military units, constituting what might be called an army, could only be formed following a decision made by the Council of War. Barma, however, explained that members of the Council of War would not become the chief military planners even though they had made the decision to go to war. Rather, it was suggested that the differing abilities and the quality of court officials dictated who did further military planning. Thus, for example, if there was trouble with tribute payment from the south and the *patcha* was a brilliant tactician, then it was likely that the *katourlil*, as the person responsible for administering southern tributaries, and the *patcha*, as the individual most likely to realize a successful campaign, would be influential in formulating military policy. A crucial decision that would have to be taken was what type of army to mobilize. In order to understand how this decision might be taken, it is important first to grasp the organization of the army.

Nachtigal observed Bagirmi's army immediately after Ab Sakin's defeat by Wadai, during a time when it would thus be small and ragtag.

> At his sides and behind Ab Sakin were his riders and foot soldiers—almost all were slaves; . . . of the former about fifty were armed with more or less complete armor for themselves and their horses, and of the latter, several hundred, of which the minority were armed with guns and the majority with hand weapons, lances, and spears, and here and there with shields.

> Toward this royal group sprang from all sides the dignitaries with those warriors they commanded and the heathen chiefs with their followers swinging their weapons in greeting. From one side came the *patcha*, the head warrior, whom I and my people had joined, followed by about thirty riders and eighty foot soldiers, and from the other side with just as many warriors came the *ngarman*, the chief of the eunuchs, who is also a high dignitary. Even smaller were the troops of the *ḳirema*, the *ḳaturlil*, and the other dignitaries. . . .[There were also soldiers from tributaries such as] the Somrai and the Gaberi; there one showed me the chief of the Phong from Ndam at the head of his contingent; I also saw a division of the Bua of Korbol, which are located east of the Shari, farther upstream, and the most numerous were the different divisions of the Sara. (Nachtigal 1889, 605)

Nachtigal's account captures the army in medias res, in the middle of the slave raiding with which I introduced this book. It appears chaotic, if colorful.

However, there was an organization beneath the hurly-burly. The army was composed of core and tributary soldiers organized into squadrons. Bagirmi called a war and a squadron of troops by the same term, *waya*. There do not appear to have been special terms for the units in the army, a squadron being called after the court official it served. Hence the *patcha*'s unit might be called *malaway patcha* or *malasinda patcha*, which meant "masters of war of the *patcha*" or "masters of horse of the *patcha*."

A squadron was normally composed of subsquadrons. These included one consisting of the court official's own staff and others consisting of his or her estate officials. There were two types of estate subsquadrons: those of core and those of tributary estate officials. Subsquadrons of core estate officials tended to be composed of the staffs of these officials. Tributary subsquadrons had whatever chain of command and types of soldiers that were particular to their ethnic group. Thus a court official's squadron might consist of three types of subsquadrons: those of his own personal staff, his core estate officials, and his tributary leaders.

The staff of the court official had two major duties within a squadron. Their first assignment was to act as liaison officers assuring communications between their squadron and others in the army as well as within their own squadron. In principle, estate and tributary subsquadrons were under the authority of the court official to whom they had been assigned; in practice, their primary loyalty tended to be to their own leaders. This meant that orders within squadrons might have to be negotiated rather than issued.

The second responsibility of a court official's staff was to serve as the major assault troops. It was they who were likely to be the armed cavalry; it was they who were asked to lead charges against the enemy; and it was they who were expected to seek out their opponent's champions, to kill them, and to seize their standards, all—of course—with great coolness.

There was considerable flexibility as to exactly what type of army, and how large, to raise. Specifically, each time the army was mobilized, decisions had to be made about which court officials' squadrons to include as well as which and how many of his estate officials to recruit. For example, on one occasion the army might include the *patcha*'s and the *galadima*'s but not the *mbarma*'s squadrons. Such flexibility allowed the army to deploy different numbers of soldiers to respond to military challenges of differing types and gravity. For example, by including the squadron of the *mbarma*, the army assured itself of riverain peoples who might be more experienced in combat along the upper reaches of the Shari River.

Discussions with Barma suggested that there were three general principles that guided mobilization. The first was that the numbers activated were a function of military objectives. This principle, however, did not translate into a simple rule that the more important the military objective, the greater the number of troops activated. It seems that when Bagirmi went on the offensive to attack another state, it sought to mobilize as many troops as it could. For example, it was said to have had nine thousand cavalry when it invaded Bornu in the 1820s (Escayrac de Lauture 1855, 68). However, when it was under attack by another state, it might choose not to recruit so many troops. Rather, on such occasions, it often kept its forces small and dispersed, retreating into areas where it could not easily be attacked. Such appears to have been the case when Bornu, in alliance with North African troops, invaded Bagirmi in response to the previously mentioned Bagirmi attack on Bornu (Rodd 1936, 160–62).

A second principle, one that was reported in chapter 6, seems to have been to keep a major military leader in reserve to defend Bagirmi when it was on the offensive; so if the *patcha* was on campaign, the *mbarma* should stay home. This principle seems to have been most applicable when Bagirmi was fighting in its tributary or predation zones against smaller polities or acephalous peoples. Under such conditions, only one or two squadrons would be activated, with the *mbang* and the *mbarma* waiting at home. This principle seems to have been directed more against internal than external threats to the state, with the *mbarma* staying behind to discourage attempts at civil discord.

A final principle of mobilization was to activate those troops that were likely to be most effective. Thus, for example, the use of Arabs would be inadvisable when Massenya was obliged to campaign against other Arabs. In such situations Bagirmi appears to have recruited troops from its southern tributaries. These were often Sara who had been raided by Arabs, and who thus had a score to settle, which motivated them to be ruthless. Arabs bitterly complained of the excesses of these troops (Carbou 1912, 2:61).

In summary, regardless of which principles of mobilization were applied, the activation of the army involved the dropping by many of the state's personnel of all their functions save their military ones. Army structure thus was state structure temporarily placed on active duty. Lanier, writing of the period immediately following 1900, said that the "army did not have a fixed organization" (1925, 472). He was both right and wrong. Bagirmi, as we have just shown, possessed two related institutions capable of delivering violence. One, the court official's staff, was fixed in composition, had policelike functions and stood permanently throughout the year. The other had armylike responsibilities, was not a permanent group, was not fixed in size or composition, and required that the state hierarchy, or at least a portion of it, stop whatever it was doing and turn itself into an army.

It made considerable sense to have a fixed police and a flexible army. The army faced major external and internal threats to the state. These could, and did, rapidly change, especially when competing polities formed alliances. Clearly, Bagirmi faced a different military threat when menaced by a Bulala-Wadai alliance in 1870 than when faced with only the Bulala, as had been the case immediately prior to 1870. Without a flexible army it would have been more difficult to respond to such changing military circumstances. On the other hand, a court official's estate remained the same size unless there was a major military success or catastrophe. This meant that policing chores were within a relatively constant area, so that a police force pegged at the size of a court official's staff was appropriate.

It is not possible to estimate the total number of soldiers Bagirmi could field during the latter part of the nineteenth century.[3] However, there are estimates of the size of four different Bagirmi armies between the 1850s and 1900. Barth, who observed a *mbang* returning from a campaign in 1852, suggested that the cavalry numbered three thousand and the infantry ten thousand (1965, 560). Nachtigal, who also directly observed Bagirmi's army, presents estimates of combined infantry and cavalry ranging from fifteen hundred (1889, 605) to two thousand (1880, 383). During Nachtigal's time, Bagirmi was experiencing civil war involving competition between Ab Sakin and a pretender, supported by Wadai, so it was to be expected that Bagirmi's armies would be smaller circa 1870 than circa 1850. Gentil was involved in the military plans to defeat Rabah, which included Bagirmi forces as auxiliaries, and was thus in a position to know force size accurately; he estimated that Bagirmi's army included at most about four thousand (1902,144). Chevalier puts the size of raiding expeditions, which would not have included the entire army, at approximately three thousand (1907, 356). Bagirmi thus, except in times of discord, seems to have fielded armies of between three and four thousand cavalry in the latter half of the nineteenth century.

These armies, at least as indicated by mid-nineteenth-century data, appear to have been smaller than those of Wadai and Bornu. Barth reports Bornuan army size on one expedition to have been between 12,500 to 13,000, most of whom were cavalry (1965, 638–40). He further reports that the strength of Wadai's army was "seven thousand horse" (1965, 658). Fresnel, writing at roughly the same time, gives Wadai a larger army of 10,000–11,000 cavalry (1849, 46).

It should be clear that most of the personnel in Bagirmi's police and armies were staff of court or estate officials. It should be equally clear that decision making within these forces was exercised by the court officials. In short, the control and application of violence in Bagirmi, as in all states, was strictly official business.

Cavalry

This section considers the equipment that Bagirmi and other central Sudanic states used when warring.[4] The role of firearms is the first question that must be dealt with when discussing instruments of war because guns became the decisive weapon in post-sixteenth-century European conflict, and they were apparently introduced into the Sudan as early as the end of the sixteenth century.[5]

Guns (*bundukge*) were certainly used by Bagirmi's armies prior to the nineteenth century, because al-Tunisi mentions their discovery in Gaurang I's palace when it was sacked by Sabun in 1801 (1851, 166). However, Fisher and Rowland have argued that firearms were not especially important to central Sudanic armies prior to the end of the nineteenth century (1971). This appears to be largely the case with Bagirmi, for in the 375-year period of Bagirmi's history, there seem to have been only two nineteenth-century conflicts whose outcomes depended upon firearms. The first conflict was during the Bagirmi-Bornuan wars of the 1820s when, following the Bornuan rout of a formidable Bagirmi army, the words on every Bornuan's lips were, according to Major Denham, who was present at the battle: "The guns! The guns! The guns! Oh, wonderful! How they made the dogs skip!" (1826, 250). Further, at the very end of the century, in the 1890s, Bagirmi was unable to defend itself against Rabah's soldiers, who were heavily armed with repeating rifles. Most Bagirmi guns prior to the 1890s were muzzle-loading flintlocks of dubious accuracy that had a nasty tendency to explode in their operators' faces. Guns were used, one old Barma slyly confided, "to make a boom"—that is, to frighten.

It should be understood, however, that the nineteenth century was a time of transition with regard to the use of guns. This was especially true for Wadai. Al-Tunisi, writing during the first years of the nineteenth century, reports that there were almost no guns in the Wadaian army (1851, 418). Fifty years later, Barth suggests that Wadai had about three hundred musketeers (1965, 658). Then another fifty years later, at the turn of the century, Carbou suggests that Wadai had ten thousand modern rifles (1912, 2:264). Bagirmi lagged far behind Wadai in this arms race. There appear to have been almost no guns circa 1800 (al-Tunisi 1851, 418), apparently still very few fifty years later (Barth 1965, 560), and only a few hundred at the beginning of the twentieth century (Gentil 1902).

Bagirmi's armies therefore had to rely upon traditional armaments. Lances and swords were used for attack, and quilted armor or occasionally chain mail for defense.[6] Bows and arrows were used but were normally an infantry weapon, often employed by *kirdi* allies, and archers never developed the ability, possessed by the English longbow archers, to bring down cavalry. Light throwing axes were also used by both cavalry and infantry. They were not, however, especially effective in stopping a cavalry charge.[7]

Al-Tunisi wrote: "Horses are, for Sudanese populations, the most precious possession, the strongest way of imposing respect and triumphing over their enemies" (1851, 444). The sale and ownership of horses were affairs of state, with different regimes trying to assure themselves of and deny others a supply of hardy horses.[8] The reason horses were important is that they were the sine qua non of cavalry; and, as Lanier said:

> as in the Age of Chivalry, it was above all with cavalry that battle was waged. . . . They charged until within a respectable distance of the cavalry upon whom they discharged their guns and then returned, generally followed by their adversaries' cavalry, who employed the

same tactics. After successive charges, the party with the most remaining tried an enveloping maneuver, while a certain number of specially armed cavalry grappled with the opposing infantry. These were *cuirassiers*, cased not in iron but in a veritable quilt sheltering them and their horses from arrows and blows of the lance. (1925, 473)

When lances and swords were used instead of guns, the same charges Lanier describes would occur, but the charge would end in a fury of hacking and thrusting.[9]

The use of cavalry in the manner described by Lanier was by no means unique to Bagirmi. Each of the central Sudanic states used it in roughly the same manner.[10] The simple fact was that a state could not compete with another unless it could compete with its cavalry. Cavalry had certainly been used in the east-central Sudan as far back as the tenth century, and perhaps earlier. It was only at the very end of the nineteenth century that Rabah, arriving from outside the central Sudan, was able to give the new and more effective repeating rifles to disciplined infantry squares, whose massed firepower simply dissolved cavalry charges, and with them the utility of the cavalry.

There has been a tendency to romanticize central Sudanic cavalries. Urvoy, for example, says, "this boasting and anarchic cavalry, . . . this hand-to-hand combat, the pillaging of hamlets, the rare and brilliant battles, . . . it is our feudal army; it is Crécy and Agincourt" (1949, 78). It should be clear that there was nothing especially "brilliant" about cavalry. The essential tactic was one of repeated charges. These used the massed weight of hundreds of horses to break opposing forces into small, isolated groups, preferably knocked to the ground—where they were in the proper posture, in the words of one old enthusiast, to be "hacked to mini-morceaux."[11] Cavalry mounted butchers on horses, hardly a romantic practice.

There does not seem to have been a prohibition against food producers owning weapons. In fact, most mature men owned a spear and a knife. But cavalry weapons were another matter. They were extremely expensive. Horses were the second most expensive commodity in east-central Sudan's markets, costing sixty to one hundred francs each in the early 1900s, which was two to three times the cost of a slave (Chevalier 1907, 362). Quilted armor and chain mail were luxury items that were usually stored in royal vaults (al-Tunisi 1851, 166). Metal armor appears to have been the only item more expensive than horses, for the price of ten slaves seems to have been necessary to acquire a suit of chain mail in the 1840s (Fresnel 1849, 46).

Cost considerations, then, precluded food producers from acquiring cavalry weapons.[12] Court officials acquired their arms through purchase from merchants or as spoils of war. Staff usually received their horse, at least their first one, as a gift when they joined a court official's retinue. Thus, although it is incorrect to say that the state enjoyed a total monopoly over weapons, it did possess an effective monopoly of the decisive weapons—those that transformed a man into a cavalry man.

Raiding and Warring

All Bagirmi conflict occurred following the November harvests, during the dry season. Such postharvest timing reflected sound tactical judgments. War was scheduled at pre-

cisely the time of year when there was the greatest amount of agricultural product awaiting distribution, when roads were passable following the rains, and when tributary and
predation zone peoples would be gathered about the fruits of their harvests. Bagirmi's
army, like those of other central Sudan states, engaged in two types of conflicts, raiding
and warring. These can be distinguished from each other in terms of the size of the
military units participating in engagements, the amount of time given over to military
operations, the nature of the opponent, the military objectives, and the political goals of
the combat.

Raiding in the francophone literature is called *razzia*. A raiding expedition in
Darfur or Wadai was called a *ghazoua* (al-Tunisi 1851, 467). Barma appear to have
no specific term for it but spoke of raids in terms of where they were generally directed,
so they would say that they would "go to pagan lands," or *ḳab ḳirdi*. East-central
Sudanic states appear to have had two major ways of organizing raids, one stressing
private and the other, state initiative. The former raids were organized by nonofficial
entrepreneurs who would be granted permission to pillage in specific areas. Such a way
of organizing raiding appears to have been popular in Darfur at the beginning of the
nineteenth century (al-Tunisi 1851, 467). Bagirmi, Wadai, and Bornu, on the other
hand, seem to have relied upon their officials and their staffs to conduct raids, at least
throughout the nineteenth century.

Raids tended to involve small military units over relatively short time periods.
Bagirmi raids typically involved one or two court officials' squadrons. They occurred for
only two or three months—with everybody planning to be home by the rains. Usually,
though by no means always, raiding was conducted in predation zones against peoples
who were acephalous and non-Muslim, against opponents who lacked standing armies.
Raiding, whether against a competing state or an acephalous people, sought not so
much to defeat an enemy as to seize as many products as possible.

The French tend to use the word *razzia* broadly, to cover any type of Sudanic military
operation. Thus different authorities have said that desert pastoralists, such as the Tubu,
conducted *razzia* (Chapelle 1957), as well as Sudanic states such as Wadai (Carbou 1912,
vol. 2). Yet Chapelle is very clear in reporting that Tubu raids involved very few people,
that members of opposing sides were usually kin, and that their purpose was to acquire
or restore honor to a body of relatives (1957, 329). Such raiding was, to paraphrase
von Clausewitz, kinship politics by another means. This was not what either Bagirmi,
Wadaian, or Bornuan raids were about. Their raids were short operations conducted by
relatively small military units of a state with the objective of accumulating booty.

Raids could be a tricky business. They were conducted far from the Bagirmi core
in areas that officials knew relatively little about, so that they could easily be directed
against regions where there would be little booty, or, worse still, where there were
numerous, well-organized opponents operating on a home terrain inhospitable to horses.
Thus an important condition that had to be satisfied if raids were to be successful was the
creation and maintenance of a safe base of operations. This meant, as one gentleman
engagingly put it, "War makes friends." Bagirmi could raid more effectively where
it had tributaries, for these provided bases that were both safe and able to provide
intelligence regarding profitable targets. Consequently, an important political goal of

raiding was the creation and maintenance of tributaries—that is, the transformation of predation zones into tributary areas.

There seem to have been two general ways in which this was done. The first would be to set up an operations center in a predation zone. Initially, these were temporary camps occupied only during actual raids. Gradually, however, they might take on a more permanent character. They would be staffed by Bagirmi officials, who would seek an informal understanding with the heads of surrounding communities concerning likely raiding targets. Such a camp appears to have been located near the town of Gundi in the late nineteenth century (Bruel 1905).[13]

The second way in which tributaries were initiated was to harass a *kirdi* community militarily until it became an ally. Its leader might then be invested as a Bagirmi official, perhaps called *mbang*, or more often *alifa* or *ngar*. He might or might not have been some sort of leader in the *kirdi* community, but regardless of his authority in his own society, he would fall under the authority of a court official, that is, become part of that person's estate. As such he would become an estate official, though as a new official in an area unfamiliar with Bagirmi tradition, he was likely to receive special tutelage from the court official's staff concerning Bagirmi governance. This was especially likely to be the case with regard to the planning and execution of raids. The area around the Sara town of Koumra appears to have become a tributary in this manner during the second half of the nineteenth century.

Warring might include raids, but it was an altogether different and more serious affair than raiding. Wars involved large numbers of military units—frequently all the squadrons that could be mobilized. They were directed against cephalous opponents, usually in one's own or in a competing state's core or tributary territories. The opponent in war was a state—with an army to be overcome. As a result, the military objective could not be solely pillage, no matter how profitable it might be. So wars were not of brief duration but were major investments of means of destruction and evolved slowly, beginning with minor skirmishes and building to major campaigns. It can be said, for example, that Wadai and Bagirmi fought a one-hundred-year war in the nineteenth century, which began with Sabun's defeat of Gaurang I circa 1800 and continued until the arrival of the French. The objective of war was to crush the opponent's army lest that army crush yours.

Wars were often against states, and states operated from urban centers. Thus in war one frequently sought to crush the cities and towns of one's opponents. Offensive war sought to take towns, and defensive war sought to protect them. Cities and towns tended to be built on naturally protected, fortified sites, so they were difficult to take. Wars, therefore, often involved intense combat.

Consider, for example, Rodd's reconstruction from Denham's notes of a single campaign in a decade-long war during the 1820s between Bagirmi and Bornu. This campaign occurred in 1819 and involved a Bornuan invasion of Bagirmi with the assistance of North African allies. The invading force was led by the ruler of Bornu, Sheikh al-Kanemi and probably numbered circa thirteen thousand men (Rodd 1936, 160). The campaign began in a tributary of Bagirmi called Babelyia in a town called in the text "Babbilla," which was probably Dal.[14]

The gates of the town which is walled were built up and everything prepared for defense. The walls were very high and showers of arrows fell on the besiegers. Lighted fire brands [and] boiling stinking liquids were poured on those who approached the walls. Their dread of firearms and the effect of gunpowder however induced them to surrender. Discharges of musketry alone caused the Bagirmi to fly from the ramparts and [they] refused to show themselves in any numbers at the close of day and the town was entered. 2000 were killed, nearly 5000 made slaves and 6000 camels taken. (Ibid., 160)

Al-Kanemi's invading force moved farther south with the fall of Dal and invested the city of Gawi in Kotoko territory, also tributary to Bagirmi, which was immediately to the north of Bagirmi's core. At Gawi:

red hot arrows were fired over their walls. In one instance when a breach had been made a sudden blaze of straw and wood prevented any attack being made and on the fires subsiding the besiegers to their dismay found the breach had been repaired. At night however the town surrendered and dreadful scenes of slaughter and worse than slaughter commenced. Several 1000 were killed and made prisoners but the females only preserved. The males were quickly put to death. (Ibid., 161)

Gawi's fall seems to have altered Bagirmi's strategy. Defense would now be flight. The *mbang* escaped "with his family and treasures" from Massenya and fled south, crossed the Shari, and disappeared into southern ķirdi country. Al-Kanemi, perhaps frustrated because his main prize had eluded him, fell upon: "a large body of fugitives. More were destroyed than my . . . [informant] could say—all the men. 2000 women and children were the plunder. . . .Here . . . [al-Kanemi] closed a campaign so shocking in details that no language can give an adequate idea of the miseries inflicted" (ibid., 162). It was earlier noted that the control and application of violence in central Sudanic states was official business. It should be clear that officials meant business when they went to war.

All commentators, whether of Bagirmi, Bornuan, or Wadaian origin, have concurred that the business of destroying competing states was usually performed to achieve a political goal—establishment of control over competing polities' revenue systems. Control was first engineered once a war had been won by securing revenues that the defeated state had previously acquired. Revenues tended to be stored as treasure, which usually included the most expensive forms of weaponry. Pillaging quickly transferred treasures from the losers to the winners.

Victors tried to collect the booty that would help them dominate more effectively. Al-Tunisi makes this point regarding Wadai's victory over Bagirmi circa 1800, saying that an "immense booty" was seized in the looting of Massenya (1851, 165). Sabun decreed that all might have their booty because they "only came from Wadai . . . in order to strive to acquire some gain." Sabun further decreed, "But that which is in money, . . . that which is in war materiels, such as swords, lances, chain mail, or uniforms, that which is the regalia of royalty or nobility, such as decorated saddles, fine harnesses—that is my domain" (al-Tunisi 1851, 166). What Sabun wanted out of the booty looted from Massenya was the means of destruction, or money to buy it. Bagirmi informants remembered that *mbang* Ab Sakin's and Gaurang II's booty preferences were identical to those of Sabun. In passing it should be noted that one of the reasons that slaves were a favorite form of booty was that merchants eagerly traded Middle Eastern or European weapons to acquire them.

Pillaging, then, was a bit like settling the accounts of an old business before setting up the new one, and once the looting was over, a new system of accounts had to be set up. This is to say, once the loser's previously acquired revenues had been disposed of, its revenue system had to be either articulated or disarticulated with that of the winner. There were generally three ways in which this was done. First, Bagirmi might defeat a state and make it its tributary, thereby diverting part of its revenues to Bagirmi as tribute. Second, existing allies might become reluctant to make tribute payments. In this case a war against the tributary might maintain or increase the flow of its tribute. The third possibility was that a state might have been articulated with Bagirmi not as a tribute giver but as a tribute taker. In this situation war might be used to defeat the competitor state and to destroy its ability to divert revenues out of Bagirmi. Ultimately, then, a political goal of war was to control other polities' revenues, thereby enhancing one's own revenues.

The Sun Kings' Sickle

The preceding analysis has suggested the intimate relationship between military action and revenues in the east-central Sudan. Public revenues in whatever form they might take—religious exactions, tribute, or booty—did not flow of their own accord. *Kirdi* did not loll about pleading with Bagirmi, "Pillage me! Pillage me! Take all that I've got!" Tributaries did not voluntarily give up tribute, thereby threatening their own welfare. Similarly food producers might be induced to meet some religious exactions, but as few as possible because, after all, they had their own kin and neighbors to support. Thus there had to be some instrument to do the work of moving taxes from food producers to officials, be they in core, tributary, or predation zones. Frequently this instrument was a violent one.

Raiding always required a few squadrons to enter into combat to do the job of collecting booty. Thus conflict was invariably necessary to secure booty. It was not always required for the acquisition of religious duties and tribute. Certain wars were over tribute flows, but not all tribute payments resulted from combat. Rather, many years—decades even—might go by and tribute payments would be made without any violence. A similar situation prevailed with religious duties. This meant that police actions were used, but only occasionally, in core areas to maintain the flow of religious duties. Consequently, fighting did not occur every time tribute or religious duties were collected. However, the potential was always there in the sense that a recalcitrant tributary or religious duty payer knew that there was always the force of so many soldiers with the potential for so much violent labor to make them pay.

A similar case can be made for warring among states, between whom there might be many years, even centuries, of peace. Eventually, however, a war would begin. This would involve campaigns and counter-campaigns until there were winners and losers; and the winner not only seized immense booty from the loser but also reduced it to a tributary initiating a flow of tribute. In sum, police actions, raids, and warring helped produce state revenues as surely as the food producers' sickle helped produce grains.

We are now in a position to appreciate why warfare was the Sun Kings' sickle. Warfare ultimately produced state revenues in the form of religious or secular taxes, tribute, or booty. These, as surplus products, surplus value, or violent labor, became official incomes. Official income was expended to replace the means of destruction, men and materiel, exhausted in the process of ruling. Thus warfare reproduced state revenues, which reproduced official incomes, which reproduced the means of destruction (see figure 8.1).

The preceding chapter argued that just as grass reproduces horses, so food producers reproduce officials. But grass will not nourish stabled horses unless there is a person with a sickle to cut it and bring it to them. Warfare was that sickle. It hacked products and labor from highly reluctant food producers so that they could be "fed" to officials stabled throughout the east-central Sudan.

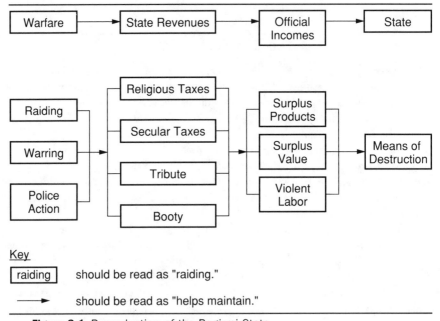

Figure 8.1 Reproduction of the Bagirmi State

PART III

PREDATORY ACCUMULATION

Chapter 9

Predatory Accumulation
in Fields of Empire

We have come a long way. Part 1 introduced the tumultuous east-central Sudan to which Bagirmi came as a relatively late but vigorous actor. The Sun Kings' realm was revealed in Part 2. Everywhere, in all places and all times, as the administrator-linguist Henri Gaden bluntly put it, "the history of Bagirmi is no more than a long list of war expeditions" (1909, 3).

It is time now to construct the model of this warfare promised in the introduction. The chapter's procedure is to present the structures of which the model is composed and then the process by which these operated. Thus the work of the chapter is a bit like that of a model airplane builder. First, all the pieces are carefully assembled—except that what is built is not a replica of a World War II fighter but an understanding of fields of empire. Then it is as if the fighter were taken outside and tried, because the second section reveals that the flight of fields of empire was powered by a predatory accumulation. The final section compares certain events of late-nineteenth-century Bagirmi history with those predicted by the model. This will make all too clear that the course of Bagirmi, as a participant in the fields of empire, was one of continual war.

Fields of Empire

Fields of empire were composed of different relations of domination. These were distinguished by hierarchies of domination, revenue systems reproducing these hierarchies, and the contradictions engendered by the revenue systems. This section first introduces the idea of relations of domination. It shows how the domestic mode of production and the state were articulated into relations of domination within Bagirmi. Next, it demonstrates that relations of domination in one area were articulated with other relations of domination in other areas into grids composed of different types of empires. Finally, it reveals that these grids were articulated into still larger fields of empire extending over vast stretches of the east-central Sudan.

Relations of Domination

The nature of both the domestic mode of production and of the state need to be reviewed before the notion of relations of domination may be introduced. Chapter 5 showed how little land, labor, or capital were employed in the production activities of the households. In addition, it noted that agricultural production occurred in a climate where rainfall was fickle and generally low, which meant that Bagirmi's domestic economies had weak productive forces characterized by low output and high uncertainty. Further, labor was the most crucial factor of production, because it was the sole factor that was both a necessary and a sufficient condition of increased agricultural output.

Farming was organized on the basis of elders and juniors working together in households. Both elders and juniors might "own" fields. However, juniors owed elders deference and so deferred to the elders' sense of how farming should occur and how the output of the various fields should be distributed. Juniors and elders may be considered the two component parts in the structure of the relations of production because, as a result of their differences with each other vis-à-vis their status as deference payers or receivers, they varied in their control over the factors of production and the distribution of the product. Thus it might be concluded that the modes of production in Bagirmi, and other east-central Sudanic societies, were domestic modes of production because their production relations were formulated on the basis of domestic kinship.

This mode of production had a tendency to be closed in the sense that its products were consumed either within the household or in the local community in which it was situated. Recall that elders tended to appropriate juniors' agricultural products. However, they tended to distribute them to other kin who were also food producers. Generally products went first to household members for their subsistence and their marriages, thereby securing their continued membership in the household. Then they went to more distant kin or nonkin, local community members who might be expected to contribute products or, more importantly, labor to the household. Elders, acting in this fashion, functioned more as circulators than as accumulators of products. This they did in order to maintain or to expand the household's labor. In short, elders exchanged products for people to reproduce the household's most crucial factor of production — labor. When products were distributed to hold existing household members within the household, they contributed to the simple reproduction of the household. When they were exchanged to add to the number of household workers, they contributed to its extended reproduction. The more a domestic mode of production was closed, the more its products circulated within community reciprocity networks facilitating a household's accumulation of labor.

In the political sphere, it will be remembered how power and authority descended from the sovereign to court officials, from these to estate officials, and from these to village and camp leaders. On the lowest rung of this ladder, individual food producers had virtually no power or authority. So each and every one of them came under the authority of some official in this hierarchy. Recall also that the Bagirmi thought of this hierarchy as the *mbang*'s household, so that it was decided in chapter 7 to call their polity a household state.

This state and domestic mode of production were two parts of a structure that may be termed the relations of domination.[1] Just as societies have certain structures that produce products, so they have others that produce domination. Domination is the exercise of power, which is the ability of an individual or a structure to control the behavior of others. Thus it is appropriate to identify as modes of domination those structures that are composed of dominators, those with power to control, and dominated, those being controlled. Similarly, just as modes of production exhibit forces and relations of production, so modes of domination have forces and relations of domination.

The notion of forces of domination refers to the set of means of control that are combined in a specific way at a specific time to produce control. It was suggested in chapter 6 that different officials had three different combinations of military, ideological, and informational powers. These were based upon different means for achieving control. Military power is based upon the means of destruction: the combination of people, resources, and instruments capable of inflicting violence. Ideological power is based upon the means of cooptation: the combination of people, resources, and instruments, that inculcate ideological notions that motivate people to accept control in certain ways. Informational power rests upon the means of knowing: the combination of people, resources, and instruments that provide information necessary for control. Taken together, the means of destruction, cooptation, and knowing are the most important means of control in societies. Clearly, the more effective and efficient these means of control, the greater the forces of domination.

The concept of relations of domination refers to the functions performed by persons and/or structures in the control process and in their relationship to the means of control. The function of some persons and/or structures is to command the means of control, while that of others is to be commanded. Persons and/or structures in the former category can be called dominators; those in the latter category can be designated the dominated. Thus relations of domination are structures; and the parties to it are the dominators and the dominated.[2] Relations of domination is a rather abstract notion, so it is helpful to descend to a less abstract level to establish what their institutional parts were in the Sun King's realm.

Clearly, Bagirmi's soldiers, performing either police actions, raids, or battles, were the institutional manifestations of the means of destruction, because they inflicted violence. Similarly, state ceremonials, such as royal burials or inaugurations, were the institutional manifestations of the means of cooptation, because all royal ceremonies communicated how the king incarnated divinity, so that deference to the Sun King and his planets was, as the old proverb had it, "like a white robe." Such rituals would justify to officials their command while at the same time motivating food producers to accept this control. Finally, the officials, their wives, and their wives' relatives involved in the door system would appear to be institutional manifestations of the means of knowing. Certainly this system, together with audiences, provided the information necessary to take action to dominate different situations.

Officials operated the means of control; food producers did not. Officials were the soldiers, the performers of state rituals, or the doors that opened and closed. Food producers, who lacked such opportunities, were controlled by these means. It was they who were the ultimate targets of the soldiers' lances, the audiences at state ceremonials and other official actions. Officials function to operate and food producers to be operated upon by the means of control. Individuals on the institutional level conceptualized their relationship to the means of control in terms of "eating." If they had "eaten" an office, their relationship to the means of control was as "eaters." If they have not done so, their relationship to them was as the "eaten."

Thus officials and food producers were institutional expressions of the state and the domestic mode of production; the former commanded the means of control, while the latter were commanded by it. This meant that the state and the domestic mode of production were substructures cohabiting in a larger structure, the relations of domination.

It is time to specify certain of the *relations* in these relations of domination. Nachtigal observed that officials spent most of their time immersed in the affairs "of court or war" (1889, 612). As a result, neither they nor their families produced food at any level in the hierarchy. Officials thus had to have food producers' foodstuffs and other products to survive—but then, so did the food producers. Chapter 7 showed how these were acquired as surplus products through the revenue system, which was the process through which, as the proverb at the end of chapter 7 expressed it, the food producers became the "grass" for the officials, who were the "horses" of state. It was the process by which the state assured itself of the material means of reproduction.

It was proposed in chapter 1 that the process of extracting resources from a structure or structures to reproduce another structure or structures results in contradictions between these articulated structures. It was further suggested that these contradictions intensify if they move toward their limits, that is, the threshold beyond which a structural change must occur. The domestic mode of production and the state were married to each other by revenue collection, and this marriage was uneasy, because the more of food producers' foodstuffs that were consumed by officials, the fewer were left for the food producers themselves. Conversely, the more of their own products that were used by food producers, the fewer could be consumed by officials. Clearly this was a contradictory situation because the reproduction of one structure, the state, was at the expense of another, the domestic mode of production, and vice versa.

When referring to contradictions, we shall place the structure doing the extracting first. Thus, for example, there is a capitalist-proletarian contradiction in capitalism. The Bagirmi state reproduced itself, through, inter alia, extraction of taxes from its core domestic mode of production. This created what can be called a state–core domestic mode of production contradiction. (Hereafter domestic mode of production will be abbreviated as DMP.)

The preceding has shown how relations of domination involve a hierarchy of domination—minimally of officials over food producers, revenue systems to reproduce such domination, and contradictions generated by these revenue systems. Different relations of domination in the nineteenth-century east-central Sudan were based upon more complex hierarchies of domination involving empires. The occurrence of imperial relations of domination seems related, at least in part, to certain limits of the state–core DMP contradiction. These are now explored.

The weak productive forces in the DMP meant that there were very often few food products for the official and food producer classes that lived in the core to consume.

Mean daily caloric intake for people resident in the most productive part of Bagirmi's habitat appeared to be about twenty-one hundred calories per person in nondrought years (Bascoulerque: n.d.). This intake plummets in drought years to below the threshold level of adequate diet for savanna African populations to reproduce. Droughts affecting large numbers of people currently occur in some area of Bagirmi at least once every ten years, and there is evidence that they have been at least as frequent ever since the sixteenth century (Nicholson 1949). This suggests that one limit to the reproduction of the relations of domination was nutritional, for these would be in jeopardy if either the food producers' or the officials' mean nutritional level declined beneath the threshold of adequate diet.

The preceding suggests that the state–core DMP contradiction exhibited an uncertain, but all too frequent, spiking toward its nutritional limits. This was experienced on the institutional level as officials grasping at food producers' products and food producers clutching after the remaining straws of their welfare. There was, however, a way to relax this situation, which is explored in the following section.[3]

Proto-Grids, Grids, and Fields

In principle, the contradiction between core officials and their food producers might have been reduced by increasing farmer productivity. This, for reasons discussed below, was simply not the way things worked. Rather, it was relaxed by increasing the number of farmers subject to a state's system of taxation, which was done by articulating relations of domination in one area with those in others into a system of contradictory grids and fields.

Barma food producers were unanimous in insisting that court officials would try to "pull" little from an area devastated by drought, while redoubling their "pulling" elsewhere, so that the revenues extracted shifted to include more tribute and booty. Raiding was especially useful in this regard. Most raiding during the nineteenth century was directed into the *kirdi* predation zone, which was in the southern parts of the Shari-Logone river system. It meant that officials raided into southern ecosystems characterized by greater and more certain production when harvests were poor in their own core. Thus tribute and booty relaxed the limits of the officials–core producers contradiction by switching to other forms of revenue collection in other habitats. This only worked, however, if officials had other environments to extract from, which obliged them to follow policies to maintain or expand their tributary and predation zones.

A result of such exigencies was that the complete revenue collection system— religious and secular taxes, tribute, and booty—articulated three sets of structures into a network of one internal and two external contradictions. Taxes linked officials to food producers in the core.[4] This created the state–core DMP contradiction discussed in the previous section. It will be recalled that a distinction was made in chapter 1, following Godelier, between internal contradictions—those within structures—and external ones— those between structures. The state–core DMP contradiction was internal, in the sense that it was between substructural units within the core's relations of domination.

Tribute linked Bagirmi's relations of domination with those of other east-central Sudanic centralized or centralizing societies. This was because tribute was given by the officials of one state to another after it had been extracted from the giving state's core DMP, its tributaries, or its predation zone. Thus, when the Kotoko gave tribute to Bagirmi, it normally originated as religious exactions extracted from its own core food producers and given to its own officials, who in turn gave them to Bagirmi officials. Such a tributary flow transferred surplus products from one set of relations of domination, those of the Kotoko, to another, those of Bagirmi. Kotoko surplus products enjoyed by Bagirmi were obviously at the expense of the Kotoko. Consequently, in a situation where one state paid tribute to another, there was an external contradiction between the core's relations of domination and those in its tributary areas.

Booty, unlike tribute, was not an official-to-official flow of surplus products. Rather, it was directly seized from the households of the raided, who were normally food producers. As such, it articulated Bagirmi with the domestic modes of production of more acephalous societies. It thus created a second, external contradiction between the core's relations of domination and the DMP in the predation zones.

When east-central Sudanic states were introduced in chapter 4, they were said to be like an archer's target, with a bull's-eye core surrounded by tributary and predation zones. It should now be seen that this target was a network of three contradictions articulating states with DMPs. Specifically, when taxes articulated states with DMPs in core areas, they created what has already been termed the state–core DMP contradiction. When tribute articulated a state with DMPs in its tributary region, it formed what might be termed the state–tributary DMP contradiction. Finally, when booty articulated a state with the DMPs in its predation zones, it in its turn formed what might be termed a state–predatory DMP contradiction. Most states in the east-central Sudan extracted taxes, tribute, and booty, so they may be said to have had such networks. Networks are grids. Those just identified were networks of contradictions, so they may be appropriately called contradictory grids.[5]

Certain polities lacked a complete set of all three contradictions. This appears to have been true of Bagirmi's southern tributaries in the nineteenth century. For example, the Bua appear to have had only the state–predatory DMP contradiction at the beginning of the nineteenth century. Such a grid, because it was incomplete, may be said to be a proto-grid. However, by the end of the nineteenth century, the Bua at Korbol extracted taxes from their own citizens while collecting tribute from neighboring populations. In short, their proto-grid had evolved into a full-fledged one.

Mature grids were not unchanging. Over time they, too, grew or shrank, which is to say that the flow of religious exactions, tribute, and booty to the core relations of domination increased or declined. As the grids of two states expanded, they eventually came into contact with each other. First, their predation zones might overlap, so that they might find themselves raiding in a common area. Both Bagirmi and Wadai, for example, raided in the nineteenth century in the Guera. Finally, the two states might war, and as a result of warring, one state might be obliged to pay tribute to the other, as occurred when Sabun defeated Gaurang I at the beginning of the nineteenth century.

When this occurred, something of structural significance had happened, because the tribute payments from one mature grid to another articulated the two and created a contradiction that was not within but between grids. This was because, to use the example of Bagirmi and Wadai, the more Wadai siphoned surplus products from

Bagirmi in the form of tribute, the less Bagirmi was able to use these to reproduce its own state, that is, the more it was pushed toward its limits. Conversely the fewer surplus products Bagirmi gave to Wadai as tribute, the less Wadai was able to reproduce its state, and it was thereby pushed toward its limits. Mature grids joined in this manner may be said to be fields.

Such fields covered vast regions of the east-central Sudan. For example, in the 1870s, Bagirmi's tribute to Wadai came from booty seized in its Sara predation zone, tribute taken from its Babelyia tributary area, and religious exactions given by Barma food producers around Massenya. Wadai received booty from its own predation zone, Dar Fertit, tribute from tributaries such as Dar Runga and Dar Zagawa, and religious duties from its own Maba core food producers. Thus tribute delivered from the court of Massenya to that at Abeche articulated the mature grid of Bagirmi with that of Wadai, thereby forming the Wadai-Bagirmi field. This was an area that extended from Lake Chad in the northwest to roughly the contemporary location of the Zagawa in the northeast, to Dar Fertit in the southeast, and to the Sara areas in the southwest.

Different fields may be distinguished in terms of different types of states found in them. Such states, however, were actually different varieties of empire. An empire "is a relationship, formal or informal, in which one state controls the effective political sovereignty of another political society" (Doyle 1986, 45). The key notion in this view is that of effective sovereignty. Doyle suggests that a state has achieved such sovereignty when it dominates the domestic and foreign policies of another polity (ibid., 44–45). Of course, whether a state controls another's foreign and domestic policies is often open to vigorous debate.

However, the process of creating and holding tributaries only occurred when one state acquired considerable domination over another polity, because the assumption of tributary obligations profoundly affected a polity's sovereignty: its domestic policies had to be sensitive to the reality that it paid tribute. This led to policies designed to create new revenue and military institutions, as, indeed, occurred among the southern tributaries that Bagirmi acquired during the nineteenth century. Equally, a tributary's foreign policies had to respond to the reality that it paid tribute: first and foremost, policy had to be designed either to pay the tribute or to suffer the consequences. For example, Bagirmi's new, southern tributaries embarked on a foreign policy of warring with their neighbors to collect tribute. A state that had made other polities its tributaries and had held on to these for a considerable period might be said to have acquired considerable domination over significant sectors of these tributaries' foreign and domestic affairs. Such a state was thus something of an empire.

There was, in fact, a hierarchy of what may be termed dominant, mature, and proto-empires within east-central Sudanic fields based upon the giving and receiving of surplus products by the component polities of the field. At the top of this hierarchy were dominant empires. These were dominant in the sense that they were militarily superior to all other polities in their field, so they took from all and gave to none. They were empires to which a portion of all revenues taken through taxes, tribute, or raiding within the field were paid and who themselves made no such payments to other states. They were thus surplus receivers. Wadai was just such an empire during the nineteenth century.

Mature empires occupied the middle rung in this hierarchy. They were mature because their military had created longstanding, centralized tributaries over which they exercised considerable domination; but they were not dominant because they had been defeated by another state and made its tributary. So they took from some and gave to others. They thus received a portion of all revenues taken as taxes, tribute, or booty within their own mature grids, but they themselves were obliged to make tributary payments to dominant empires. Mature empires were both givers and receivers of surplus products. Bagirmi was such an empire throughout much of the nineteenth century.

Then there were proto-empires. These states had more rudimentary military machines, so they received revenues from booty in their predation zone. However, they received none in taxes from their own core or tribute from other states. Their proto-grids included a state articulated with a predation zone through raiding and, perhaps, an incomplete tributary zone that derived tribute not from other states but from acephalous populations. The Bua appear to have had just such a proto-empire by the middle of the nineteenth century. Such polities normally were revenue givers to other states.

It may be concluded that the political economy of the precolonial east-central Sudan was substantially organized by a regional structure called the field of empire. This was composed of different relations of domination, which were distinguished by the type of empire they possessed, the revenue system they operated, and the grid of contradictions such revenue systems generated. There were three types of relations of domination: proto-, mature, and dominant empires. Proto-empires had incomplete revenue systems. They took booty, but they had not yet gotten the knack of taxing or tribute. As a result they had proto-grids, characterized only by the state–predatory DMP contradiction. Mature empires had complete revenue systems. They took taxes, tribute, and booty, and thus had a mature grid of the state–core DMP, the state tributary DMP, and the state–predatory DMP contradictions. However, though they received tribute from some, they also gave it to others. This act of giving made them mature, not dominant, empires. Then there were dominant empires. This last relation of domination involved an empire that had its own mature grid that extracted revenues from the grid of a mature empire that in turn extracted surplus products from grids of other mature and proto-empires — thereby weaving a veritable field of empire.

Fields of empire thus were a bit like redistributive systems run awry. Products were transferred from direct food producers to redistributive centers in both redistributive systems and fields, but hereafter similarity ceased. In redistributive systems these products then tended to be recirculated back to their producers. In fields, however, a further distribution followed, but one that moved the products even farther away from their original producers to officials in distant mature and dominant empires in remote relations of domination.

The relations between the empires in fields of empire in some respects resembled those supposed to obtain between certain venerable Bostonian families where the Lowells spoke only to the Cabots and the Cabots only to God—except that in the east-central Sudan, when they "spoke," it was with revenues. So the Bua gave to Bagirmi, and Bagirmi gave to Wadai, and Wadai was a dominant empire—and there was war when they spoke in the fields of empire. Why this was so will only be appreciated after we fly the model that has just been constructed.

Predatory Accumulation

Electric fields are galvanized by the charges of the bodies in the field. Matter may be negatively or positively charged. Like-charged bodies obey a dynamic of repulsion; unlike-charged bodies conform to the reverse dynamic. Bodies in fields of empire similarly acted in a dynamic of attraction and repulsion. This involved predatory accumulation—a process of the development of the means of destruction by the empires—as they acted upon certain policy imperatives of the second and the third contradictions. Bodies in electrical fields are either attracted or repelled; bodies politic in fields of empire were simultaneously both attracted and repelled. Analysis of how this might be the case begins by revealing these policy imperatives.

The second contradiction was that between a state and its tributaries. As was shown in chapter 8, the size of revenues an empire gave or received as tribute controlled in part the amounts of surplus products, surplus value, and violent labor available as official incomes, and bigger incomes meant a larger and more easily maintained officialdom, that is, more easily reproduced relations of domination. Therefore, the more revenues a dominant or mature empire received as tribute, the easier it was to reproduce their relations of domination; and the fewer revenues a mature or proto-empire surrendered as tribute, the easier it was to reproduce their relations of domination and vice versa.

The preceding implied that dominant, mature, and proto-empires operated under utterly different imperatives with respect to tribute. For dominant and mature empires, as revenue receivers, it was better to receive as much tribute as possible, while for mature and proto-empires, as revenue givers, it was better to give as little tribute as possible.

The development of the means of destruction, however, was necessary to implement such imperatives because, as established in chapter 8, tribute ultimately flowed as a result of war. Specifically, it flowed to winners of wars and away from losers. As a result, dominant and mature empires, acting as revenue receivers, sought to augment their means of destruction to win wars to increase the tribute received; and mature and proto-empires, as revenue givers, sought to augment their means of destruction to win wars to decrease the tribute given.

This implied that if states increased their means of destruction, then the more of these they could expend on military success, which would increase tribute, thus making it easier to reproduce themselves; and the better they reproduced themselves, then the greater their official incomes, so the more means of destruction they could expend. Thus the second contradiction implied that a process of accumulation of forces of domination facilitated the accumulation of revenues necessary for reproduction, and vice versa.

The third contradiction was between a state and its predation zone, and it had accumulation consequences similar to those of the second contradiction, because the size of the booty an empire gave or received influenced its revenues and, as was just emphasized, the size of its revenues determined the sizes of official incomes, which in turn controlled the reproduction of the relations of domination. Thus the more revenues a dominant, mature, or even proto-empire acquired as booty, the easier it was to reproduce their relations of domination; and equally clearly the fewer revenues predation zones lost as booty, the easier it was to reproduce their DMP. Conversely, the fewer revenues a dominant, mature, or proto-empire received as booty, the harder it was to reproduce their relations of domination; while the more revenues predation zones surrendered as booty, the harder it was for them to reproduce their modes of production.

Consequently, dominant, mature, and proto-empires operated under radically different imperatives with respect to booty than did their prey. For the empires, as revenue receivers, it was far better to take as much booty as possible, while for all revenue givers, it was essential to give as little booty as possible.

The preceding has implied that the vaster empires' raids were, the grander their booty, so they could better reproduce themselves; and the better they could reproduce themselves, the more officials they could field as soldiers, so the more they could raid successfully. Thus the third contradiction, like the second, implied that the accumulation of forces of domination increased the accumulation of revenues necessary for the reproduction of relations of domination, and vice versa.

The third contradiction had a special consequence for acephalous populations in predation zones, because the accumulation of their own means of destruction decreased the loss of products and labor necessary for their reproduction. This reality was expressed on the less abstract, institutional level by movements toward larger, more elaborate official hierarchies, because these provided the larger cavalries necessary to frustrate their imperial predators. So acephalous peoples were moved toward a centralization of their power if they marshaled their forces of domination in conformity to the imperatives of the third contradiction.

Thus there was an iron logic to the final two contradictions: if the reproduction of dominant, mature, or proto-empires, as well as that of acephalous populations, was to occur at higher levels, then their polities would have to accumulate and expend means of destruction. This, of course, meant war.

The concept of field position provides a useful way of thinking about this predatory logic of empires reproducing their relations of domination in fields of empire. Field position was the share of the total revenues in a field annually possessed by an empire. Empires enhanced their field position by increasing the size of their core, tributary, and predation zones. If the affairs of east-central Sudanic polities were consistent with the exigencies of the second and third contradictions, at time A an empire would expend some of its means of destruction to conduct warfare to enhance its field position, which meant that at time B it would have a greater sum of means of destruction at its disposal than it had had at time A. It would then expend more of these at time B to conduct war to increase its field position further, which meant that at time C it would have a still greater sum of forces of domination at its disposal than it had had at time B. This suggests a tendency toward positive feedback between forces of domination—especially means of destruction, revenues, and field position—as empires and raided populations warred over field position.

However, when empires successfully increased their forces of domination in a field, they did it at the expense of others in that field. This pushed losers toward their limits, because they lost products and labor vital to their own reproduction. Losers had only one response. They, in their turn, would try to enhance their means of destruction to defeat their predators, thereby reducing the revenues extracted from them, thus increasing their field position.

The preceding suggests that empires in a field were in so contradictory a relationship to each other that what they did to hold themselves together pulled them apart from other polities in the field. This was because relaxation of contradictions inherent in the second and third contradictions in some empire's favor intensified these very same contradictions for some other polity or polities somewhere else in the field—which allows us to return to the comparison of electric fields and fields of empire. Polities successful in war might be thought of as positively charged; those that were unsuccessful might be seen as negatively charged; and a current of revenues flowed from negatively to positively charged polities. However, this very force of attraction was one of repulsion, because revenues lost in one war could be regained only as a result of others.

The different warring parties in this process resembled competing firms, except that the competition was ultimately over revenues, not market shares, so the competitive edge went to those who—in the terms of al-Maglili quoted at the beginning of the second chapter—had more "daring birds of prey" rather than bold captains of industry. This suggests that the operation of the forces of domination, instead of those of the market, distributed much surplus. If this was true, it meant that control over the forces of production, especially economic capital, in order to control market position was irrelevant to the reproduction of relations of domination and to the dynamics of east-central Sudanic history. At last one is able to grasp a grim necessity for the war woven into the imperial tapestry of the east-central Sudan. The process of reproduction of relations of domination in fields of empire was: war in order to accumulate (means of destruction), and accumulate (means of destruction) in order to war. This was certainly predatory accumulation.

Expected Events

This conception of the east-central Sudan as, in part, a set of polities reproducing themselves through predatory accumulation might be assigned the status of a tentative theoretical model. How useful is it?

One way such a judgment may be made is to evaluate the degree to which events observed to have occurred in Bagirmi's late nineteenth-century history were those that would be expected if the predatory accumulation model were correct. This can be done by offering certain propositions derived from the model and then observing whether what they say would occur in the late nineteenth century actually came to pass.

Perhaps a most fundamental conclusion of this model is that the better a polity's field position, the more it can relax the limits of its contradictions and thus the better reproduce itself. This suggests a first proposition:

> Polities in fields will seek to enhance their field position. Hence dominant, mature, and proto-empires, as well as raided populations, will conduct their affairs to prevent decreases and stimulate increases in their total annual supply of products and labor.

This is precisely how the Sun Kings conducted their affairs between 1870 and the arrival of the French, for during this period they conducted a two-front military strategy. First there was a northern front against Wadai and its tributaries, which flared into open warfare in the 1870s and sputtered on and off through 1897 and the arrival of the French. Then there was a second, southern front against Sara, Chadic, and Adamawan speakers, which involved occasional wars and continual raids. This two-front policy was designed to transform Wadai into a tributary of Bagirmi while adding new southern tributaries, both of which would have vastly enhanced Bagirmi's field position.

In fact, however, the strategy had only achieved partial success by 1897. There were, indeed, three new Sara tributaries, but Bagirmi had been unable to defeat Abeche in the north and east and had, as a result of trying to do so, suffered a devastating defeat circa 1871 at the hands of Wadai. However, the policy remained intact as late as 1902, when the French discovered that Gaurang II "dreamed of the empire of Wadai" while he raided to the south (Dubois 1968, 34).[6]

Four corollaries of this proposition may be inferred.

1. Dominant empires, to improve their field position, will expend means of destruction to increase field size.

Wadai was the dominant empire in Bagirmi's contradictory grid. Its rulers had warred so successfully that by the early 1870s the empire was at its greatest extension. The final phases of this expansion occurred under the sovereign Ali (1858–74), whose armies appear to have added "the Bahr Salamat, the Runga and the Kuti" (Carbou 1912, 2:123). Such affairs are consistent with corollary 1.

2. Mature empires, to improve their field position, will expend means of destruction to decrease product and labor payments to dominant empires and to increase product and labor payments from tributary and predation zones.

Bagirmi was a mature empire, and the affairs just recounted are precisely those expected by this corollary.

3. Proto-empires, to improve their field position, will expend means of destruction to decrease product and labor payments to dominant or mature empires and to increase product and labor payments from tributary and predation zones.

The Bua at Korbol were a southern tributary in Bagirmi's grid who had formed a proto-empire by the 1870s. They later improved their military capacity and were said to be able to place a substantial force in the field. By the 1890s they had become such redoubtable adversaries of Bagirmi that they only irregularly paid their tribute (Prins 1900, 182). They also fought both to secure booty and to create their own tributaries, their troops operating over a wide territory ranging from the Guera (Gabe, n.d.) to the Niellim, who may at this time have been reduced to tributary status (Chapelle 1980, 55). These affairs are those predicted by corollary 3.

4. Raided populations, to improve their field position, will expend means of destruction to decrease product and labor payments to any form of empire.

When Sara, Chadic, or Adamawan speakers were attacked throughout the southern predation zone in Bagirmi's contradictory grid, they often learned to counterattack. Sometimes the defenses were feeble, as at Kimre; at other times there was flight before counterattack; but invariably the warred-against learned to war. The Bua, who had been attacked for hundreds of years, had created a formidable thousand-man cavalry by 1900 (Gabe, n.d.). The Niellim, who had been subjected to similar attacks for a similar time, had developed a "numerous cavalry " (Prins 1900, 179). Farther south, where the predations were more recent, Brown describes the rise of a new type of leader called the *ngol* among certain Sara (1975), who led bands of fighters. These were a new military institution formed as a response to raids by Bagirmi and other states. Such developments seem entirely consistent with those predicted by corollary 4.

Finally, if the affairs of the east-central Sudanic polities were governed in part by predatory accumulation, then the history of the region should be one of gradual evolution of fields of empire between the time of the first centralized polity and the arrival of the French. This does not mean that there would never be times and places when states weakened and fields declined. It does mean that the trend between circa A.D. 900 and 1900 would be for increased field position. This might be our second proposition:

> The dynamics of fields will be one where empires use their forces of domination to improve their field position, promoting increases in their revenues, facilitating increases in their means of destruction, permitting this same cycle to recur so that the polities will enjoy greater forces of domination.

The period roughly from A.D. 900 through 1248 saw the origin and first expansion of the east-central Sudanic state in what is today the desert and subdesert in the Kanem and Equei. This was the epoch of the Zagawa and the first Saifwa empire that came to its apogee under *mai* Dunuma circa 1248. Then in the period between 1248 and the 1500s, states warred southward into the dry Sudan. At this time the Bulala created their empire in the Kanem, driving the Saifwa to create a new one in Bornu. It was the period when the Sao-Kotoko states emerged. It was also the epoch when Magna Kuka, which we speculated may have been Gaoga, was astir with the centralization that produced Kuka, Medogo, Babelyia and the first and second kingdoms of Bagirmi. It was also the time when the Tunjur created a centralized polity in Wadai, only to be driven westward by Abd el Kerim, whose descendants forged what was to be the dominant empire in the east-central Sudan in the nineteenth century. Finally, the nineteenth century saw centralized polities spill out of the dry and into the moist Sudan, for during this time proto-empires seem to have emerged among the Niellim, the Somrai, the Bua, and perhaps among certain Sara, to mention only those polities within Bagirmi's grid.

Thus a first proto-grid probably began at some small point in space and time in the Kanem or Equei around A.D. 900. A thousand years later, circa 1870, the mature grids of empires like Bagirmi, the Kotoko, and Bulala were woven into the fields of empire of Bornu and Wadai. Clearly, during this time the means of destruction at the disposal of these empires had enormously increased from perhaps a few hundred horsemen circa A.D. 900 to the thousands upon thousands of cavalry of the different empires. Similarly in A.D. 900 religious and secular taxes, tributes, and booty were seized from some small area in the Kanem or Equei, and by 1900 these same revenues were "pulled" from almost the entire east-central Sudan. This means that the revenues that the empires extracted had enormously increased between A.D. 900 and 1900, and thus means of destruction, fields, and revenues had vastly enlarged during that period. Such increases are compatible with a cycle in which polities employed their means of destruction to increase field position, promoting increases in their revenues, facilitating increases in their means of destruction.

What the two propositions and the four corollaries say should theoretically occur did, in fact, happen in the grids and fields into which Bagirmi was woven, all of which strengthens the view that certain affairs of the Sun Kings and other empires in the east-central Sudan were ones where they warred in order to accumulate and accumulated in order to war.

Chapter 10

Epilogue

The precolonial east-central Sudan was likened to a vast pointillist landscape in chapter 4. Now it can be seen that each point was a polity within a field of empire. The particular point we have examined, that of the Sun Kings, suggests that a dynamic of predatory accumulation was the creative force responsible for the entire landscape. Clearly, far too few points have been examined for far too little time to suggest that such an attribution is anything other than exceedingly tentative.

However, if it was true that the precolonial east-central Sudan was dominated by polities reproducing themselves in fields through predatory accumulation, then we might suggest why there was little economic development in the region. Our argument begins with another explanation for the underdevelopment of the Sudan. Abdoulaye Bara Diop expressed this position when he noted that "the weakness of the means of production . . . was the factor which prevented the development of large plantations and primitive capital accumulation" (in Rey 1976, 121). What Diop was proposing was that weak productive forces, especially the means of production, helped restrain the development of the precolonial Sudan. It was entirely true that farming was characterized by low productive forces, as was documented in chapter 5, so Diop's suggestion that an underdeveloped productive sector was due to underdeveloped means of production seems entirely sensible. However, this raises the question, Why the low productive force? To answer this we turn to "double mills."

Capitalist accumulation, according to Marx, reproduced the productive relations between the capitalists and their workers, because it threw the latter on a "double mill" (in Balibar 1970, 266). On the one hand, the worker was required to sell his or her labor to subsist; on the other, in so doing, he or she produced the products that the capitalist in turn sold, thereby realizing surplus value that was necessary for the capitalists' reproduction. Predatory accumulation may have placed many food producers on a different type of double mill.

Officials used their incomes to feed themselves and their dependents, to secure and maintain weapons, and to purchase sumptuary and other goods required in the performance of official duties. The costs of cavalry weapons and sumptuary goods, as has been shown, were exceedingly high. There is not a single account, from either informants or the literature, of officials investing in any productive enterprise, with the exception of their slave villages. This is probably because they had very little income left after meeting the costs of their means of destruction. Food producers also had very little income to invest. It will be remembered how al-Tunisi had suggested that food producer investment potential was restricted to buying "a goat here, a sheep there" (1851, 360). These hardly constituted massive investments in agriculture or any other productive enterprise.

Thus predatory accumulation was a double mill. First, it threw food producers back into extensive farming by removing so much product for state revenues that there was little left to invest in other productive activities. Second, it circulated these products to officials, providing them with the means they required to invest in the means of destruction, which allowed them to continue extracting from the farmers. Seen in this light, the underdevelopment of productive forces was a consequence of the development of those destructive ones required by predatory accumulation.

Certain readers may be anxious to learn whether this analysis has been Marxist. My sense is that such a question is not particularly germane to the research's utility. More to the point is whether the facts of east-central Sudanic history are consistent with a model of predatory accumulation in fields of empire; whether this model can account for other historical facts in other climes and times; and whether other models might do the job better. Nevertheless, the argument is not Marxist in one important respect: the model it proposes does not rely upon modes of production as the "motor" of history. The argument further implies that explanations of greater scope may be expected if models are formulated of the articulation of entire regions' political and economic dynamics.

In another sense, though, this work owes a lot to Marx. A particularity of humanity is that people fabricate their own hells; or rather, more accurately, to satisfy their own needs they construct hells for others. It was noted in chapter 4 that certain Barma thought deference, especially to officials, "was like a white robe." Perhaps we are finally now in a position to appreciate a meaning of this proverb. It introduced into the consciousness of ordinary people the view that officials were like family elders: benevolent folk whom you respected because they had your interests at heart. This trope would help nudge out other, contrary ones by helping to coopt dangerous, rebellious impulses, thereby aiding officials to go about their business of extracting things from people. Thus, analytically, the proverb was part of the means of cooptation that were themselves part the forces of domination. More bluntly, the proverb cloaked a reality of predatory accumulation. You deferred to those "daring birds of prey" because, if you did not, they would rip your entrails out, just as Nachtigal had watched them do that dawn in the village of Kimre.

Raids, police actions against recalcitrant taxpayers, and wars against tributaries or competing states all had to occur for the fields of empire to endure. But raided peoples learned to raid. Recalcitrant taxpayers and tributaries revolted. States warred against returned the favor. Thus predatory accumulation reproduced the Sun Kings' realm in the fields of empire by generating "wars . . . without end" (Nachtigal 1880, 405) and the hells of Kimre.

Marx grasped that humans create hells for others, and more than any other social scientist he sought to make the explanation of these hells the central task of social thought. *Wars without End* has followed Marx in this concern.

Appendix: Sources

Wars without End draws on my own fieldwork and on published and unpublished accounts of the region. The nature of these is explored here. I conducted research in Bagirmi in 1969–70 and again in 1973–74. The first fieldwork took place in what had been one of the historically important towns of Bagirmi—given the pseudonym Be Ngollo—which for a brief period in the nineteenth century had been its capital. Be Ngollo was inhabited by Barma.

Information gathered during this time provided a general picture of Barma social and economic life around Be Ngollo. Though concentrating on fertility, I retained a strong interest in the old Bagirmi polity and asked questions concerning the precolonial state of anyone I could. Looking back at my notebooks, I see that everyone—from a group of nuns to old Bagirmi warriors—was asked political questions. There were, however, four informants who consistently provided me with the richest political information. Three of these were elderly and had ties with the state in Massenya: one was the grandson of a sovereign, and the other two were descended from officials who governed during this sovereign's reign. The state at Massenya grew by adding other political entities. One of the major polities that was so incorporated was centered at the town of Bousso in Bagirmi's extreme south. The fourth informant was an offspring of Bousso's royal house.

I found that people simply could not give very much information if I posed questions about the distant past—years that Barma called *lua kakge* ("years of ancestors"). However, if questions were asked about the years of the reign of Gaurang II (1883–1912), who ruled at the time the French arrived, answers could be given that included the names of actors and the approximate dates when actions occurred. This was probably the case because the four informants had been raised to rule and had thus been given information by their relatives about the state they were to direct. In general, Barma whose families had not provided officials to the precolonial state knew little about its organization and operations except where these directly touched their lives. Such families, however, were often touched by war or taxation. Barma reckoned years in terms of the number of dry seasons that had passed since an event occurred. I was struck one afternoon when I asked one person how many years it had been since Bagirmi went to war. Instantly the answer came: "Sixty-three years."

In 1973–74 I returned to Chad as the anthropologist for the Assale-Serbewel Livestock Development Project. This fieldwork was conducted during the Sahelian drought of 1972–74 among Abu Krider Arabs in a region that had once been northern

Bagirmi. I lived in the household of the *sheikh*, whose family—as the dry season progressed—fed my thatched hut to their starving animals. The consumption of my residence publicly displayed my privacy; and as I became an increasingly open figure, Abu Krider told me more of themselves—and in telling more of themselves, they revealed more of Bagirmi.

Ethnologists have tended to study states by going to the old capital and gathering information there. However, political systems have outer boundaries that can be as crucial to the systems' operation as the center. Abu Krider territory had been just such an outer province, and their history was very much influenced by this position. Abu Krider were Bagirmi's allies and were raided by Wadai to enrage Bagirmi prior to the nineteenth century. Then they became Wadai's tributary and were harassed by Bagirmi in order to menace Wadai. Such knowledge made it clear to me that political cores were linked with allied areas, which were tied to other cores; and gradually I began to see that these sorts of relationships might be central to understanding the structural dynamics of the entire east-central Sudan. Thus, from my fieldwork, there are remembrances of things Bagirmi both from the vantage of the core and from that of a former tributary.

There are nine different literatures concerning Bagirmi. The first of these is archeological. Archeological research in the central Sudan is limited. None has been performed at Bagirmi sites. However, there is useful work by J. P. Lebeuf in Chad (1962; 1964) and Graham Connah in Nigeria (1981), which deals with the period roughly between 1500 B.C. through A.D. 1500. Their studies help us to understand the economy and society out of which Bagirmi originated.

There is an environmental literature for the east-central Sudan that is stronger than might be expected. The work of plant scientists (Harlan and Stemler 1976), and of climatologists (Maley 1973) allows speculation about the role of environmental factors in state formation.

Considerable linguistic work has been performed concerning the region (Dalmais 1961; Lukas 1939). There is a useful grammar of Tar Barma, the language of the Barma, written at the beginning of colonial rule by H. Gaden (1909). Archeological, environmental, and linguistic evidence all facilitate conjecture concerning Barirmi origins and early history.

The published works of Muslim scholars and travelers are also a source of information. There are two Islamic literatures relevant to Bagirmi. The first of these includes the accounts of medieval Arab geographers and historians, some of whom visited the Sudan while others composed their accounts based upon travelers' experiences. The most important of these were al-Ya'qubi (died c. 891), al-Muhallabi (died c. 990), Ibn Sa'id (died c. 1286), al-Maqrize (died c. 1442) and Leo Africanus (died c. 1549). Their observations provide a picture of the central Sudan from the ninth through the sixteenth century, when Bagirmi was founded. Many of their works have been translated into French and published in a common volume edited by Joseph Cuoq (1975).

A second Islamic literature comes from the central Sudan itself: works derived from Bornuan and other central Sudanic sources. The Bornuan literature includes chronicles of rulers' lives, especially that of *imam* Ibn Fartwa, who described the reign of the ruler Idris Alaoma (c. 1564–96); king lists (*girgam*), including one that covers A.D. 900 through the 1850s called the *diwan*; and praise songs, which also tend to chronicle rulers' lives. This literature is most useful for reconstructing society and history prior to the founding of Bagirmi. However, its reliability, especially in the work of both Arkell and Palmer, is unknown. Nevertheless, it provides cryptic clues about events in the area that was to become Bagirmi during the medieval period.

Three nineteenth-century accounts of the east-central Sudan were collected by Europeans from Muslim informants. The first is that of Mohammad ibn al-Tunisi, who visited Darfur and Wadai between 1803 and 1811 at a time when a decisive war flared between Bagirmi and Wadai. Al-Tunisi described his travels to a French Arabist, Dr. Perron, who compiled them in a number of works, the most useful for our purposes being *Voyage au Ouaday* (1851). This book describes in detail the Bagirmi-Wadai conflict at the beginning of the nineteenth century. The sources for *Voyage au Ouaday* are unclear. Perron says that it was a translation of a text written by al-Tunisi. This manuscript has never been found. There is speculation that al-Tunisi was not the only source of his information (Bjorkelo 1976, 25). Whatever the sources, the *Voyage* is distinguished by graphic and detailed accounts of Bagirmi's imbroglio with Wadai.

Following in the tradition of Perron, Escayrac de Lauture, another French Arabist scholar, began to interview Sudanese students at El Azhar University in Cairo in the 1840s. These interviews resulted in certain publications of which the most useful for our purposes is *Mémoire sur le Soudan* (1855). A major informant for this work was a Bagirmi who claimed to be of the royal family, and the account vividly describes warfare between Bagirmi and Bornu in the 1820s. At about the same time, M. Fresnel (1849), a French diplomat, conducted similar inquiries in Jidda among pilgrims from the central Sudan. Most of Fresnel's information concerns Wadai, but there is some interesting information that bears upon Bagirmi from its eastern rival.

The fifth information source is the publications of nineteenth-century European explorers. A British team lead by Denham and Clapperton was first on the scene between 1822 and 1825 and spent considerable time in Bornu. They had hoped to visit Bagirmi but were prevented from doing so by the same hostilities that are described by Escayrac de Lauture's informant. Though having a Bornuan bias, Denham's account (1826) of the Bornu-Bagirmi conflict is important for the details of the fighting it presents and its revelation of the political consequences of this conflict.

Twenty-five years later, from 1850 through 1855, the German explorer Heinrich Barth continued the explorations of Denham and Clapperton. Barth was a gifted observer, and the volumes of *Travels and Discoveries in North and Central Africa*, first published in English in 1857 and 1858, are one of the most important sources on the Central Sudan in the nineteenth century. Barth, the first European ever to visit Bagirmi, went there during 1852, when, for at least part of the time, the sovereign was campaigning to the east. Barth presented Bagirmi economy, society, and government as it appeared at mid century. He also compiled the first Bagirmi history: this account is relatively brief, only about nine pages (1965: 547–56).

Approximately twenty years after Barth, the second great German explorer, Gustav Nachtigal, visited Bagirmi. Nachtigal arrived under far different conditions than did Barth, for the latter visited during a time of Bagirmi military success, whereas the former visited in 1872, immediately following grave defeat at the hands of Wadai. Massenya had been sacked, and the sovereign, Ab Sakin, was involved in a campaign against a

Wadaian pretender while at the same time trying to extract slaves from southern allies. Nachtigal left the richest nineteenth-century accounts of Bagirmi government (1880; 1889, 571–625, 659–85) and history (ibid., 691–721). Nachtigal's major source of information was the official known as the *alifa moyto* (1889: 692).

There would have been more incentive for the Bagirmi to present their history to Nachtigal than to Barth. Historical traditions were preserved in a document called a *dabcar*, which appears to have resembled Bornuan king lists. One of my informants had at least one *dabcar*, but is was only a few torn sheets of paper that contained relatively little information. It appears that when Wadai sacked Massenya in 1870, they destroyed a major *dabcar* (Devallee 1925, 27). As the *dabcar* was a document that above all told what territories and ethnic groups belonged to Bagirmi, and accordingly from which tribute might be expected, there would have been some incentive to tell Bagirmi history to justify Bagirmi claims to different peoples and places.

Further, because Nachtigal's principal historical informant was the *alifa moyto*, there may have been an additional, personal incentive on this gentleman's part to provide a detailed account of events, for his had been an important office prior to the nineteenth century. However, the loss of northern territories in the nineteenth century made him a fifth wheel. Thus, if he was to impress Nachtigal with his importance, he had to describe fully the earlier, pre-nineteenth century periods of Bagirmi history. Whatever the reason, Nachtigal's is the fullest account we have of Bagirmi history.

The last explorers of the nineteenth-century came between 1880 and 1892, after France was committed to the inclusion of the east-central Sudan into its empire. A number of missions were sent out from the south in the French Congo, where a logistical base had been built to hasten this process. Two publications resulted from these missions: one by C. Maistre (1895) and a more useful one for Bagirmi by P. Brunache (1894). Maistre and Brunache spent most of their time in the territory of Sara ethnic groups, who reside to the south of Bagirmi. Certain Sara were in the process of incorporation into Bagirmi during the nineteenth century, and Brunache provides direct observations of this process. Hence the fifth source of information, European explorers' publications, provided samplings of Bagirmi history roughly once every twenty years throughout the nineteenth century, while also providing compilations of Bagirmi's earlier historical traditions.

French colonial rule began in 1897. There were a number of colonial officials of different professions who left accounts of Bagirmi at the turn of the century. The official directing French expansion into the Chad region from the 1890s through the first years of the twentieth century was E. Gentil. His account (1902) of these years, where it pertains to Bagirmi, contains largely political information, especially relating to Gaurang II, the sovereign of the time. In 1897, Gentil engineered the signing of a treaty of protection between Bagirmi and France and left a M. Prins as his representative to Gaurang. Prins has left an account of his year with Gaurang (1900). In 1900 the French defeated Rabah, their major military competitor for hegemony in the central Sudan. This presented them with the task of assessing the economic significance of the lands they had just won. The Mission Oubangi-Chari-Tchad, headed by the agronomist A. Chevalier, was sent to make this assessment between 1902 and 1904. Chevalier was a meticulous observer whose work, *L'Afrique centrale française* (1907), included

accounts of Bagirmi's environment, farming systems, relations with tributaries, and
military operations at a time when these all still functioned more or less as they had
in precolonial times.

Chad was a military colony at the beginning of the twentieth century. So its
administrators were often officers. *M. le capitaine* Dubois was the French *resident* in
Bagirmi in 1902, and he has left an account of the country at that time (1968).
M. le capitaine Cornet spent from 1904 through 1906 blasting away at big game and
rebels in Chad. Though never posted to Bagirmi proper, he described certain Bagirmi
affairs in southern allied territories (1911). Another, far richer source for this time and
area is G. Bruel, who was a nonmilitary administrator in southern Chad following 1900.
His observations (1905; 1935) bear upon Bagirmi's southern affairs during this time.

The final administrator of significance during this earliest period of colonization was
H. Carbou. His postings were largely in eastern and northern Chad between 1900 and
1910. He, Gaden, and Chevalier are the most scholarly observers of this period, but
where Gaden's and Chevalier's passions ran to linguistics and natural history, Carbou's
were for history. He was familiar with the works of both Barth and Nachtigal, and
he extended the collection of historical traditions to include the peoples of eastern and
northern Chad. The two volumes of *La Région du Tchad et du Ouadai* (1912) are
useful because they provide information about precolonial Bagirmi military affairs from
the perspective of northern and eastern neighbors such as the Bulala and Wadaians.

There are two final works by colonial administrators that date from the second
decade of the twentieth century. The earliest of these was by *M. le lieutenant* Lanier,
who resided in Bagirmi between 1913 and 1916. He left an account of Bagirmi history
and government (1925). Lanier's historical speculation should be used with caution, for
he does not describe who his informants were, nor does he indicate if he was familiar with
the work of either Barth or Nachtigal. His accounts of events prior to the eighteenth
century seem especially suspect. However, Lanier was both an officer and a colonial
administrator and consequently had experience in both soldiering and taxing, so his
descriptions of the precolonial state's military and revenue affairs are more convincing.

The final and most thorough account of Bagirmi from a colonial administrator was
that of M. Devallée, who administered Bagirmi in the late teens and early 1920s. His *Le
Baguirmi* (1925) discusses environment, history and government. It is the most complete
account of Bagirmi history. He was familiar with the work of Nachtigal, Carbou, and
Gaden and appears to have read Barth. However, he does not seem to have performed
a great deal of historical investigation for the period prior to 1877, preferring, he
says, to use information from the French translation of Nachtigal (ibid., 29). Devallée's
account of events following Nachtigal's visit is the most complete currently available, his
reconstruction of Bagirmi government offers more detailed material than was presented
by his colonial predecessors, and there is considerable information concerning military
affairs. Thus the colonial officials' publications provide rich information concerning
Bagirmi political and military affairs around 1900. They also provide a second round
of compilation of precolonial historical traditions.

I reviewed the colonial archives concerning Bagirmi for the years 1900 through
1940. This seventh source of information was especially revealing regarding the jockeying
for control between Bagirmi officials and colonial administrators, which in turn provided

insight into the way the precolonial state had operated. The archives also contained considerable economic information.

The publications of other ethnologists who have studied Bagirmi are an eighth information source. Annie M.-D. Lebeuf (1967) and Viviana Pacques (1967; 1977) have both conducted research in Bagirmi. Pacques's work is the more extensive and, in certain ways, complements my own. Her information appears derived from fieldwork in Massenya and in Barma towns along the Chari south of Bugoman; my information comes from near Bugoman, Bousso, and N'Djamena. My emphasis has been upon social organization and economics; Professor Pacques's work emphasizes cosmology, religion, and political ideology. She has also collected considerable information concerning historical traditions.

The final source of data about Bagirmi is from published accounts of other central Sudanic societies. I have sought to use all the major sources available. To the east the work of Rex O'Fahey (1980) has been useful, especially for documenting Bagirmi links with Darfur in the period before the nineteenth century. In the south the work of Denis Cordell (1985) permits us to explore Bagirmi relations with Dar Kuti during the nineteenth century. There have been a number of ethnographies of southern acephalous populations with whom Bagirmi interacted, the most useful being E. Brown's study of the Sara Nar (1975; 1983), J. Fortier's study of Sara Madjingay sacred "kingship" (1982), B. O'Loughlin's analysis of Mbum political economy (1973), and Dumas-Champion's study of Masa (1983).

Annie M.-D. Lebeuf's (1969) work upon "sacred authority" in Kotoko principalities provides information concerning these important pre-nineteenth-century tributaries of Bagirmi as far back as the eighteenth century. Further, to the west, the labors of the historians Palmer (1970a; 1970b; 1967), Y. Urvoy (1949), and L. Brenner (1973), in conjunction with those of the ethnologist R. Cohen (1967; 1970; 1966a; 1966b; 1984) give us an idea of Bagirmi's relations with Bornu as far back as the sixteenth century.

Four conclusions might be drawn from this survey of the information available to students of Bagirmi. First, the most thoroughly documented period in which the precolonial state still functioned is that which began with the arrival of Nachtigal around 1870 and ended with the destruction of political autonomy around 1912. This is a period remembered by my informants and described by explorers, colonial officials, archives, and other historians and ethnologists of Bagirmi and the central Sudan. Second, there is a fair amount of military information for the entire nineteenth century, with observations occurring in 1803–11 (al-Tunisi), 1822–25 (Denham, Clapperton, and Escayrac de Lauture), 1850–55 (Barth), 1872 (Nachtigal), and the 1890s (Brunache and Maistre). Third, the information from the founding of Bagirmi in the sixteenth century to the nineteenth century is weaker. The major source is Nachtigal—with Barth, Lanier, Pacques, and Reyna providing some information, and students of other central Sudanic societies providing other observations. Fourth, the vast bulk of the available historical information concerns affairs of state, especially those having to do with war.

NOTES

Chapter 1   Introduction (pp. 1–12)

1. The term *Bagirmi* has two meanings in this book. It is sometimes used as shorthand for the "society of Bagirmi." It is also used to refer to *all* the people of Bagirmi, regardless of their ethnic affiliation. In the latter case it means "people of Bagirmi."

2. Immediately south of the Sahara and north of the forest is a vast savanna stretching from the Atlantic in the west to the Red Sea in the east. Islamic scholars called this land the *bildan es-Sudan*. The central Sudan roughly corresponds to Nigeria and Chad. The east-central Sudan is Chad's corner of the Sudan. The nation called Sudan will always be referred to as the Republic of Sudan.

3. The east-central Sudan is bounded to the north by the Sahara and to the south by the forests of the Zaire River Basin. It was one of the last areas of the world to be explored, largely in the second half of the nineteenth century, and one of the last to be colonized—only after 1900. Chad is the major country in this area. It remained isolated and tumultuous throughout its colonial period (1897–1960) (cf. Gide 1937; Moran 1934). The postcolonial era has been dominated by civil and other forms of warfare, which began in 1965 and continues to the present (Buijtenhuijs 1978; Bouquet 1982). Given such conditions, it is remarkable that there has been as much social science research in the Chad region as there has been. A guide to this work can be found in Moreau and Stordeur 1970 and De Calo 1977.

4. The handful of useful works that do exist concerning Sudanic warfare include Bazin's (1982) and Aubin's (1982) more general surveys; Cohen's (1984) essay concerning nineteenth-century Kanuri warfare; Smaldane's (1977) monograph about Sokoto's nineteenth-century wars; and Law's (1980) as well as Fisher and Rowland's (1971) analyses of weapons.

5. Useful discussions of English and French anthropological research traditions in Africa can be found in Kuper 1973 and Alexandre 1973.

6. Insistence upon participant observation as the central source of information in ethnological analyses partially explains the neglect of warfare by sociocultural anthropologists, because war is an exacting phenomenon to participate in or observe. The wars of archaic states ultimately were suppressed by colonial rule, so these conflicts were largely nonexistent when there were anthropologists to observe them. Thus, though there have been brilliant anthropological monographs seeking to understand warfare in colonial and postcolonial Third World states (Wolfe 1969; Durham 1979), there have been no studies of warfare in archaic states by sociocultural anthropologists with the exception of Hassig's (1988) Aztec monograph. Ferguson and Farragher (1988) published a useful bibliography of warfare that emphasizes anthropological sources.

7. There are those who would disagree with the assertion that Marxism of any variety is healthy—
see, for example, Kowlakowski 1978. My view on this matter resembles that of Foucault,
who saw the debates between Marx and his opponents as "no more than storms in a childrens'
paddling pond" (1970, 262). The paddling pond is nineteenth-century social theory, and
taming of the storms involves navigating around the absurd to the useful in both Marxist and
non-Marxist thought. Such navigation demands careful scientists, not zealous prophets.

8. Glucksmann's (1974) work is still an especially useful introduction to French structuralism.
Benoist provides an important interpretation in *La Révolution structurale* (1975). Scheffler
(1970, 56–79) and Rossi (1982, 3–23) present two decades of anthropological responses
to structuralism.

9. Scope is more technically defined as "the substantive range of reference, and the spatiotemporal
range of reference" of concepts (Wallace 1971, 106). Abstractness is "the length of the
reduction chain connecting the theoretical terms to observable ones" (Kaplan 1964, 301).

10. The definition of *institution* in the text resembles Malinowski's usage of the term, which was
as "definite groups . . . united by a charter, following rules of conduct" (1973, 291).

11. Other commentators have noted other similiarities between Althusser and the structural-
functionalism of which Durkheim was a founding father (Smith 1984, 166).

12. A useful review of the notion of process in anthropology can be found in Moore 1983,
42–48.

13. Bhaskar says that the dialectic is "possibly the most contentious topic in Marxist thought"
(1983, 122). What was so innovative in the work of Althusser and Godelier was their
insistence upon treating the dialectic as a realm of social structure. Their dialectic had nothing
to do with *Geist* and the unfolding of ideas and everything to do with how economic and
political organizations' interactions might be conceptualized. The approach taken in the text
largely derives from Godelier's version of this dialectic, one that attacks Hegel while claiming
kinship to systems theory.

14. Though the analysis in this book is not quantitative, readers with a mathematical background
will realize, as did Friedman (1974), that the situation that has just been described is
analogous to one of mutually limiting functions in a set of equations that impose inequality
side-conditions on each other. Here, the mathematical functions, which describe the behavior
of the structures, are autonomous, though the range of values that they can take is limited by
the other functions.

15. Translations from French, German, Italian, Chadian Arabic, Tar Barma, and Sara, unless
otherwise noted, are my own. Material derived from the Chadian national archives will be
cited as "NA: W, 8, 7." "NA" refers to the national archives; "W" to the series in which
a file is located; "8" to the box in which a file is located; and "7" to the actual file. Works
1976:261–62 discusses these archives.

Chapter 2   The East-Central Sudan (pp. 13–40)

1. Useful introductions to the geography of the east-central Sudan can be found in Chapelle
1980, 8–17 and Cabot and Bouquet 1972 and 1974. More specialized work can be found
on soils in Dabin 1969 and on vegetation in Pias 1970.

2. The following sources are useful for reconstructing the paleoecology of the Chad Basin: Maley
1973 and 1977; Nicholson 1977; Pias 1967; Schneider 1967.

3. Maley's proposal of a final desiccation in the central Sudan appears to corroborate Arkell's proposal of a similar trend at a similar time in the eastern Sudan (1952, 261).

4. Useful heuristic classifications of east-central Sudanic peoples can be found in Chapelle 1980 and Cabot and Bouquet 1972.

5. There is an interesting literature concerning the camel pastoralists in the east-central Sudan. The most important source for the nineteenth century is Nachtigal 1974. Baroin 1985, Chapelle 1957, Cline 1950, and Le Coeur 1950 and 1953 are useful recent sources.

6. Camel pastoralists, especially Teda, are frequently described as possessing "castes" (cf. Cline 1950, 42). It was certainly true that "servile" individuals (freed slaves and slaves) were found in Teda households. These were supposed to marry endogamously but do not appear to have done so any more frequently than "noble" (*maina*) individuals. There was no religious system that assigned different forms of purity to the different occupations.

7. Presentation of the Wadaian state hierarchy can be found in Barth 1965, 654–63, Nachtigal 1971, 172–84, and Carbou 1912, 2:239–72.

8. Useful accounts of cereal producers include Adler 1966, Adler and Zempleni 1972, Brown 1975 and 1983, Dumas-Champion 1983, Fortier 1967 and 1982, Garine 1964, Jaulin 1971, Kokongar 1971, O'Laughlin 1973, and Pairault 1966. A classic account of farming among cereal producers can be found in Guillard 1965.

9. An introduction to Yedina can be found in A. M.-D. Lebeuf 1959, 103–7. Useful information is in Barth 1965, 60–70, Landeroin 1911, Talbot 1911, Konrad 1963, and Verlet 1967. Bouquet 1974 and Verlet et al. 1965 describe Yedina farming, herding, and fishing.

10. Certain Yedina had begun to centralize by the nineteenth century. However, very little is known about this process (Landeroin 1911, 332; Bouillie 1937, 233).

11. Excellent studies of Hadjeray can be found in Fuchs 1960 and 1970, Pouillon 1975, and Vincent 1975.

12. Hadjeray intensive agriculture has never been thoroughly studied. However, it is described, and placed in a comparative perspective, in Froelich 1968.

13. Arkell suggest that the name *Zagawa* may have been a generic designation for all the peoples in the Kanem (1952, 270).

14. A useful overview of the literature concerning the trans-Saharan trade in the central Sudan may be found in Bjorkelo 1976, 17–77. Law argues that this trade existed in classical times (1967). An opposing view is taken by Swanson (1975). Martin discusses the role of states in the trade over the period c. A.D. 900–1600 (1969).

15. Palmer suggests that the Bulala were formed from a rival "tribe" of the Saifwa (Palmer 1967, 2:39); Carbou has them being a rival lineage to the ruling Saifwa lineage (Carbou 1912, 1:301).

16. Arkell places the first Dajo kingdoms in Darfur, which he thinks were an offshoot of the Zagawa, about A.D. 1200 (1952, 269). He further speculated that the "Tunjur 'kingdom' of Darfur was a province of the Nubian kingdom of Mukurra." Tunjur Wadai was "but another province of Christian Mukurra," and both provinces became "lost to Nubia in the 13th century with the advance of . . . Kanem" (1963, 315).

17. Urvoy (1949) accepts Palmer's interpretation of the term *ḳaiga*.

18. O'Fahey and Spaulding do not believe Leo's Gaoga was in the Fur region (1974, 204). Their view is based upon the late-medieval geographer d'Anania's clear distinction between an Uri state and Gaoga. Uri was a city in the Jebel Marra that has been identified as the

capital of Tunjur Darfur (Arkell 1952). If this was the case, it means that Gaoga was not in Darfur.

19. Leo does not name the slave who founded Gaoga. Kuka traditions report that Hassan el Kuk was their founder (Carbou 1912, 1:339). Nachtigal and Carbou recount nothing of Hassan's life. Thus, it is possible that Hassan was Leo's slave, though no evidence other than Leo's assertion that a slave founded Gaoga and Kuka traditions that the name of their founder was Hassan support this view.

20. Review of the central Sudan's regional trade literature can be found in Bjorkelo 1976, 164–70. Lovejoy and Baier (1975) and again Baier (1980) have shown how in the west-central Sudan the exchanges between Tuareg and Hausa were, indeed, exchanges of "necessaries."

Chapter 3 Origins and Other "Impressive Things" (pp. 41–56)

1. Descriptions of Bagirmi's geography can be found in Chevalier 1907, Devallée 1925, and Pias 1964.

2. It was suggested by some that the Hittites or the Egyptians brought civilization to the east-central Sudan (Boulnois 1943; Griaule 1943).

3. The following linquistic analyses of Bongo-Bagirmi languages are useful: (Dalmais 1961, Fortier 1971, Gaden 1909, Palayer et al. 1970, Stevenson 1962, and Vandame 1962 and 1968. It should be noted that the southernmost Sara languages have been the most carefully analyzed. There are no studies of either the Kuka or Bulala languages.

4. Other work conducted at the Crop Evolution Laboratory places the domestication of the first sorghums, s. bicolor, in the savanna somewhere between the headwaters of the Nile and Lake Chad circa 3000 B.P. (Harlan and Stemler 1976, 473). Bicolor is a cereal adapted to arid conditions. Caudatum is even more resistant to drought. These domestications may have been a subsistence response to desertification after 4000 B.P. Perhaps—and what follows is speculation—as the central Saharan environment became inhospitable, the most seriously affected northern peoples, who would have been Saharan speakers, domesticated s. bicolor. Then, at a latter date a more southerly and easterly group, the Bongo-Bagirmi speakers took bicolor and developed it into caudatum.

5. According to Palmer the three *mais* were Daud Nigalemi (1377–86), buried at Jitwa; Othman Daudumi (1387–90), buried at Bursilim; and Kore Laga (1399–1400), buried at Gugawan or Kukawan. Palmer explicitly states that all three were buried in Fitri territory (1929, 3:43). The *diwan* which he later published in *The Bornu Sahara and Sudan*, gives their places of death respectively as Malfe, Bursilim, and Ngurlulu (Palmer 1970a, 93). A place of death is not invariably a place of burial, so it is not necessary that the towns in the two documents exactly overlap. Malfe, however, appears to have been near Jitwa in the Fitri. Bursilim seems to have been close to Njimi, the Saifwa capital in the Kanem. It is not clear where Gugawan or Kukawan or Ngurlulu were. Certainly Gugawan and Kukuwan sound as if they have something to do with the Kuka, which suggests a possible location in the Fitri.

6. The view that Bagirmi commerce played a significant role in the east-central Sudan is at odds with that of A. M.-D. Lebeuf, who believed that Massenya was never an important commercial center (1967, 215). Lebeuf, however, provided no evidence for her position which ignores Burkhardt's report of an important Bagirmi textile trade in the eastern Sudan at the end of the eighteenth century, Cordell's (1985) documentation of the importance of

Bagirmi merchants in Dar Kuti during the nineteenth century, and above all the very large Bagirmi slave trade.

7. This dating is that of Nachtigal (1889, 712–13).

Chapter 4   The Social Landscape (pp. 57–71)

1. The understanding of Bagirmi conceptualization of the *mbang* and his association with supernatural forces is largely derived from Pacques 1967 and 1977. These notions can be conflicting and unclear. For example, the *mbang*'s first two wives are associated with the moon (Pacques 1977, 130); but, then, so is the *mbang* (Pacques 1967, 207), which poses the question, Who is associated with the moon? Such unclarities may be because the ethnographer has not fully comprehended Barma thought, or because this thought is unclear, or both. There is one area where I believe native thought was unclear. Bagirmi simply did not know what the force was that animated things. They spoke of it in metaphors, as being like whirlwinds; or in terms of its manifestations, as being a falling star. One fellow said that *mao* and *ḳarḳata* created animal forms, but he assured me that he did not know how. "Maybe," he thought, turning on his feeble flashlight, "*mao* making animals is like electricity."

2. Gaden glosses *jili* as "family" or "tribe" (1909, 78). This appears misleading. When my informants used the word it referred to a "kind." So that one would say that different animals, plants, rocks, etc. were different *jili* of things. When one spoke of one's family as "my *jili*," one was in effect saying they were "my kind of people."

3. Both A. M.-D. Lebeuf (1959) and Pacques (1967, 185) mention the Barma conception of themselves as *barma ba* and *barma ḳubar*. I do not, however, believe that this distinction was of major structural significance, at least in the mid twentieth century. A number of my informants were unfamiliar with it. When it was used, it usually meant no more than that some people live by the streams and others live inland. Certainly, the distinction did not refer to a moiety that organized Barma activities. This might well, however, have been the case in the past.

4. The historical relationship between the Kenga and Bagirmi needs exploration. Older accounts of the origin of the second kingdom of Bagirmi have the founders coming from Kenga territory (Barth 1965, 448; Nachtigal 1889, 694–96). These are not absolutely clear as to whether the founders were or were not Kenga. At least one scholar, however, believes that Bagirmi was founded by Kenga (Fuchs 1961).

5. My informants never used the term *tarpo* to mean "family." Furthermore, Chadians have a tendency to use the French word *famille* when they are talking about descent groups. Pacques appears to have learned the word *tarpo* from the head of the village of Erla, who told her that it "was composed of ten families, *tarpo*"(1977, 8). Erla was an important eastern Bagirmi village. It is in an isolated area of Bagirmi, one likely to retain survivals. Erla was, and is, too large a place to have only ten families. It was, however, just the right size to have ten patrilineages.

6. The word *ḳambe* is of Kanuric origin (Lukas 1937, 208). This suggests that Barma thought in Kanemi or Bornuan terms when they were obliged to conceptualize unequal social categories. People tend to think in somebody else's terms only when they are familiar with them. This supports the view proposed in the preceding chapter of considerable intimacy between Kanuric speakers and Barma at the time of Bagirmi's founding.

7. Elderly polygynists appear to have been especially vulnerable to being labeled *gada*. This is because husbands were expected to sleep each and every night with a different wife in rotation. I was asked by one such gentleman to provide him with pep pills. These were of a brand called *Gawa* that pictured a lusty red bull on the cover.

8. Barth's Massenya is today a wilderness roughly 20 kilometers northeast of the town presently marked on maps as Massenya. Barma call this town Chekna. A. M.-D. Lebeuf has made an interesting comparison of the old and new Massenya (1967).

9. *Ngars* are found among different Bongo-Bagirmi speakers in Chad. The term is often translated as "chief," which suggests that all *ngars* were the same and that the English word *chief* catches this similarity. Not all *ngars* were alike. This can be understood if one compares the Sara *ngar* (Brown 1975, 44–60) with that found among the Kenga (Fuch 1973–74, 261–63). Palmer has speculated that the term was a "caste title" among the Bulala 1970, 106). This seems improbable as the Bulala lacked castes.

10. My guess is that there were two types of village-level leaders in Barma villages. This is because we know that there were *ngars*, who had purely political functions. Then Pacques mentions that there are still "land chiefs" in some villages. She calls these *ngolbe* and says that they are believed to be held by descent lines that "created a pact with the earth" (1977, 59). Barma thus appear to have used three terms to refer to village-level leaders—*ngolnange*, *ngolbe*, and *ngar*. I suspect, however, that the first two terms were different ways of referring to the same type of leader.

11. Shenton and Freund have argued that Lovejoy's suggestion of a plantation society among the precolonial Hausa is false (1978).

12. Barma and Bornuans refer to Arabs as *shuwa*. This term often has a pejorative connotation, similar to calling somebody a "nigger." The term *shuwa* is occasionally found in the scholarly literature. Given its meaning, its continued use seems inappropriate.

13. The Arabs among whom I conducted fieldwork, the Abu Kirder, used the term *nafar* rather than *ḳabila*, to refer to a tribe. Many knew the word *ḳabila* but said it was used by those in North Africa or the Arabian Peninsula. *Nafar* resembled the Tar Barma word *jili*, for both had a root meaning of "a kind of thing."

14. Summaries of what is known about the Fulani in Bagirmi can be found in Works 1976 and Cordell 1985. Cordell speaks of there being a "Fulani-Bagirmi religious class" (1985, 41). Use of the term *class*, with all of its different definitions, is a bit confusing. The Fulani were an ethnic group who often married Barma. Religious officials often came from this class of people, with *class* here understood to mean "category."

15. Pacques suggests that there were three original Fulani migrations to Bagirmi. These were of groups that she calls "famillies" that included the Forkobe, who settled at Bideri, the Djobto, who went to Darkan, and the Kamumudji, who located at Abgar (1977, 14). What these groups were (families, lineage segments, or unrelated pilgrims) is unknown. When they arrived is equally unclear, though at least for some of them it may have been prior to the founding of the second kingdom.

16. In Tar Barma the *ge* suffix indicates a plural. *Maladonoge* is thus the plural of *maladono*.

17. When Bagirmi was incorporated into the French colonial empire following 1897, the old *maladonoge* offices ceased to function, because they were replaced by those of the French colonial administration. This meant that food producers were no longer attached to *maladonoge*, meaning, in effect, that there were culturally no longer any *tashḳipage*. These structural changes appear to have been accompanied by a change in the term denoting a food producer,

NOTES

179

because by the late 1960's many Bagirmi, especially the younger ones, tended to call food producers *meskin*. This is an Arabic term that means "poor person," and increasingly food producers seem to be thought of as just another category of poor person.

18. Gaden glossed the word *hormo* as "respect" (1909, 52). However, Gaden was French, and the French term *respecter* at the turn of the century was far stronger than the American term *respect* is at present. A respectful nineteenth century French person would strike his twentieth-century American counterpart as too deferential.

Chapter 5 Food Producers and Their Households (pp. 72–91)

1. A 1970 survey of two Barma villages indicated that about 25 percent of the households had either father-son or brother-brother extended families (Reyna 1972).

2. Barma expressed this individualism by naming enterprises or their products after the person who was responsible for them. Consider, for example, a household consisting of Bugar and his wife Mymuna, where the former cultivated sorghum and the latter had peanuts. The household would be referred to as *be Bugar*, or "Bugar's place." Its fields would be called *baya jarto Bugar*, or *baya buli Mymuna*, i.e., "Bugar's sorghum field" and "Mymuna's peanut field."

3. My guess is that household members provided somewhat over 70 percent of all labor used in Barma households in 1970. Similar findings are reported elsewhere in the dry savanna (Delgado 1978; Echard 1964; Guillard 1965).

4. French colonial population figures were derived from village censuses that were repeated on an annual basis. This information has its biases, but it is better than earlier nineteenth-century accounts.

5. Barth adds a type of grub, which he said was called *hallu wendi*, as a source of uncertainty, because one of his informants told him that these "worms . . . were devouring crops" and threatening "starvation" (1965, 483).

6. Yield figures reported in the text are for 1970. There are earlier estimates from colonial sources. For example, it was reported that the Korbol area experienced harvest of 600–700 kilograms per house of red and white millets in 1913 (NA W, 15, 2). It was reported that the region of Bousso experienced yield of 1,200 to 1,600 liters per hectare in the same year (NA W, 15, 4). It is difficult to know the accuracy of such estimates. They are, however, of the same general order of magnitude those made at mid century.

7. The higher productive forces found in medieval Europe or imperial China were in part due to their development of different forms of agricultural capital that was absent in the east central Sudan. These were the heavy plow in the case of Europe (White 1962) and irrigation systems in that of China (Buck 1937).
Certain readers might be concerned with the use of Gambian agricultural production statistics. After all, the Gambia's place in the Sudan is a considerable distance from Chad's. Why not use production statistics from Chad's western neighbor, northern Nigeria? However, geographic proximity does not insure farming system similarity. Northern Nigerian agricultural research, while excellent, has been conducted, beginning in the 1970s, under conditions of far greater population density and commercialization than prevailed in precolonial Bagirmi. Haswell's agricultural research in the Gambia, whose quality is unparalled, was performed much earlier, under conditions which a bit more closely approximated those of precolonial Sudanic farming systems.

8. Farmers at mid twentieth century in southern Chad employed 2.8 workers on 3.1 hectares using 3.5 hoes, 2 axes, 1 sickle, and 0.5 machetes (INSEE 1967).

9. It was estimated that throughout Chad only about 10 percent of a harvest was marketed at mid twentieth century (BCEOM 1961).

Chapter 6   The Sun King and His Court (pp. 91–118)

1. The use in the central Sudan of the "household" as a trope for other aspects of social life was first emphasized by Cohen (1967, 111). O'Fahey says that in "the *fashir*" in Darfur which was the royal palace, "was the Fur household writ large" (1980, 24). Certain Chinese emperors also regarded their empire as a household (McNeil 1982).

2. This surrounding of an important official with a staff was common in central Africa. Denham, for example, while on a Bornuan raiding expedition in the Mandara region, noticed that "chiefs . . . are accompanied by as many personal followers as they think proper to maintain . . . some of them form the band, if I may so call it" (1826, 105). It would be interesting to compare these "bands" to Tacitus' *comitatus*, the "band of companions," which in different forms was common in Celtic and Germanic polities.

3. *Agids* were relatively minor administrative personnel in Bagirmi. This was not the case in Wadai, where they were allotted large "provinces" to administer (Barth 1965, 656).

4. There seem to have been a fair number of *alifa*s in late nineteenth-century Bagirmi. Most of these were estate officials, such as the *alifa miltu* and the *alifa korbol*. The *alifa ba* and the *alifa moyto* were also probably originally estate officials. However, by the nineteenth century both officials had come in from the outside and been given court functions.

5. Pacques too indicates that she does not know when the practice of purchasing office began (1977, 60).

6. It is significant in this respect that, while Gaden has a word for gifts in his dictionary, one for payments is lacking. This may be merely an oversight on Gaden's part, or it may indicate that the notion of "paying" is relatively recent to Barma.

7. Certain Barma speculated that this process of buying office became more marked following the arrival of the French. This was because colonial policies led to a drastic reduction of state revenues, which forced the *mbang* to seek larger investiture gifts as a means of replacing lost revenue.

8. Bornuan estates, as was the case in Bagirmi, are reported to have been scattered in different areas in the nineteenth century (Brenner 1973, 105).

9. The approach to policy formation taken in the text is generally that expressed in Almond and Powell 1966.

10. It should be noted that the door system was probably not as effective a way of articulating the interests of non-Barma either in the core or in tributary zones. This was because far fewer wives were taken from ethnic groups that were not Barma. Thus Arabs and Fulani may have found their concerns unexpressed at court more often than Barma.

    It might be observed that some other central Sudanic ethnic groups also thought of women as doors under certain social circumstances, though in ways that varied from how this was conceptualized in Bagirmi (Meek 1925, 1931; Cohen, personal communication.)

11. Bagirmi's senior counselors appeared to resemble Bornu's senior counselors in the sense that in both cases they were supposed to have originally come from groups, variously spoken of

as "kingdoms" or "tribes," out of which the state coalesced. The difference seems to have been in the number of these groups. Bornu was believed to have emerged out of twelve such groups (Brenner 1973, 12–13). Bagirmi was believed to have had only eight "master-of-the-earth" groups that formed the core of the second kingdom.

12. The *mbang*'s political actions were further constrained by the fact that he was obliged to observe both Barma and Islamic notions of sovereign rule (cf. Pacques 1977, 23).

13. Descriptions of the *mbang*'s staff are inadequate. Useful, however, are Pacques 1977 and Nachtigal (1889, 614–15). A fair portion of the staff seems to have been given over to persons with responsibilities over horses. There was a *kadamasinda*, who was in overall charge of the horses, a *warnak*, who saddled the *mbang*'s horse, and the *katamutmane* who watered horses.

14. Barth reported that there were "from 700 to 800 horsemen" (1965, 526) when *mbang* Abd el Kader returned to Massenya following a military expedition. He was surprised at the small numbers of these horsemen but was assured by a source, whose judgement he valued, that the number of cavalry in Massenya was "at least 2,000" (ibid., 526). Perhaps there were seven hundred or eight hundred cavalry in the 1850s who were the *mbang*'s personal soldiers, and another twelve hundred or so who belonged to the other court members' staffs.

15. Pacques discusses the supernatural meaning of the *mbang*'s lances, his fly whisk, his drums and his investiture (1977, 192–93; 39; 26–27; 25–37).

16. Pacques links Nyonnyon with the Muslim world, especially that of the Fulani (1967, 197). Escayrac de Lauture, however, suggested another alternative when he reported that "the part of the Shari which waters their country is called, in Sara, BaNyon, that is to say river (*ba*) of the termites [*nyon*]" (1855, 51). The important point is that when de Lauture wrote, the Sara were not part of any Muslim world. Pacques says that *nyon* also means termite in Tar Barma (1967, 197), just as de Lauture said it did in Sara. This suggests that, perhaps, Nyonnyon was linked to non-Muslim cultural notions prevalent in certain Bongo-Bagirmi speakers.

17. Speculation is in order about the Mweymanga. Escayrac de Lauture reported that a word that he spelled as *mae* meant "pond" in Tar Barma (1855, 24). *Mae* appears to have been *mwey*. *Manga* means cattle (sing.) in Tar Barma. This means that *mwey manga* means "pond of the cattle," which suggests that the Mweymanga might have originated as a community around some pond.

18. Pacques makes contradictory statements about the origins of the *alifas ba* and *moyto*. At one point she says they were from servile, presumably slave, origins (1977, 45). At another she says that the *alifa ba* was of "noble origin" (ibid., 48). My informants suggested that the offices were for free persons.

19. Pacques says the office of the *alifa moyto* was a "relatively recent" one (1977, 45). Nachtigal says that it was an old one originating at the time that Bagirmi and Bulala were fighting in the 1500s or 1600s (1889, 611–12). Nothing my informants said suggested that it was a new office.

20. Gaden suggests that the Bagirmi began specializing in eunuchs under *mbang* Hadji (1757–83) (1907, 441). This is considerably later than Malo.

21. Whether the *patchas* had larger personal followings of soldiers than other court members is not certain. The most famous *patcha*, Araueli, who lived at the end of the eighteenth and the beginning of the nineteenth century, appears to have built a personal army of circa 3,500 soldiers (Devallee 1925, 49). This may have been exceptional, but it was likely that most *patchas* had slightly larger staffs, and hence more soldiers, than fellow court members.

22. *Magira, gumsu, chiroma, chiḳotima, galadima, mbarma* are titles that originally came from either Bornu or Kanem.

Chapter 7 Revenue Collection and Allocation (pp. 119–134)

1. Royal officials were the mother, wives, sons, and daughter of the *mbang*. This suggests that royal court offices may have evolved out of the early *mbangs'* households, with different relatives promoted to different offices as the need arose. This is another reason for thinking of the state as a household state.

2. Analysis of taxation in precolonial central Sudanic states is in its infancy. Two proclivities in the existing literature tend to hinder its study. First, certain accounts confuse revenues with reciprocity. Thus O'Fahey, in *State and Society in Dar Fur*, presents thirty-seven different nineteenth-century revenues collected in Darfur (1980, 103–4). One of these was "assistance"('*ana*). However, the reader was never informed whether assistance involved transfers of products and/or to money to officials, thus classifying them as a tax, or to private persons such as kin, thereby classifying them as some form of reciprocity. Failure to distinguish the former from the latter makes it difficult to distinguish taxation from reciprocity. A second hindrance to the study of precolonial taxation is that many accounts of these fiscal systems were made by colonial officials, who often reported that precolonial revenue systems extracted more from peasants than their colonial counterparts (cf. Lanier 1925, 468). Such assertions should be treated with caution because colonial officials were in the business of justifying their domination.

3. The main nineteenth-century core taxes in Wadai and Darfur are reported to have been the *zakhat* and *fitr* (Julien 1904; O'Fahey 1980, 101). Those in Bornu were the *sataga*, apparently a Bornu term for the *zakhat*, and the *binumram* (Brenner 1973). Of these, only the *binumram* does not appear to have been a religious obligation. Thus most taxes in the east-central Sudanic states seem to have been religious exactions.

4. Wadai's ruler had slaves cultivating for him on lands surrounding Abeche. However, as suspected for Bagirmi, the revenue derived from these lands was a very small amount of Wadai's total revenues (Julien 1904, 140–41).

5. Devallee reports the destruction of a "history" of Bagirmi by the Wadaians subsequent to their defeat of Bagirmi circa 1870 (1925, 27).

6. Some raiders appear to have conceived of booty as a form of reciprocity. Normal protocol when meeting a person throughout the east-central Sudan was to feed them. This was a form of generalized reciprocity because people you fed were under an obligation to feed you. Clearly those who fled raiders shattered this reciprocal politesse, so Denham reported that "a *sheikh* and a *marabut* assured me it was quite lawful [*hallal*] to plunder those who left their tents instead of supplying travellers" (1826, 41).

7. Nachtigal reported that the Somrai, the "largest and most centralized" of Bagirmi's southern tributaries, had "rendered tributary their closest neighbors" (1872, 379). This statement is consistent with my informants' memories of an expanding Somrai and further suggests that the Kimre raid may have been to help the Somrai extend their control among the Gaberi.

8. At least one nineteenth-century tax in Darfur appears to have been responsive to climatic fluctuation. This was the basic tax, the *zaka* (O'Fahey 1980, 102). No *zaka* appears to have been collected if a household's harvest was beneath a certain amount. However, because harvest size depended upon climate, this meant that in poor rainfall years taxation was reduced.

9. One of the rationales for French imperialism in Chad was the suppression of slavery, so a number of sources mention the numbers of individuals acquired as slaves in southern Chad at the beginning of the twentieth century. These sources are reviewed in Azevado 1980. My estimate, following a review of this literature, is that Chevalier's suggestion that Bagirmi captured five-thousand slaves a year is possible, but high.

10. Bagirmi was, in principle, a tributary of Bornu circa 1900. However, Bornu had been conquered by Rabah at this time, and Bagirmi had been warring with Rabah since 1892. This made it unlikely that any tribute was still being paid to Bornu (Urvoy 1949, 121).

Chapter 8   Warfare (pp. 135–148)

1. Certain persons in Darfur remember that Ahmad Jurab al Fil was one of the greatest exponents of the chivalric ethos. Ahmad, at the end of the eighteenth century, brilliantly quelled a major civil disturbance in Darfur. What is interesting about this remembrance is that Ahmad was a Bagirmi (O'Fahey 1980, 39).

2. The term *means of destruction* appears to have been introduced by Goody, who did not formally define it (1971, 39–57).

3. The total number of soldiers that Bagirmi could mobilize would consist of everybody on all the staffs of the court officials, plus all those on the staffs of core estate officials, plus the total number of tributary soldiers. Such information is simply unavailable. The available data cited in the text refer to particular army sizes. The relationship between army size and the total numbers available to be mobilized in unknown. There is some suggestion, however, that Wadai, at the beginning of the nineteenth century, may have sought to field about one half of its potential soldiers (Bjorkelo 1976, 135).

4. A most helpful discussion of east central Sudanic military technology in the nineteenth century can be found in Bjorkelo 1976, 111–31.

5. The famous *Mai* Idris Alaoma, who ruled at the end of the 1500s, is reported to have used Turkish "musketeers" in his campaigns (Palmer 1970, 42).

6. Quilted armour was the east-central Sudan's most ingenious contribution to military technology. It was "made of cotton" and was "like a large overcoat which also covered part of his legs, and his head and neck were covered in the same manner. The head, neck, back and sides of the horse were covered and the padded armour reached almost to its hooves" (Bjorkelo 1976, 112). A description of the chain mail can be found in Nachtigal (1971, 4:196).

7. Throwing axes were used as an end-of-combat weapon to bring down someone who was fleeing or to throw at an attacker and then flee oneself.

8. Al-Tunisi devotes an entire chapter to horses (1851, 444–65). Paul Brunache, writing in the 1890s of Bagirmi's southern tributary and predation zones, describes how people there refused to sell horses in order to preserve their military advantage (1894, 248).

9. Cavalry must have good saddles, stirrups, and reins to be effective. Different nineteenth-century travelers tended to be impressed by what they observed of these. Barth, for example, preferred his Sudanic to his English stirrups, saying , "if I had made use of English stirrups, I should have lost both my legs" (1965, 324).

10. Al-Tunisi describes Darfurian cavalry and infantry tactics (1851, 420–24). Nachtigal mentions those of Wadai (1971, 4:184).

11. Goody, referring to the nineteenth-century western Sudan, said that "often the horse was just a means of transport to war" (1971, 47). If Goody is correct, then different tactics were used

in the western and east-central Sudan, with the former relying upon infantry and the latter upon cavalry. However, it does appear that horses were relegated to the role of transport vehicles once guns were adopted as the principal weapon. Carbou reports this to have been the case for Wadai at the beginning of the twentieth century (1912, 2:265).

12. Bjorkelo argues that "peasants or artisans," in addition to lacking the wealth to purchase cavalry weapons, also lacked the time to learn how to use them (1976, 124).

13. The role of Gundi in Bagirmi raiding is excellently described in an unpublished document written by Sargent Say in 1910, which can be found at the *Institut Tchadien pour les Sciences Humaines* in N'Djamena.

14. There is no record of a town in Babelyia named Babelyia. The capital, however, of Babelyia was called Dal.

Chapter 9 Predatory Accumulation in Fields of Empire (pp. 149–164)

1. Rey (1973) employs the term *relations of domination*. However, he does so without explicitly defining it. The use of the term here is different from Rey's.

2. The concepts of forces and relations of domination presented in the text are developed in a manner similar to Godelier's presentation of forces and relations of production (1972b, 335). The concept of relations of domination employed is not identical to that of the state. States are official hierarchies that do the dominating. They are not also the structures dominated. These are different, deserving of analysis in their own right, and often ignored. Relations of domination, conceptualized as both dominators and dominated articulated by a process of control, makes such oversights less likely.

3. Other scholars might treat the official–food producer relationship in the Sudan far differently than I have done. O'Fahey, for example, refers to officials as elites (1980, 37–46) and to their relationship to food producers as one between patron and clients (ibid., 49). Such characterizations are entirely correct as far as they go, but perhaps they don't go far enough.

Bagirmi officials were certainly set apart from the rest of society by their preeminent authority, achievement, and reward; and, as such, they qualified in Bottomore's (1964) terms as an elite. However, Bagirmi officials enjoyed revenues from food producers, and classifying them as an elite says nothing about this relationship. Saying that the official elite was in a patron-client relationship with food producers appears to address this concern. However, patron-client relationships, as they classically occur in Latin America, are between private persons, a landowner on his hacienda and a peasant seeking access to some of the landowner's resources. The official–food producer relationship in the east-central Sudan was an official-citizen relationship, and so to classify it as patron-client seems inappropriate.

4. It should be remembered from chapter 7 that not all core taxes were religious exactions. However, most seem to have been.

5. There is an approach called network theory in the social sciences whose problematic is different from that in the text. The term *contradictory grid* is proposed instead of *contradictory network* in order to help distinguish these different approaches from each other.

6. Descriptions of Bagirmi-Wadai relations subsequent to 1870 can be found in Carbou 1912, 2: 124–27; Devallee 1925, 58ff.; and Nachtigal 1889, 726ff. Descriptions of Bagirmi-southern relations can be found in Brown 1975, 21–73; and Fortier 1982, 71–82.

References

Adams, W. Y. 1986. *Ceramic Industries of Medieval Nubia.* Lexington: University of Kentucky Press.

Adler, A. 1966. *Les Day de Bouna. Etudes et documents tchadiens.* Fort Lamy: Institut National Tchadien pour les Sciences Humaines.

———. 1969. Essai sur la signification des relations de dépendence personelle dans l'ancien système politique des Moundang du Tchad. *Cahiers d'Etudes Africaines* 9(35):441–60.

Adler, A., and A. Zemplini. 1972. *Le Baton de l'aveugle.* Paris: Hermann.

Alcock, L. 1971. *Arthur's Britain.* Harmondsworth: Penguin.

Alexandre, P. 1973. *French Perspectives in African Studies.* London: Oxford University Press.

Allan, W. 1965. *The African Husbandman.* New York: Barnes and Noble.

Almond, G., and G. B. Powell. 1966. *Comparative Politics: A Developmental Approach.* Boston: Little, Brown.

Althusser, L. 1969. *For Marx.* London: New Left Books.

———. 1970. The Object of Capital. In L. Althusser and E. Balibar, eds., *Reading Capital.* London: New Left Books.

Anthony, K., B. A. Johnston, W. O. Jones, and V. C. Uchendu. 1979. *Agricultural Change in Tropical Africa.* Ithaca, N.Y.: Cornell University Press.

Arkell, A. K. 1952. The History of Darfur: 1200–1700 A.D. *Sudan Notes and Records* 33:129–155, 244–273.

———. 1963. The Influence of Christian Nubia in the Chad Area A.D. 800–1200. *Kush* 9:315–319.

Aubin, C. 1982. Croissance économique et violence dans la zone soudanienne, du XVIe au XIXe siècle. In J. Bazin and E. Terray, eds., *Guerres de lignages et guerres d'états en Afrique.* Paris: Editions des Archives Contemporaines.

Azevado, M. J. 1980. Pre-Colonial Sara Society in Chad and the Threat of Extinction Due to the Arab and Muslim Slave Trade 1870–1917. *Journal of African Studies* 7(2):99–109.

Baier, S. 1980. *An Economic History of Central Niger.* London: Oxford University Press.

Bakker, E. M. van Zinderen. 1976. Paleoecological Background in Conjunction with the Origin of Agriculture in Africa. In J. R. Harlan, J. de Wet, and A. Stemler, eds., *Origins of African Plant Domestication.* Paris: Mouton.

Balibar, E. 1970. The Basic Concepts of Historical Materialism. In L. Althusser and R. Balibar, eds., *Reading Capital.* London: New Left Books.

Bannock, G., R. E. Baxter, and R. Rees. 1972. *Dictionary of Economics.* Harmondsworth: Penguin.

Baroin, C. 1985. *Anarchie et cohésion sociale chez les Toubou: Les Daza Keserda (Niger).* London: Cambridge University Press.

Barth, F. 1966. Models of Social Organization. *Occasional Papers of the Royal Anthropological Institute* 89:5–21.

Barth, H. 1965 (1857). *Travels and Discoveries in Northern and Central Africa.* Vol 2. London: Frank Cass.

Bascoulerque, M. n.d. *Enquête nutrionnelle dans les régions du Chari-Baguirmi (Bousso) et le Moyen Chari (Kyabe). Février à Avril 1957.* Brazzaville: Section de Nutrition du SGMHP de AEF.

Bazin, J. 1982. Etat guerrier et guerres d' états. In J. Bazin and E. Terray, eds., *Guerres de lignages et guerres d'états en Afrique.* Paris: Editions des Archives Contemporaines.

BCEOM. 1961. *Rapport General.* N'Djemena: BCEOM.

Benoist, J. M. 1975. *La Révolution structurale.* Paris: Grasset.

Benton, T. 1984. *The Rise and Fall of Structural Marxism: Althusser and His Influence.* New York: St. Martin's Press.

Berre, H. 1984. Daju. In R. V. Weekes, ed., *Muslim Peoples: A World Ethnographic Survey.* Westport, Conn.: Greenwood Press.

Bhasker, R. 1983. Dialectics. In T. Bottomore, L. Harris, V. G. Kiernan, and R. Miliband, eds., *A Dictionary of Marxist Thought.* Cambridge, Mass.: Harvard University Press.

Bjorkelo, A. 1976. *State and Society in Three Central Sudanic Kingdoms: Kanem- Bornu, Bagirmi and Wadai.* Bergen: Hovedoppe i histoire hosten, Universitetet i Bergen.

Bottomore, T. 1964. *Elites and Society.* London: Watts.

Bouillie, R. 1937. *Les Coutumes familiales au Kanem.* Etudes de Sociologie et d'Ethnologie Juridiques 24. Paris: Domat-Montchrétien.

Boulnois, J. 1943. Migrations des Sao au Tchad. *Bulletin IFAN* 7:80–120.

Bouquet, C. 1974. *L'Homme et les plaines alluvialles en milieux tropicales. Iles et rives du sud-Kanem (Tchad). Etude de géographie régional.* Travaux et documents de géographie tropicale. Bordeaux: Centre d'Etudes de Géographie Tropicale, Université de Bordeaux.

———. 1982. *Tchad: Genèse d'un conflit.* Paris: Harmattan.

Bovill, E. W. 1968. *The Golden Trade of the Moors.* London: Oxford University Press.

Brenner, R. 1973. *The Shehus of Kukawa: A History of the al-Kanemi Dynasty of Bornu.* London: Oxford University Press.

Brewster, B. 1980. Glossary. In L. Althusser and E. Balibar, *Reading Capital.* London: New Left Books.

Brown, E. P. 1975. Family and Village Structure of the Sara Nar. Ph.D. dissertation. Cambridge University, Cambridge.

———. 1983. *Nourrir les gens, nourrir les haines.* Paris: Société d'Ethnographie.

Bruel, G. 1905. *Le Cercle du Moyen-Logone.* Paris: Publication du Comité de l'Afrique Française.

———. 1935. *La France équatoriale africaine.* Paris: Larose.

Brunache, P. 1894. *Le Centre de l'Afrique, Autour du Tchad.* Paris: Félix Alacn.

Buck, J. L. 1937. *Land Utilization in China.* Nanking: University of Nanking.

Buijtenhuijs, R. 1978. *Le Frolinat et les révoltes populaires du Tchad, 1965– 1976.* The Hague: Mouton.

Bunting, A. H. 1975. Time, Phenology and the Yield of Crops. *Weather* 30(10):312–26.

Burkhardt, J. 1968 (1822). *Travels in Nubia*. Westmead, England: Gregg International.

Cabot, J., and Bouquet, C. 1972. *Atlas pratique du Tchad*. Paris: IGN.

———. 1974. *Géographie: Le Tchad*. Paris: Hatier.

Callinicos, A. 1976. *Althusser's Marxism*. London: Pluto Press.

Carbou, H. 1912. *La Region du Tchad et du Ouadai*. Vols. 1 and 2. Paris: Leroux.

Carniero, R. 1970. A Theory of the Origin of the State. *Science* 169:733–38.

Chapelle, J. 1957. *Nomades noires du Sahara*. Paris: Plon.

———. 1980. *Le Peuple Tchadien: Ses racines et sa vie quotidienne*. Paris: Harmattan.

Chevalier, A. 1907. *L'Afrique centrale française*. Paris: Challamel.

Clark, C., and M. Haswell. 1964. *The Economics of Subsistence Agriculture*. New York: Macmillan.

Cline, W. 1950. *The Teda of Tibesti, Borku and Kawar in the Eastern Sahara*. General Series in Anthropology. Menasha, Wisc.: Banta Publishing Co.

Cohen, R. 1962. The Just-So So: A Spurious Tribal Grouping in Western Sudanic Culture. *Man* 12.

———. 1966a. The Bornu Kinglists. *Boston University Papers on Africa* 2:41–83.

———. 1966b. The Dynamics of Feudalism in Bornu. *Boston University Papers on Africa* 2:87–105.

———. 1967. *The Kanuri of Bornu*. New York: Holt Rinehart and Winston.

———. 1970. The Kingship in Bornu. In M. Crowder and O. Ikime, eds., *West African Chiefs*. New York: African Publishing Corp.

———. 1978. State Foundations: A Controlled Comparison. In R. Cohen And E. R. Services, eds., *Origins of the State: The Anthropology of Political Evolution*. Philadelphia: ISHI.

———. 1984. Warfare and State Formation: Wars Make States and States Make Wars. In R. B. Ferguson, ed., *Warfare, Culture and Environment*. New York: Academic Press.

Connah, G. 1981. *Three Thousand Years in Africa: Man and His Environment in the Lake Chad Region of Nigeria*. Cambridge: Cambridge University Press.

Cordell, D. 1985. *Dar al-Kuti and the Last Years of the Trans-Saharan Slave Trade*. Madison: University of Wisconsin Press.

Cornet, C. 1910. *Au Tchad, trois ans chez les senoussistes, les ouaddaiens et les kirdis*. Paris: Plon.

Crognier, E. 1969. Données biometriques sur l'état de nutrition d'une population africaine tropicale: Les Sara du Tchad. *Biometrie Humaine* 4:37–55.

Cuoq, J. M. 1975. Receuil des sources Arabes concernant l'Afrique Occidental du VIIIᵉ et XVIᵉ siècles. Paris: CNRS.

Dabin, M. 1969. *Etude générale des conditions d'utilization des sols de la cuvette tchadienne*. Travaux et Documents de l'ORSTOM no. 2. Paris: ORSTOM.

Dalmais, P. 1961. *Catalogue systématique de la bibliothêque du l'archevêque de N'Djamena*.

d'Anania, G. L. 1582. *L'Universale Fabrica del Mondo, Overo Cosmografia*. Venice.

Decalo, S. 1977. *Historical Dictionary of Chad*. London: Scarecrow Press.

Delgado, C. L. 1978. *Livestock versus Foodgrain Production in Southern Upper Volta: A Resource Allocation Analysis*. Ann Arbor, Mich.: Center for Research in Economic Development.

Denham, D. 1826. *Narrative of Travels and Discoveries in Northern and Central Africa in the Years 1822–1823*. London: John Murray.

Devallée, M. 1925. Le Baguirmi. *Bulletin de la Société des Recherches Congolaises* 7:3–76.

Doyle, M. W. 1986. *Empires*. London: Cornell University Press.

Dubois, G. 1968 (1902). *Le Baguirmi en 1902*. Etudes et Documents Tchadiens, serie B. Fort Lamy: INTSH.

Dumas-Champion, F. 1983. *Les Masa du Tchad: Bétail et Société*. London: Cambridge University Press.

Dumont, R. 1970. *Types of Rural Economy*. London: Methuen.

Dupré, G. 1985. Une Mise en perspective. *Canadian Journal of African Studies* 19(1):46–50.

Durham, W. H. 1979. *Scarcity and Survival in Central America: Ecological Origins of the Soccer War*. Stanford, Calif.: Stanford University Press.

Echard, N. 1964. Socio-Economic Study of the Ader Doutchi Majya Valleys. *Etudes Nigériennes* no. 15. Niamey, Niger: Institut Fondamental d'Afrique Noire.

Eldridge, M. 1975. Khalifu ou l'émirat Peul de Baguirmi et les Tooribbe de Sokoto. *Afrika Zamani* 4(49):67–113.

Engels, F. 1940. *Herr Eugen Dühring's Revolution in Science (Anti-Dühring)*. London: Lawrence and Wishart.

Escayrac de Lauture, S. 1855. *Mémoire sur le Soudan, redigé d'après des renseignements entièrement nouveaux*. Paris: Imprimerie de L. Martinet.

Evans-Pritchard, E. 1929. The Bongo. *Sudan Notes and Records* 12:459–63.

Fartwa, A. 1970 (1926). *Mai Idris of Bornu 1571– 1583*. London: Frank Cass.

Ferguson, R. B., and L. Farragher. 1988. *The Anthropology of War: A Bibliography*. New York: Harry Frank Guggenheim.

Firth, R. 1967. *Elements of Social Organization*. Boston: Beacon Press.

Fisher, H. J. 1975. The Central Sahara and Sudan. In R. Gray, ed., *The Cambridge History of Africa*, vol. 4. London: Cambridge University Press.

———. 1977. The Eastern Maghrib and the Central Sudan. In R. Oliver, ed., *The Cambridge History of Africa*, vol. 3. London: Cambridge University Press.

Fisher, H. J., and V. Rowland. 1971. Firearms in the Central Sudan. *Journal of African History* 12(2):215–39.

Fortier, J. 1967. *Le Mythe et les contes de Sou*. Paris: Juilliard.

———. 1971. *Grammaire Mbaye-Moissala (Tchad, Groupe Sara)*. Lyon: Afrique et Language.

———. 1982. *Le Couteau de jet sacre*. Paris: Harmattan.

Fortier, J., and Y. Villeon. 1977. *Proverbes Mbay*. Sahr, Tchad: Centre d'Etudes Linguistiques, Collège Charles Lwanga.

Foster-Carter, A. 1978. Can We Articulate Articulation? In J. Clammer, ed., *The New Economic Anthropology*. New York: St. Martin's Press.

Foucault, N. 1970. *The Order of Things: An Archeology of the Human Sciences*. New York: Vintage.

Fresnel, M. 1849. Mémoire de M. Fresnel, consul de France à Djeddah, sur le Waday. *Bulletin de la Société de Géographie*. Janvier-Février, 7–75.

Fried, M. H. 1967. *The Evolution of Political Society: An Essay in Political Anthropology*. New York: Random House.

Friedman, J. 1974. Marxism, Structuralism and Vulgar Materialism. *Man* 9(3).

Froelich, J. C. 1968. *Les Montagnards paléonigritiques.* Paris: Berger-Levrault.

Fuchs, P. 1960. Der Margai-Kult der Hadjerai. *Mitteilungen der Anthropologischen Gesellschaft in Wien.* Vienna. 90:85–97.

————. 1961. Entwicklungen und Veranderungen der Institution des Priesthäuptling in Sud-Wadai, Sudan. *Sociologus* 2:174– 86.

————. 1970. *Kult und Autorität: Die Religion der Hadjerai.* West Berlin.

————. 1973–74. Bagirmi und Kenga. Die Geschichte einer Zentralsudanesischen Staatsgründung. *Paideuma* 19–20:258–79.

Gabe, M. n.d. *Les Bouas de la région de Korbol.* Paris: Mémoire pour l'Ecole des Hautes Etudes d'Administration Musulman.

Gaden, H. 1907. Les Etats musulmans de l'Afrique centrale et leurs rapports avec la Mecque et Constantinople. *Questions Diplomatiques et Coloniales* 24:436–47.

————. 1908. Note sur le dialect Foula parlé par les Foulbé du Baguirmi. *Journal Asiatique* 10(2):5–7.

————. 1909. *Manuel de la langue baguirmienne.* Paris: Leroux.

Garine, I. de. 1964. *Les Massa du Cameroun: Vie économique et sociale.* Paris: Presses Universitaires de France.

Gearing, F. 1964. *Priests and Warriors.* Washington, D.C.: American Anthropological Association Memoir no. 93.

Gentil, E. 1902. *La Chute de l'empire de Rabah.* Paris: Hachette.

Geras, N. 1972. Althusser's Marxism: An Account and Assessment. *New Left Review* 71:57–89.

Gide, H. 1937. *Le Retour du Tchad.* Paris: Gallimard.

Gluckman, M. 1948. *Essays on Lozi Land and Royal Property.* Lusaka: Rhodes-Livingstone Institute.

Glucksmann, A. 1972. A Ventriloquist Structuralism. *New Left Review.* 72:68–92.

Glucksmann, M. 1974. *Structuralist Analysis in Contemporary Social Thought, A Comparison of Claude Lévi-Strauss and Louis Althusser.* Boston: Routledge and Kegan Paul.

Godelier, M. 1972a. *Rationality and Irrationality in Economics.* New York: Monthly Review Press.

————. 1972b (1966). Structure and Contradiction in Capital. In R. Blackburn, ed., *Ideology in Social Science.* London: Fontana.

Goody, J. 1971. *Technology, Tradition and State in Africa.* London: Oxford University Press.

Griaule, M. 1943. *Les Sao légendaires.* Paris: Gallimard.

————. 1965. *Conversations with Ogotemmeli.* London: Oxford University Press.

Guillard, J. 1965. *Golonpoui: Analyse des conditions de modernisation d'un village du Nord-Caméroun.* The Hague: Mouton.

Hagenboucher, F. 1968. Notes sur les Bilala du Fitri. *Cahiers ORSTOM, Série Sciences Humaines* 5(4):39–77.

Harlan, J. R. and A. Stemler. 1976. The Races of Sorghum in Africa. In J. R. Harlan, J. De Wet, and A. Stemler, eds., *Origins of African Plant Domestication.* Paris: Mouton.

Harries, P. 1985. Modes of Production and Modes of Analysis: The South African Case. *Canadian Journal of African Studies* 19(11):30–37.

Harris, M. 1968. *The Rise of Anthropological Theory: A History of Theories of Culture.* New York: Crowell.

Hassig, R. 1988. *Aztec Warfare: Imperial Expansion and Political Control.* Norman: University of Oklahoma Press.

Haswell, M. R. 1963. *The Changing Pattern of Economic Activity in a Gambian Village.* Overseas Research Publication no. 2. Department of Technical Cooperation. London: HMSO.

Hiernaux, J. 1969. Investigations anthropologiques au Moyen Chari (République du Tchad), préliminaires à des recherches multidisciplinaires. *Homo* 20:1–11.

————. 1975. *The People of Africa.* New York: Scribner's.

INSEE. 1967. *Enquête agricole au Tchad 1960–1961.* Paris: Secrétariat d'Etat aux Affaires Etrangères. Chargé de la Coopération.

Jaulin, R. 1967. *La Mort Sara.* Paris: Plon.

Julien, E. 1904. Le Dar Ouadai. *Bulletin du Comité de l'Afrique Française, Renseignements Coloniaux.* 14(2):51–62; 14(3):87–92; 14(4):108–10; 14(5):138–43.

Kalck, P. 1972. Pour une localisation du royaume de Gaoga. *Journal of African History.* 13(4):529–48.

Kaplan, A. 1964. *The Conduct of Inquiry.* New York: Chandler.

Khayar, I. H. 1984. *Tchad, Regards sur les élites ouaddaiennes.* Paris: CNRS.

Kokongar, G. 1971. Introduction à la vie et à l'histoire pré-coloniale des populations Sara du Tchad. Thèse du doctorate du 3ᵉ cycle. Paris: Université de Paris.

Kolakowski, L. 1978. *Main Currents of Marxism.* Vols. 1–3. London: Oxford University Press.

Konrad, W. 1963. Neue Beitraege zur Kentoris der Buduma. *Zeitschrift für Ethnologie.* 88(2):332–36.

Kowal, J. M., and A. H. Kassen. 1978. *Agricultural Ecology of the Savanna: A Study of West Africa.* London: Oxford University Press.

Kuper, A. 1973. *Anthropologists and Anthropology: The British School 1922–1972.* New York: Pica Press.

Lacan, J. 1966. *Ecrits.* Paris: Editions du Seuil.

Landeroin, M. A. 1911. *Notice historique. Documents scientifiques de la mission Tilho 1906–1909, onzième partie.* Paris: Imprimerie Nationale.

Lange, D. 1972. L'Intéresse de l'Afrique occidentale d'après Giovanni Lorenzo Anania (XVIᵉ siècle). *Cahiers d'Histoire Mondiale* 14(2):299–350.

————. 1977. *Chronologie et histoire d'un royaume africain.* Wiesbaden: Franz Sterner Verlag.

Lanier, H. 1925. L'Ancien Royaume du Baguirmi. *Renseignements Coloniaux de l'Afrique Française* 10:457–74.

Lanne, B. 1977. Histoire de frontières. *Tchad et Culture.* 104(Nov.):9–18.

Law, R. C. C. 1967. The Garamantes and Trans-Saharan Enterprise in Classical Times. *Journal of African History* 8(2):181–200.

Law, Robin. 1980. *The Horse in African History.* London: Cambridge University Press.

Lebeuf, A. M. D. 1959. *Les Populations du Tchad au nord du dixième parallèle.* Paris: Presses Universitaires de France.

————. 1967. Boum Massenia: Capital de l'ancien royaume de Bagirmi. *Journal de la Société des Africanistes* 37:214–44.

————. 1969. *Les Principautés Kotoko*. Paris: Presses Universitaires de France.

Lebeuf, J. P. 1962. *Archéologie tchadienne: Les Sao du Caméroun et du Tchad*. Paris: Hermann.

————. 1964. Contribution à l'étude de l'histoire de la région Tchadienne et considerations sur la méthode. In J. Vansina, ed., *The Historian in Tropical Africa*. London: Oxford University Press.

Lebeuf, J. P., and A. M. D. Lebeuf. 1950. *La Civilisation du Tchad*. Paris: Payot.

Le Coeur, C. 1950. *Dictionnaire ethnographique Teda*. Paris: Larose.

————. 1953. Le système des clans au Tibesti. *Etudes Nigériennes* 1.

Le Cornec, J. 1963. *Histoire politique du Tchad de 1900 à 1962*. Paris: Pichon, Durand-Auzias.

Leo Africanus, J. 1956 (1526). *Description de l'Afrique*. Paris: Adrien-Maisonneuve.

Lévi-Strauss, C. 1973. Social Structure. In P. Bohannan and M. Glazer, eds., *High Points in Anthropology*. New York: Knopf.

Lewicki, T. 1974. *Arabic External Sources for the History of Africa to the South of the Sahara*. London: Oxford University Press.

Lovejoy, P. E. 1978. Plantations in the Economy of the Sokoto Caliphate. *Journal of African History* 19(3):341–68.

Lovejoy, P. E., and S. Baier. 1975. The Desert-Side Economy of the Central Sudan. *International Journal of African Historical Studies* 8:553-63.

Lowie, R. H. 1920. *Primitive Society*. New York: Liveright.

Lukas, J. 1937. *A Study of the Kanuri Language*. London: Oxford University Press.

————. 1939. Linguistic Research between Nile and Lower Chad. *Africa* 12(3):335–49.

Maistre, C. 1895. *A travers l'Afrique centrale du Congo au Niger, 1892–1893*. Paris: Hachette.

Maley, J. 1973. Méchanisme des changements climatiques aux basses altitudes. *Paleogeography, Paleoclimatology, Paleoecology* (Amsterdam) 14:193-227.

————. 1977. *Analyses polliniques et paléoclimatologiques des derniers millénaires du Bassin du Tchad (Afrique Centrale)*. Birmingham, England: Comité Français pour le Dixième Congrès de l'INQUA.

Malinowski, B. 1973 (1929). The Group and the Individual in Functional Analysis. In P. Bohannan and M. Glazer, eds., *High Points in Anthropology*. New York: Knopf.

Mandel, E. 1968. *Marxist Economic Theory*. Vol. 1. New York: Monthly Review Press.

Marchal, Y. 1983. *Yatenga: Nord Haute Volta*. Paris: ORSTOM.

Martin, B. G. 1969. Kanem, Bornu and the Fazzan: Notes on the Political History of a Trade Route. *Journal of African History* 10(1):15–27.

Marx, K. 1906 (1867). *Capital*. Vol. 1. New York: Kerr.

————. 1981 (1894). *Capital*. Vol. 3. New York: Vintage.

————. 1973 (1939). *Grundrisse, Foundations of the Critique of Political Economy*. New York: Vintage.

Matlock, W., and E. Cockrun. 1974. *A Framework for Agricultural Development Planning*. Cambridge, Mass.: Center of Policy Alternatives, MIT.

McNeill, W. 1982. *The Pursuit of Power*. Chicago: University of Chicago Press.

192 REFERENCES

Meek, C. K. 1925. *The Northern Tribes of Nigeria, An Ethnological Account of the Northern Provinces of Nigeria together with a Report of the 1925 Decennial Census*. London: Oxford University Press.

————. 1931. *Tribal Studies in Northern Nigeria*. London: K. Paul, Trench and Trubner.

Meillassoux, C. 1964. *Anthropologie économique des Gouro du Côte d'Ivoire*. Paris: Mouton.

————. 1977. *Femmes, greniers et capitaux*. Paris: Maspero.

Meillet, A., and M. Cohen. 1952. *Les Langues du monde*. Paris: Centre Nationale de la Recherche Scientifique.

Modat, Capitaine. 1912. *Une Tournée en pays fertyt*. Paris: Comité de Afrique Française.

Moore, S. F. 1983. *Law as Process: An Anthropological Approach*. London: Routledge and Kegan Paul.

Moran, D. 1934. *Tchad*. Paris: Gallimard.

Moreau, J., and D. Stordeur. 1970. *Bibliographie du Tchad*. Etudes et Documents Tchadiens, serie A. N'Djamena: Institut Tchadien pour les Sciences Humaines.

NA. 1913. Chadian National Archives. W,15,2. N'Djamena: Musée Nationale.

————. 1913. Chadian National Archives. W,15,4. N'Djamena: Musée Nationale.

————. 1924. Chadian National Archives. W,15,36. N'Djamena: Musée Nationale.

————. 1931. Chadian National Archives. W,33,13. N'Djamena: Musée Nationale.

Nachtigal, G. 1880. Voyage du Bornu au Bagirmi. *Le Tour du Monde*. 40:337–416.

————. 1879–81. *Sahara und Sudan*. Vols. 1–2. Berlin: Weidmann.

————. 1889. *Sahara und Sudan*. Vol. 3. Leipzig: Brockhaus.

————. 1971 (1889). *Sahara and Sudan: Wadai and Darfur 1872–1873*. Vol. 4. Los Angeles: University of California Press.

————. 1974 (1879). *Sahara and Sudan: Tripoli and Fezzan, Tibesti or Tu*, vol. 1. New York: Barnes and Noble.

Nadel, S. F. 1942. *A Black Byzantium: The Kingdom of Nupe in Nigeria*. London: Oxford University Press.

Nicholson, S. E. 1976. A Climatic Chronology for Africa: Synthesis of Geological, Historical and Meteorological Information and Data. Ph.D. dissertation. University of Wisconsin, Madison.

————. 1979. The Methodology of Historical Climate Reconstruction and Its Applications to Africa. *Journal of African History* 20(1):31–49.

Norman, D. W., M. D. Newman, and I. Ouedraogo. 1981. *Farm and Village Production Systems in the Semi-Arid Tropics of West Africa: An Interpretative Review of Research*. Andhra Pradesh, India: ICRISAT.

Norman, D. W., B. J. Buntjer, and A. Goddard. 1970. Intercropping Observation Plots at the Farmers' Level. *Samaru Agricultural Newsletter*. 12:97–101.

O'Fahey, R. S. 1980. *State and Society in Dar Fur*. New York: St. Martin's Press.

O'Fahey, R. S., and J. L. Spaulding. 1974. *Kingdoms of the Sudan*. London: Methuen.

O'Laughlin, B. 1973. Marxist Approaches in Anthropology. *Annual Reviews of Anthropology*. Palo Alto, Calif.: Annual Reviews Inc.

Otterbein, K. 1973. The Anthropology of War. In J. Honigmann, ed., *Handbook of Social and Cultural Anthropology*. Chicago: Rand McNally.

Pacques, V. 1967. Origine et caractères du pouvoir royal au Baguirmi. *Journal de la Société des Africanistes* 30:183–214.

———. 1977. *Le Roi pêcheur et le roi chasseur.* Strasbourg: Travaux de l'Institut d'Anthropologie de Strasbourg.

Pairault, C. 1966. *Boum le grand: Village d'Iro.* Paris: Institut d'Ethnologie.

Palayer, P., M. Fournier, and E. Moundo. 1970. Elements de grammaire Sar (Tchad). *Etudes Linguistiques* 2(36).

Palmer, H. R. 1929. *Gazetteer of Bornu Province.* Lagos: Government Printer.

———. 1967 (1928). *Sudanese Memoirs.* Vols. 1–3. London: Frank Cass.

———. 1970a (1936). *Bornu, Sahara and Sudan.* New York: Negro University Press.

———. 1970b (1926). *History of the First Twelve Years of the Reign of Mai Idris of Bornu, 1571–1583.* London: Frank Cass.

Pias, J. 1964. Notice explicative: Cartes pédologiques de reconnaissance au feuilles de Fort Lamy, Massenya, et Mogrom. No. 14. Paris: ORSTOM.

———. 1967. Chronologie du dépôt des sédiments tertiares et quaternaires dans la cuvette tchadienne (République du Tchad). *Comptes Rendus des Séances de l'Académie des Sciences.* Serie D:2432–35.

———. 1970. *La Végétation du Tchad: Ses rapports avec les sols. Variations paléobotantiques au quaternaire.* Travaux et Documents de l'ORSTOM. Paris: ORSTOM.

Pouillion, J. 1975. *Fétiches sans fétichisme.* Paris: Maspero.

Preitze, R. 1914. Bornulieder. *Mittheilungen des Seminars für Orientalische Sprachen, Afrikanische Studien* 17:134–260.

Prins, P. 1900. Une Année de résidence auprès de Mohamed Abd-er-Rhaman Gaurang, Sultan de Baguirmi. *La Géographie* 3(13):177–92.

Radcliffe-Brown, A. R. 1965. *Structure and Function in Primitive Society.* New York: Macmillan.

Rey, P.-P. 1973. *Les Alliances de classes.* Paris: Maspero.

———. 1976. *Capitalisme négrier, La Marche des paysans vers le prolétariat.* Paris: Maspero.

Reyna, S. P. 1972. *The Costs of Marriage.* Ph.D. dissertation. Columbia University, New York.

———. 1976. The Extending Strategy: Regulation of the Household Dependency Ratio. *Journal of African Research* 32(2):182–95.

———. 1984. Chadian Arabs. In R. V. Weekes, ed., *Muslim Peoples: A World Ethnographic Survey.* Westport, Conn.: Greenwood Press.

———. 1987. Wars without End: Reproduction of Class Relations through Predatory Accumulation. In R. W. England, ed., *Economic Processes and Political Conflicts.* New York: Praeger.

Rodd, F. 1936. A Fezzani Military Expedition to Kanem and Baguirmi in 1821. *Journal of the Royal African Society* 35:153–168.

Rossi, I. 1982. On the Assumptions of Structural Analysis. In I. Rossi, ed., *The Logic of Culture.* South Hadley, Mass.: J. F. Bergen.

Sahlins, M. 1968. *Tribesmen.* Englewood Cliffs, N.J.: Prentice-Hall.

———. 1972. *Stone Age Economics.* Chicago: Aldine.

Say, Sergent. 1910. Renseignements sur la rive gauche du Bahr Sara. Unpublished report. N'Djamena: INTSH.

Scheffler, H. K. 1970. Structuralism in Anthropology. In J. Ehrman, ed., *Structuralism*. Garden City, N.Y.: Anchor.

Schneider, J. L. 1967. Evolution du dernier lacustre et peuplements préhistorique aux pays-bas du Tchad. *Bulletin de Liaison, Association Sénégalèse pour l'Etude du Quaternaire de l'Ouest Africain* 14–15:18–23.

SEDES. 1966. *Enquête démographique au Tchad, 1964. Résultats Définitifs*. Paris: Secrétariat d'Etat aux Affaires Etrangères. Chargé de la Coopération.

Shea, R. J. 1975. The Development of an Export Oriented Dyed Cloth Industry in Kano Emirate in the 19th Century. Ph.D. dissertation. University of Wisconsin, Madison.

Shenton, R., and W. Freund. 1978. The Incorporation of Northern Nigeria into the World Capitalist Economy. *Review of African Political Economy* 13:8–31.

Smaldane, J. 1977. *Warfare in the Sokoto Caliphate: Historical and Sociological Perspectives*. Cambridge: Cambridge University Press.

Smith, M. G. 1960. *Government of Zauzau*. London: Oxford University Press.

———. 1978. *The Affairs of Daura*. Los Angeles: University of California Press.

Smith, S. B. 1984. *Reading Althusser*. Ithaca, N. Y. : Cornell University Press.

Spaulding, J. 1985. *The Heroic Age in Sinnar*. East Lansing: African Studies Center, Michigan State University.

Stemler, A. B. L., J. R. Harlan, and J. M. J. Dewet. 1975. Caudatum Sorghums and Speakers of Chari-Nile Languages in Africa. *Journal of African History* 16(2):161–83.

Stenning, D. 1959. *Savannah Nomads*. London: Oxford University Press.

Stevenson, R. C. 1962. *Baguirmi Grammar*. Khartoum: Sudan Research Unit, Faculty of Arts, University of Khartoum.

Swanson, J. T. 1975. The Myth of Trans-Saharan Trade during the Roman Era. *International Journal of African Studies* 8(4):582–600.

Tahir, I. A. 1975. Scholars, Sufis, Saints and Capitalists in Kano, 1904–1970. Ph.D. dissertation. Cambridge University, Cambridge.

Talbot, P. A. 1911. The Buduma of Lake Chad. *Africa* 12(9):12–32.

Temple, O. 1912. *Chiefs and Cities of Central Africa, Across Lake Chad by way of British, French and German Territories*. London: Blackwood and Sons.

Therborn, G. 1976. *Science, Class and Society: On the Formation of Sociology and Historical Materialism*. London: New Left Books.

Thompson, E. P. 1978. *The Poverty of Theory and Other Essays*. New York: Monthly Review Press.

Tilly, C. 1975. *The Formation of National States in Western Europe*. Princeton, N.J.: Princeton University Press.

al-Tunisi, M. 1851. *Voyage au Ouaday*. Paris: Duprat.

Turney-High, H. 1949. *Primitive War: Its Practice and Concepts*. Columbia: University of South Carolina Press.

Urvoy, Y. 1949. *Histoire de l'empire du Bornou*. Mémoires de l'Institut Française d'Afrique Noire. Paris: Larose.

Vandame, C. 1962. *Le Ngambay-Moundou*. Dakar: Mémoires de l'IFAN.

———. 1968. *Grammaire Kenga*. Lyon: Afrique et Language.

Verlet, M. 1967. Le Gouvernement des hommes chez les Yidena du lac Tchad dans le courant du XIXe siècle. *Cahiers d'Etudes Africaines* 7(1):190–93.

Verlet, M., P. Blanchet, and J.-P. Delegarde. 1965. *Aspects humains de la pêche au lac Tchad: Etude socioeconomique*. 6 vols. Paris: Bureau pour le Développement et la Promotion Agricoles.

Vincent, J.-F. 1975. *Le Pouvoir et le sacre chez les Hadjeray du Tchad*. Paris: Anthropos.

Vivien, A. 1967. Essai du concordance de cinq tables généalogiques du Baguirmi (Tchad). *Journal de la Société des Africanistes* 37(1):25–39.

Wallace, W. 1971. *The Logic of Science in Sociology*. Chicago: Aldine.

Weber, M. 1968. *Economy and Society: An Outline of Interpretive Sociology*. Vols. 1–3. New York: Bedminster Press.

White, L. 1962. *Medieval Technology and Social Change*. London: Oxford University Press.

Wolfe, E. 1969. *Peasant Wars of the Twentieth Century*. New York: Harper and Row.

Wolpe, H. 1980. *The Articulation of Modes of Production*. London: Routledge and Kegan Paul.

Works, J. 1976. *Pilgrims in a Strange Land, Hausa Communities in Chad*. New York: Columbia University Press.

Zeltner, J.-C. 1980. *Pages d'histoire du Kanem, pays Tchadien*. Paris: Harmattan.

INDEX

Note: names of societies and polities are given in **boldface**; page numbers followed by *M* and *T* indicate Maps and Tables.

Ab Sakin, *mbang*, 102, 126, 139, 141, 146, 169–70
Ab Tujur peak, 26
Abd Allah, *mai* of **Bornu**, 49, 51
Abd Allah, *mbang*, 69
Abd el Kader, *mbang*, 54, 102, 103, 181n. 14
Abd el-Karim, 31, 36, 163
Abeche, 69, 181n. 4
Abgar, 51, 178n. 15. *See also* Durbali
Ability of officeholder, 94
Abstractness, conceptual, 5, 6, 174n. 9
Abu Krider, 23; Arabs of, 167–68, 178n. 13
Abughern region, 63
Acacia, 84, 85, 88
Accumulation: of capital, 9, 82; of forces of domination, 159; of labor, 85–86, 152; predatory, 10, 11, 40, 159–61, 165, 166
Acephalous populations, 24, 25, 137, 144, 158, 160
Achilles, 137
Adamawan-speakers, 18, 20*T*, 21*M*, 25, 69, 162
Administration, 106: according to *hada*, 120–21. *See also Jojigi (ga)*
Afrique centrale française, l' (Chevalier), 170–71
Agbar, 50
Age differences, within family, 74
Agela ("outside"), 93
Agid: **Bagirmi** staff officer, 93, 120, 125, 180n. 2; **Wadai** official, 23
Agriculture, 24–25, 48, 63, 64, 70; cooperation in, 76–77; cycle, and raiding, 144; double

cropping, 36; of Fitri region, 35–36; forces of production, 79–85; productivity, 82, 152, 155, 179nn. 6–7; relations of production, 73–79; risk-aversive practices, 82–84, 88 (*see also* Uncertainty); tools, 179n. 7. *See also* Production; *individual crops*
Ahl ("patrilineal descendant," Ar.), 23, 64
Ahmad Jurab al Fil, 183n. 1
Ahmet Mbassa, 121
Ahmet Ngollo, 120–21, 136–37
Aid, *see Kuma*
Ali, sultan of *Wadai*, 162
Alifa (viceroy), 145, 180n. 4; *ba*, 93, 113–14, 180n. 4, 181n. 18; *korbol*, 94, 180n. 4; *miltu*, 180n. 4; *moyto*, 113, 114–15, 117, 119, 170, 180n. 4, 181nn. 18–19
Aljema (**Bagirmi** court official's staff), 93, 104
Allies, 68; marriage of princesses to heads of state of, 110
Althusser, L., 4–10 passim, 174n. 11
An Sakin, *mbang*, 99
Anakazar (ibn Sa'id's southern pagans), 29, 30
Ancestor, *see Jid*
Anga feast (**Tikopia**), 6
Animals, marauding, and agricultural uncertainty, 84–85
Animism, 25, 26, 59, 100, 177n. 1
Anthropology: literature on warfare, 3–4; paleo-botanical, 45–46; participant observation in, 173n. 6; role of process in, 8
Aouni, 41
Arabia, migration from, as **Bagirmi** tradition, 44
Arabic-speakers, 18, 20*T*, 21*M*, 179n. 17
Arabs, 22, 37, 53, 60, 64–66, 98, 111, 117, 123, 135, 140, 167–68, 178n. 13, 180n. 10
Araueli, *patcha*, 117, 181n. 21
Archaeological literature on Chad and Nigeria, 168

Yesiye Arabs, 65
Yoweo ("seasonal farm hamlet"), 63

Zagawa, 27–28, 29, 51, 59, 69, 163, 175n.13
Zaire River Basin, 173n.3
Zaka/zakhat ("tax to support pilgrims"), 122, 127, 128, 182n.3, 182n.8
Zawila, 27–28

Zeltner, J.-C., 27
Ziber Pacha, 54
Zones of concentric influence and authority, 67–70; core, 67, 68, 121–24, 127–28, 154; predatory, 67–68, 69, 125–27, 144, 155, 156, 158, 162; tributary, 67, 68, 69, 102, 113, 124–25, 126, 144–45, 155, 158, 182n.7